S0-CJN-380

TRANSPORTATION IN TECHNOLOGY EDUCATION

EDITORS

Dr. John R. Wright
Professor and Dean
School of Technology
Central Connecticut State University

Dr. Stanley A. Komacek
Associate Professor
California University of Pennsylvania

41st Yearbook, 1992

Council on Technology Teacher Education

GLENCOE

Macmillan/McGraw-Hill

Lake Forest, Illinois   Columbus, Ohio   Mission Hills, California   Peoria, Illinois

Send all inquiries to:
GLENCOE DIVISION
Macmillan/McGraw-Hill
3008 W. Willow Knolls Drive
Peoria, IL 61615

Printed in the United States of America.

Orders and requests for information about cost and availability of yearbooks should be addressed to the company.

Requests to quote portions of yearbooks should be addressed to the Secretary, Council on Technology Education, in care of the publisher, for forwarding to the current Secretary.

This publication is available in microform.

University Microfilms International
300 North Zeeb Road
Dept. P.R.
Ann Arbor, MI 48106

ISBN 0-02-677127-6

FOREWORD

Transportation is a fundamental technological system which enables our society to change the location of people, goods, and services to meet human needs. Transportation technology enriches our lives by enhancing our personal mobility and by providing ready access to an amazing array of products from around the world. As a major technological system, transportation is a fundamental area of study in technology education. However, the successful implementation of technology education programs is a challenging undertaking. The Authors of this volume have set out to assist educators accomplish this goal.

This yearbook is the second of a series on the implementation of communication, transportation, manufacturing, and construction in technology education programs. Yearbook 40, *Communication in Technology Education*, appeared in 1990. The implementation of manufacturing and construction will be consided in future yearbooks.

The current series is designed to build upon earlier yearbooks which dealt with general implementation and instructional strategies for technology education programs. Yearbook 35, *Implementing Technology Education*, dealt with the realization of programs in technology education from the elementary schools through graduate study. The 1988 volume, *Instructional Strategies for Technology Education*, covered the variety of methodological approaches and delivery systems which facilitate instruction in technology education.

This volume deals with the content of transportation technology and provides working examples for teaching transportation technology and reviews the impact of transportation upon our culture. Readers will find it useful in planning, organizing, implementing, and evaluating transportation technology education programs.

On behalf of the members of the Council on Technology Education, I commend John Wright and Stan Komacek for their vision in conceptualizing this yearbook, for their organizational leadership in selecting the authors and organizing its preparation, and for their editorial skill in bringing this valuable resource to the profession. The outstanding scholarly contributions of the chapter authors are also recognized and gratefully acknowledged.

Appreciation is expressed to the Glencoe Division of Macmillan/McGraw-Hill for continuing the long-term tradition of support for the publication of the CTTE yearbooks.

Daniel L. Householder
President, Council on Technology Teacher Education

YEARBOOK PLANNING COMMITTEE

Terms Expiring in 1992

Donald Maley
University of Maryland
Ronald E. Jones
University of North Texas

Terms Expiring in 1993

Paul W. DeVore
West Virginia University
Everett N. Israel
Eastern Michigan University

Terms Expiring in 1994

Anthony E. Schwaller
St. Cloud State University
Robert Wenig
North Carolina State University

Terms Expiring in 1995

Richard Henak
Ball State University
James E. LaPorte
Virginia Polytechnic Institute and State University

Terms Expiring in 1996

Roger Betts
University of Northern Iowa
Jane Liedtke
Illinois State University

Chairperson

R. Thomas Wright
Ball State University

OFFICERS OF THE COUNCIL

President

Daniel L. Householder
Department of Educational Human Resource Development
Texas A&M University
College Station, TX 77843-3256

Vice-President

Anthony E. Schwaller
Department of Industrial Studies
St. Cloud State University
St. Cloud, MN 56301

Recording Secretary

Betty L. Rider
College of Education
The Ohio State University
Columbus, OH 43210

Membership Secretary

Gerald L. Jennings
Department of Business and Industrial Education
Eastern Michigan University
Ypsilanti, MI 48197

Treasurer

Emerson Wiens
Department of Industrial Technology
Illinois State University
Normal, IL 61761

Past President

R. Thomas Wright
Department of Industrial Technology
Ball State University
Muncie, IN 47303

YEARBOOK PROPOSALS

Each year, at the ITEA International conference, the CTTE Yearbook Committee reviews the progress of yearbooks in preparation and evaluates proposals for additional yearbooks. Any member is welcome to submit a yearbook proposal. It should be written in sufficient detail for the committee to be able to understand the proposed substance and format. Fifteen copies of the proposal should be sent to the committee chairperson by February 1 of the year in which the conference is held. Below are the criteria employed by the committee in making yearbook selections.

CTTE Yearbook Committee

CTTE YEARBOOK GUIDELINES

A. Purpose:

The CTTE Yearbook Series is intended as a vehicle for communicating education subject matter in a structured, formal series that does not duplicate commercial textbook publishing activities.

B. Yearbook topic selection criteria:

An appropriate Yearbook topic should:

1. Make a direct contribution to the understanding and improvement of technology teacher education.
2. Add to the accumulated body of knowledge of the field.
3. Not duplicate publishing activities of commercial publishers or other professional groups.
4. Provide a balanced view of the theme and not promote a single individual's or institution's philosophy or practices.
5. Actively seek to upgrade and modernize professional practice in technology teacher education.
6. Lend itself to team authorship as opposed to single authorship.

Proper yearbook themes *may* also be structured to:

1. Discuss and critique points of view which have gained a degree of acceptance by the profession.
2. Raise controversial questions in an effort to obtain a national hearing.
3. Consider and evaluate a variety of seemingly conflicting trends and statements emanating from several sources.

C. The yearbook proposal:

1. The Yearbook Proposal should provide adequate detail for the Yearbook Planning Committee to evaluate its merits.
2. The Yearbook Proposal should include:
   a. An introduction to the topic
   b. A listing of chapter titles
   c. A brief description of the content or purpose of each chapter
   d. A tentative list of authors for the various chapters
   e. An estimate of the length of each chapter

PREVIOUSLY PUBLISHED YEARBOOKS

*1. *Inventory Analysis of Industrial Arts Teacher Education Facilities, Personnel and Programs,* 1952.
*2. *Who's Who in Industrial Arts Teacher Education,* 1953.
*3. *Some Components of Current Leadership: Techniques of Selection and Guidance of Graduate Students; An Analysis of Textbook Emphases;* 1954, three studies.
*4. *Superior Practices in Industrial Arts Teacher Education,* 1955.
*5. *Problems and Issues in Industrial Arts Teacher Education,* 1956.
*6. *A Sourcebook of Reading in Education for Use in Industrial Arts and Industrial Arts Teacher Education,* 1957.
*7. *The Accreditation of Industrial Arts Teacher Education,* 1958.
*8. *Planning Industrial Arts Facilities,* 1959, Ralph K. Nair, ed.
*9. *Research in Industrial Arts Education,* 1960. Raymond Van Tassel, ed.
*10. *Graduate Study in Industrial Arts,* 1961. R. P. Norman and R. C. Bohn, eds.
*11. *Essentials of Preservice Preparation,* 1962. Donald G. Lux, ed.
*12. *Action and Thought in Industrial Arts Education,* 1963. E. A. T. Svendsen, ed.
*13. *Classroom Research in Industrial Arts,* 1964. Charles B. Porter, ed.
*14. *Approaches and Procedures in Industrial Arts,* 1965. G. S. Wall, ed.
*15. *Status of Research in Industrial Arts,* 1966. John D. Rowlett, ed.
*16. *Evaluation Guidelines for Contemporary Industrial Arts Programs,* 1967. Lloyd P. Nelson and William T. Sargent, eds.
*17. *A Historical Perspective of Industry,* 1968. Joseph F. Luetkemeyer, Jr., ed.
*18. *Industrial Technology Education,* 1969. C. Thomas Dean and N. A. Hauer, eds. *Who's Who in Industrial Arts Teacher Education,* 1969. John M. Pollock and Charles A. Bunten, eds.
*19. *Industrial Arts for Disadvantaged Youth,* 1970. Ralph O. Gallington, ed.
*20. *Components of Teacher Education,* 1971. W. E. Ray and J. Streichler, eds.
*21. *Industrial Arts for the Early Adolescent,* 1972, Daniel L. Householder, ed.
*22. *Industrial Arts in Senior High Schools,* 1973. Rutherford E. Lockette, ed.
*23. *Industrial Arts for the Elementary School,* 1974. Robert G. Thrower and Robert D. Weber, eds.
*24. *A Guide to the Planning of Industrial Arts Facilities,* 1975. D. E. Moon, ed.
*25. *Future Alternatives for Industrial Arts,* 1976. Lee H. Smalley, ed.
*26. *Competency-Based Industrial Arts Teacher Education,* 1977. Jack C. Brueckman and Stanley E. Brooks, eds.
*27. *Industrial Arts in the Open Access Curriculum,* 1978. L. D. Anderson, ed.
*28. *Industrial Arts Education: Retrospect, Prospect,* 1979. G. Eugene Martin, ed.
*29. *Technology and Society: Interfaces with Industrial Arts,* 1980. Herbert A. Anderson and M. James Benson, eds.
*30. *An Interpretive History of Industrial Arts,* 1981. Richard Barella and Thomas Wright, eds.
*31. *The Contributions of Industrial Arts to Selected Areas of Education,* 1982. Donald Maley and Kendall N. Starkweather, eds.
*32. *The Dynamics of Creative Leadership for Industrial Arts Education,* 1983. Robert E. Wenig and John I. Mathews, eds.
*33. *Affective Learning in Industrial Arts,* 1984. Gerald L. Jennings, ed.
*34. *Perceptual and Psychomotor Learning in Industrial Arts Education,* 1985. John M. Shemick, ed.
*35. *Implementing Technology Education,* 1986. Ronald E. Jones and John R. Wright, eds.
*36. *Conducting Technical Research,* 1987. Everett N. Israel and R. Thomas Wright, eds.
*37. *Instructional Strategies for Technology Education,* 1988. William H. Kemp and Anthony E. Schwaller, eds.
38. *Technology Student Organizations,* 1989. M. Roger Betts and Arvid W. Van Dyke, eds.
39. *Communication in Technology Education,* 1990. Jane A. Liedtke, ed.
40. *Technological Literacy,* 1991. Micael J. Dyrenfurth and Michael R. Kozak, eds.

---

*Out-of-print yearbooks can be obtained in microfilm and in Xerox copies. For information on price and delivery, write to Xerox University Microfilms, 300 North Zeeb Road, Ann Arbor, Michigan, 48106.

CONTENTS

PREFACE

Transportation is a vitally important part of the web of technological systems in our society. It is one of the basic tools required by civilized people just to survive. Basic necessities, such as food, clothing, and water are provided by transportation systems. One indication of the magnitude of our dependence on transportation is the number of miles of travel per year in the United States. According to the U.S. Department of Transportation, Americans logged almost 3.5 trillion passenger miles, or about 11,000 miles of travel per person, in 1987. Also, manufacturing, construction, and communication technologies are dependent upon reliable forms of transportation for their efficient operation. For example, raw material resources are transported between work stations within the plant, and finished products are transported to stores where they are purchased and carried home in the cars of consumers. In short, modern society and technology cannot exist without transportation.

Despite its importance, transportation also poses important challenges for the future of our technological society. Included among these challenges are: (a) the high cost of purchasing and maintaining transportation systems and their supporting infrastructures, (b) the political constraints placed on our national government by the dependence of transportation on crude oil reserves, (c) the possible long term affects of transportation-related air pollution, and (d) the unacceptable number of fatalities each year due to transportation accidents.

In the field of technology education, transportation is developing slowly as a content organizer. Annual surveys of the number of course offerings in various areas show transportation lagging other technological systems course offerings and most of the more common traditional course titles. This CTTE yearbook was developed to help change this situation. It provides technology educators with an orientation to the field of transportation and how it might be taught at various levels in technology education.

The first chapter initiates the examination of transportation in technology education. It provides an introduction to the contributions of transportation to the education of citizens in a technological society. Also identified are several research agendas in transportation education, which set the stage for the chapters that follow.

Chapter two addresses three basic questions; (a) why teach transportation?, (b) what should be taught about transportation?, and (c) how should transportation be taught? The third chapter examines the most recent developments and state-of-the-art in transportation technology.

Chapter four provides an interesting perspective on the technical, social, and biological-impacts-of-transportation from a person outside the technology education field.

Chapters five through eight address what might be taught about transportation, and how it might be taught, at the elementary, middle school, high school, and teacher education levels. These chapters provide excellent, practical information on content and learning activities for transportation technology education curriculum.

Finally, the last chapter (10) is on assessment and how to determine if instruction is making a contribution to the improvement of technological literacy for students. At each level, the goals and outcomes change while the field of transportation is presented and students engage in action-based activities to solve technological problems.

John R. Wright
Stanley A. Komacek

ACKNOWLEDGMENTS

We wish to express our sincere appreciation to those individuals who made this yearbook possible. Most importantly, we thank the authors who contributed considerable time and effort to put their knowledge and experience into words that others may find useful. Without dedicated and committed authors, yearbooks such as this would not be possible. Next, we would like to thank the members of the CTTE Yearbook Committee for their insight and guidance during the planning and development of this yearbook.

Finally, a very special thank you to our families for support and encouragement during the three years of this project. It is our hope that this yearbook will make a significant contribution to the literature base in Technology Education.

John R. Wright
Stanley A. Komacek

CHAPTER 1

Introduction to Transportation Technology

By Dr. Paul W. DeVore
(Professor at West Virginia University)

Education in a Technological Society

Technical Means: A Critical Variable in Human Adaptive Systems

The foundation of human adaptive systems was developed over centuries through a long, slow process of creative intellectual effort. By human adaptive systems we mean those created elements humans added to the environment that enabled them to survive, progress and establish settled communities. Humans created the technical means to provide the basic needs of survival; food, clothing, and shelter and the foundational technological base of modern civilization. Today, when we discuss human adaptive systems we mean those systems that enable humans to: (1) transform the resources of the earth into useful products; (2) transport themselves, raw materials and finished products throughout the earth and into outer space as well; and to (3) transmit, receive, store, retrieve and use information in various forms in the operation and management of their technological enterprises. Through the many intellectual efforts required to create what never existed before humans have been able to gain emancipation from the bondage and restrictions of the natural environment, to enhance their potential as humans and to change themselves socially and culturally.

The creation and use of technical means and adaptive systems have been the critical variables in the quality of the human condition and a major factor in human evolution during the last fifty thousand years. Ingenuity in selecting among the many options, together with numerous endeavors in the creation of tools, techniques and technical systems, enabled humans to transcend the lengthy organic process of evolution and to evolve socially, by choice, through creative intellectual endeavors in the technologies. Humans did not depend entirely on the environment to set the pace. They have not evolved by adapting to the environment biologically in the manner of other animals. Rather, humans through the discovery of the means to create tools, coupled with the unique human attributes of the ability to learn (the capacity for abstract thinking, generalizing and symbolizing) and the ability to perceive their activities and other events in relation to each other, were able to transition the limitations set by the natural environment.

Creativity in the Technologies. The creation of early technical means was directed toward the primary needs of survival: food gathering, clothing construction, shelter construction and the design and making of tools for these activities. These early efforts in the creation of technical means established the base for a continuous technological evolution from hunting and gathering, to horticultural, irrigation, agrarian, agricultural, industrial and post-industrial societies. These transitions from one form of technological base to another were major turning points in the history of human civilization. Today, the continued creativity in the technologies by humans portends a future that will be more technological, not less; a future where the criteria for the design of new and alternative technical means will include issues of population growth and resource limitations, environmental impact, and energy supply and conversion.

The successful creation of adaptive systems and technical means has been a complex human activity dependent on numerous factors, many of which must be present concurrently in a society. Successful creation of adaptive systems and technical means has required overcoming, throughout history, a number of constraints; constraints that limit the potential for the creation and adoption of new or alternative means within any given society. Among the constraints are:

1. the size of the information and knowledge reservoir;
2. the intellectual and social climate in which the inventor lives and works;
3. the level of technical talent and expertise available;
4. the level of development of associated technical means and adaptive systems;
5. the social compatibility of the new technical means, invention, or innovation; and
6. the interest and economic capability of the society in supporting the new technical means, invention or innovation.

Technical means and adaptive systems exist because there are humans that create and use them. In the natural order of things humans do not have the guarantee of continued existence, nor the guarantee of becoming fully human. In nature humans have the potential for existence, but not the guarantee. To be fully human requires that humans extend their potential through the creation of tools, technical means and adaptive systems that are compatible with humans and the natural environment. Today, the relation of the creations of humans in the technological realm are at a critical point. The technical means of today are totally different from the means of earlier eras, including the recent era of industrialization. To understand the differences and the problems and issues facing humans as they pursue the creation and development of technical means is the role of the discipline and science of technology. This yearbook presents an analysis of the field of transportation, one of the major adaptive systems[1] that have enabled humans to evolve and develop the civilization we have today.

Technical Means[2] and Society

Changes in technical means and the evolution of human adaptive systems have been constants in the civilization process. The difference today is in the pace and magnitude of the changes brought about by more complex, abstract, and in some ways an all encompassing technical means. In earlier times most technical means could be understood by the average human. Control was vested mostly in the group or at the local level. Today, the increasing complexity of the technical means and the interlinking of multiple subsystems has increased the amount of ignorance and misunderstanding of the very technical means that are essential to life and the social order.

New and more sophisticated technical means have decreased the level of understanding by the general population of the basic and essential technical systems of our global society. The issues of society have become more intertwined with issues of a technological nature. These in turn have become more intertwined with issues related to the life-giving and life-sustaining environment of the Earth.

---

[1]*Communication systems; production systems including manufacturing, construction and processing; and transportation systems.*

[2]*Technical means is used as a descriptor rather than technology which is the name of the discipline or field of study. Technical means are the tools, machines, techniques and technical systems that enable humans to survive and prosper in all climates and outerspace as well.*

Technical Means and Literacy. The level of political and social understanding has been affected and the inequality between the haves and have-nots has increased. This increase in inequality has been in direct relation to the decreased ability of people to participate in and contribute to the creation, use and management of the new technical means. The growing threat to society today concerns the fact that the complexities of the created technical means not only raise the level of knowledge and know-how required of the average citizen; they also increase the possibility of less involvement by citizens who are not literate about the technologies and the relation of technical means to human affairs and social purpose. *A technologically illiterate citizenry will promote the demise of democracy and place in control a group of elite people who, by default, will control the processes of public and private life.*

A Changing World. We live in an interdependent, ever-changing world, a world of accelerating industrialization, rapid population growth, wide-spread malnutrition, increasing depletion of non-renewable sources of minerals and energy, the misuse of technical means for the destruction of other humans and a deteriorating environment.

Some people believe that most technological problems have been solved. Not so. Problems of energy, environment, and the design and development of sustainable and quality human societies on our finite planet are serious and challenging problems. There has been an illusion of progress but in actuality real progress in improving the human condition of all people throughout the world remains our most serious and rewarding challenge.

Our futures are linked irreversibly to the rest of the world. People of the world are more dependent on each other than ever before, whether the context is the environment, raw materials, energy supply, finished products, food supply, or knowledge and know-how. The advent of television and communication satellites and the resulting rising expectations of people throughout the world, coupled with the microprocessor and its potential for accelerating the pace of technological change, portend a future far different from the present. We are at one of the many crossroads in the process of human civilization.

Intelligent Human Action. Our future and the future of succeeding generations will depend on intelligent human action, action based on knowing; knowing about the Earth and the behavior of humans and the natural, technological and social systems. We have discovered that placing our faith in inappropriate technical solutions is the road to disaster and that technically driven social purposes bring forth unimagined and unplanned for consequences.

The human future here on Earth will be determined by human choices. Our collective human destiny will depend on how well we prepare ourselves and how well we work together toward a common, interrelated global destiny. Our public policies and individual actions will require new levels of responsibility and a reassessment of our ethics.

A New Role for Knowledge. New levels of knowledge and responsible action are mandated by the creation of technical means that occupy such a central place in the human world and are of such a scale and whose consequences are of such magnitude that the potential of the destruction of civilization and the human species exists. The current ethic that supports individual and collective violence against nature and humans, with the objective of short-term monitary gain, brings about detrimental and destructive long-term consequences throughout the Earth. Hans Jonas reminds us that "when the *realm of making* (technical means) has invaded the *space of essential action*, then morality must invade the realm of making, from which it has formally stayed aloof, and must do so in the form of public policy." In Jonas' view there is a new role for knowledge in morality. He believes that under the circumstances *acquiring the knowledge required for intelligent human action becomes a duty beyond anything claimed for it (knowledge) heretofore*. Jonas makes the point that knowledge must be commensurate with the causal *scale* of our (technological) actions (p. 11). Thus, the very act of creating technical means has brought about the necessity of reassessing what it means to be educated in the world today. The imperative for understanding and controlling the design, development and use of technical means mandates a new form of literacy for citizens throughout the world. *The new form of literacy is a technological literacy.*

Technical Means and the Wealth of Nations

The creation of technical means has played a central role in economic and social development. Robert M. Solow, 1987 recipient of the Nobel Prize for Theory of Economic Growth, asserted some thirty years ago that invention and innovation were the keys to economic growth. Robert U. Ayres in an analysis of the question of how wealth is created concluded conclusively that wealth is derived from technological innovation (p. 200).

Conventional wisdom has been that wealth consisted of the possession of gold, silver, precious jewels, oil, timber, and land. Ayres reminds us that because of this belief *people and nations have focused on exploiting others to gain wealth rather than pursuing the creation of new technical means*. Many public policies have been formulated on this belief. Yet, when the history of significant gains in wealth by nations in the last 200 years is reviewed it is found that Britain, the United States, Japan and West Germany found their wealth in technological invention and innovation. The British failed to realize that their creativity in the machine tools of production was the basis of their wealth and dissipated their energy and wealth on their colonial empire. Their wealth declined proportionally. A similar situation developed in the United States in the latter part of the 20th Century, namely, a decline in wealth and the attainment of the rank of the largest debtor nation in the world. Today, there is an on-going search as to why the United States has lost its leadership; why the United States is not competitive in many fields. The reason is that the United States has lost its technological leadership. *The human resource base is not adequate nor the public policies appropriate to provide the context for creativity in the technologies.* We have forgotten that the driving force that made the United States a world leader was technological innovation by entrepreneurs seeking ways to earn high profits by creating new businesses (Ayers, p. 195). Understanding and acting on this knowledge is a part of the technological literacy required today.

Enhancing Technological Capabilities

It is becoming clear that the intellectual capabilities and technological understanding of our citizens must be enhanced if we are to compete successfully internationally and if we are to manage successfully the interrelated technical, social and environmental issues in our own society. The potential for creating new wealth and addressing the critical problems of the world in areas such as energy, environment, food supply and distribution, housing, and transportation, among others, through technological invention and innovation in the major adaptive systems* is high. However, knowledge and know-how are not geographic or nation specific as we are discovering. In the last several decades other nations have taken leadership in a number of developing technical fields and are gaining worldwide markets. Primary examples include Germany, Japan, South Korea, and Taiwan.

The Roles and Responsibilities in a Democratic Society

A fully functioning quality democracy requires intelligent, well educated and responsible citizens. As the complexity of the society increases socially

---

**Communication and information systems; production systems, including manufacturing, construction and processing; and transportation systems.*

and technologically there is a corresponding increase in the requirements for basic literacy in social and technological realms.

It is not possible to select, design, operate appropriately or control technical means and systems without a thorough knowledge and understanding of the behavior of the technological systems and their relation to humans, their society and the natural environment. A truly human future will require a high level of literacy and performance skills in communication and information systems; production systems including manufacturing, construction and processing; and transportation systems. The type and level of technological literacy required must be based not only on *knowing about* technical means but, more important, *being involved with* the technical means and the technological environment. The goal is a predictive understanding of the behavior of technological systems so we can select, design, develop and control our technical means so as to create sustainable and quality technological systems compatible with the natural environment. The design and/or operation of the technical means required for the transformation of our present non-sustainable technical means to a sustainable and preferable future mandates a highly educated and responsible populace. In general, the technological systems of the future will be more complex because of criteria requiring that they be designed to interrelate appropriately with other technological elements and systems, and more importantly with humans *and* the natural environment. Our systems will of necessity also be more diverse with the goal of meeting the compatibility requirements of bioregionalism which will impact on the nature, type and technical characteristics of our energy, food and shelter elements. The self-conscious, intelligent management of the living earth will be our most important challenge and responsibility. This vision of the world and technological development is based on the realization of the impact of individual decisions that often culminate in inappropriate collective human actions. Today, the actions of unknown individuals and groups can have significant impacts on others. Through collective human actions based on individual decisions, made at different times and places, serious consequences of great magnitude have been the end result. Urban sprawl, coastal development, ground water pollution, acid rain and urban congestion and air pollution in urban areas, resulting from automobile ownership are examples.

We are beginning the transition to a new era because, in looking backward and gaining insight through critical distance, we have discovered that the problems and crises born of the twentieth century have been problems and crises of perception, not ability or capability. We have discovered that laws and legislation alone could not solve the problems; that armed conflict could not resolve our differences; nor could technical means and a succession of technical fixes solve our problems and give us hope of a sustainable and quality future.

We have found that our perceptions and vision were cloudy and our knowledge and understandings limited. These limits resulted from our continued pursuit of education programs that have been grounded in the antiquated philosophies and content of a previous era. We found we were not *adequate* to the task. We did not have *adaequatio**. The requirements for responsible citizenship had changed. We were illiterate and strangers in our own world.

Literacy Requirements in a Technological Society

There are two driving forces behind change in thinking about education in our democratic-technological society. One concerns the impact of technological illiteracy on the United States. The other is a shift in the cultural paradigm which requires not only a new perception of the meaning of literacy in a technological society but also a greater emphasis on technological literacy.

From a social perspective today the technological illiteracy of citizens affects a community or a nation in many ways. Among the more critical are:

1. an increasing drain on the resources of a society or community by citizens unable to function effectively or contribute in a meaningful and productive way to their society in an increasingly technological world;
2. a loss of competitive economic potential by businesses and industries unable to obtain employees capable of functioning effectively in highly complex, ever changing, technological environments;
3. a lessening of defense and disaster response potential during times of national emergency, when citizens who should be able to contribute are unable to do so because of their lack of knowledge and know-how in the technologies; and
4. a growing number of citizens disfranchised economically as well as politically from participating effectively in the governance and management of their communities, states, and nation because of the increasing technological component of the society.

---

*Adaequatio: *That which enables us to know and comprehend anything at all about the world, our society, ourselves, and our technical means. (E. F. Schumacher, p. 39).*

A Shifting Paradigm

The shift in the cultural paradigm has brought about a reevaluation of the very essence of what it means to be literate and what the role and responsibility of technology education should be.

The evolving cultural paradigm emerged from the realization of how complex and interrelated the natural and created worlds really were. Our faith had been shaken many times in the past by the failure of technical systems to meet the needs of humans and be compatible with the natural environment. A new perspective and a new ethic have been evolving from an increasing awareness that *the Earth is not large enough nor the resources plentiful enough to tolerate, for any long-term future, the escalation of the current anthropocentric and aggressive technical behavior on the part of humans.* The new reality is one that recognizes the need for new global patterns of cooperation as well as the establishment of new relations among people and between humans, their technical systems and the environment. This new awareness places into context the question of education for the citizens of the world, namely, the question of knowledge and understanding of the relation of technical systems to biological and social systems and the behavior of the Earth as a total living system.

The alternative cultural paradigm that is evolving is one that is being influenced significantly by the question of the sustainability of life on Earth and the quality of human life. The predominant world view in the West has been based on a technocratic, industrial-scientific, or industrial-capitalistic paradigm. This paradigm perceives nature as a mechanistic system which can be understood via its simple components and their external relations. The belief is that nature should be controlled for the benefit of humans and that only minor adjustments are necessary in technological systems to protect the Earth's ecosystem from harm (Drengson, p. 63). When tested against the criteria of sustainability, this perception has been found to be lacking. The evidence is mounting of extensive, and at times irreversible, damage being done to the ecosystems that sustain and nourish life. People are realizing that there are limits; that it may be best if we slowed the process and reassessed our values and our social goals. Discussions are focused more today on the design and development of technical means and systems that are appropriate to the long-term well-being of *all* life on Earth. A shift is taking place from viewing life in an instrumental way to perceiving the intrinsic worth of *all* life. The challenge to education, and to technology education specifically, is to address this vision.

The Design of Technical Systems

The new ethics and morality with respect to the creation and use of technical means focus attention on the design of technical systems that have a long-term compatibility with humans and the natural environment. The emphasis is on an integrated technological, human and environmental design process. The creative technologists of the future will be searching for solutions to problems associated with the critical elements of food, health, energy, shelter, transportation, resource utilization and environment at the micro and community level. They will also be asked to direct their talents to working with people in their communities in the design of self-reliant, self-sufficient, sustainable communities where appropriate and meaningful citizen roles are identified and enhanced. The goals that will be emphasized will be the development of technological diversity and the decentralization of technological enterprises globally. The challenge of technology educators will be to develop and deliver education programs that will prepare people for full participation in the development of their communities based on *a reaffirmation of hypothesis of the living earth (GAIA) and the concept of design with nature and bioregionalism.* These concepts must be reaffirmed because of the many ethical problems we face as a human society—population size, food supply, appropriate shelter, health and wellness, meaningful roles in society, conservation of nonrenewable resources, diversity of the gene pool of life, diversity of the technological gene pool, and environmental quality.

Barriers to Change

We face many barriers to change as we attempt to carry out our responsibilities in the new era of complexity. Among the more critical are our own ignorance, diverse religions and belief systems, political power, folk knowledge and beliefs, myths and cultural heritages. The context in which the problems associated with designing, developing and operating sustainable and preferred communities is multifaceted. Besides these obvious barriers to change we face the stark realization that we inhabit a living planet where there are limits to fossil fuels, natural fresh water, food-productive land, habitable environments, the waste-absorbing capacity of the natural environment and the resilience of the life-support ecosystems of the living Earth (Harman, p. 7). Our technological challenges in the *physiotechnologies* and *biotechnologies* are greater at this stage of our transition to a truly human society than at any other time since the beginning of civilization. Technology educators have a critical role in serving the needs of the nation and the need of future generations. They are responsible for developing *adaequatio* among the youth; that essential intellectual and knowledge foundation in the technologies required to address the critical problems of the present and the future.

The Study of Technology

The nature and character of technical means have evolved over many centuries. During this evolution a vast body of information and knowledge about the creation, use and impact of technical means has been created, codified and preserved. Evolving from these creative endeavors was a new discipline, the discipline of technology. As with other disciplines, as the practitioners of the field (technologists) obtained more information and insights into their practice, the discipline has evolved from a skilled practice to *a science with the goal of developing greater predictive understanding of the behavior of the created human adaptive systems and their relation to humans and the natural environment.* This reservoir of knowing and doing is a field of study called technology.

Perceptions of the importance and meaning of technical means have changed as the technical means have changed. Perceptions about technology have also changed. Viewpoints about technology range all the way from technology as things or tools only, to technology as a major component of the adaptive systems of society. The word technology brings to mind such concepts as skill, craftsmanship, artifacts, technique, work, or a system of work, engineering, a body of knowledge, a discipline, a system of means, or an effect. Each of these viewpoints has contributed to a more complete understanding of the nature of technology as well as adding to the confusion. Even the standard definitions of technology tend to cloud the issue. The numerous dictionary definitions of the word technology range from: (1) the branch of knowledge that deals with the industrial arts, applied science, and engineering; (2) the science of the application of knowledge to practical purposes; to (3) the totality of the means employed by a people to provide the material objects of their culture. Others define technology from the perspective of their discipline. Economists define technology in reference to production; sociologists from the perspective of social relations and political structures; and engineers in terms of physical structures or technical systems. If there is an agreement, it is that the created technical adaptive systems are woven into the entire fabric of society.

The Science of Technology

The diverse and conflicting viewpoints about technology are of little help to those concerned with public policy, education, and technological literacy. They only increase the confusion and dissonance. With no common agreement on meaning, it is not possible to pursue intelligent public policy, develop valid education programs and curricula, or establish programs to attain desired levels of technological literacy.

Most unabridged dictionaries define the word *science* as a branch of knowledge or study dealing with a body of facts or truths *systematically* determined, or as *systematic* knowledge of the physical, material or natural world. There is general agreement that science means not one branch of knowledge, but numerous branches of knowledge such as psychology, anthropology, geology, biology, and other -ologies. Each of these branches of knowledge or sciences, including technology, share a common factor, the *systematic determination* of facts, truths and knowledge. The goal of most sciences is the predictive understanding of the behavior of the phenomenon being studied.

The intellectual endeavors involved in the choice, creation and control of the technical means of today are of a different order from those of the craft and trade era of the past. The new modes of thinking have established the base for the new discipline and the new science. *Those involved in the science of technology are concerned with investigating the processes of creating technical means and the evolution of technical means and society and in determining and understanding the predictive behavior of tools, machines, and technical systems and the relation of these elements to humans, their societies and the life-giving and life-sustaining environment.* Today, technologists base their work on information about the behavior of multiple variables and dynamic environments. Their goals are *predictability, replication, reliability, optimization* and the *efficiency* and *conservation of system operations*. Rules and systematic predetermined procedures are based on objective knowledge. Emphasis is on logical, instrumental, orderly, and disciplined approaches. The development of the "knowing base" of *the science of technology involves a number of intellectual processes including identifying and defining problems, designing, creating, observing, analyzing, visualizing, computing, communicating* using special words and symbols, *measuring, predicting, questioning and hypothesizing, interpreting data, constructing mathematical and physical prototypes, experimenting, testing, and managing*. These are the goals and behaviors of technologists. These goals and behaviors are the core of the science of technology. An analysis of these goals and behaviors provides insight into the critical importance of the science of technology as a central component in the education of the youth of our global community. They also provide insight into the critical elements that must form the foundation for the development of appropriate and valid programs of education for the preparation of technologically literate citizens for a global society.

Structure of the Discipline: Evolution and Rationale

The goals, scope and structure of the science of technology have evolved over time. As have all disciplines, the science of technology has evolved into sub-disciplines and fields of investigation including micro and macro systems. The primary adaptive systems of human societies have been identified as those concerned with (1) the *transformation of natural resources* into useful products, (2) the *movement of physical mass*—materials, products and people—by various technical means within the several natural environments and (3) the *movement of information* including the technical means of coding, transmitting, receiving, recording, storing and retrieving of information. *Transformation activities are classified as production systems* and consist of extracting, growing, processing, manufacturing and constructing. Those activities associated with *movement of physical mass are classified as transportation systems*. Those technical activities associated with the *movement and use of information are classified as communication systems*.

These three systems are extant in all human societies and contain the fundamental elements that provide the technological base of any society. These are the universal technological endeavors essential to the civilization process. *These cultural universals provide the foundation for the common learnings essential to understanding the behavior of our technological culture*. And, understanding the behavior of these systems is central to being culturally literate and capable of participating in a responsible way in a democratic technological society.

In this context, *the science of technology is the science whose practitioners are involved in the systematic study of the creation, utilization, and behavior of adaptive systems* (tools, machines, materials, techniques, physical and biological *processes* and technical means) *and the behavior of these elements and systems in relation to humans, their societies and the life-giving and life-sustaining environment*. Given this context, a technologist might be involved in any number of activities ranging from:

(1) creating technical devices, means or systems utilizing specific technical means;

(2) studying the behavior of various technical systems; to

(3) identifying the impact of various technical means on humans, their society and the natural environment.

One of the critical factors that affects the comprehension and understanding of human endeavors in the technologies is that everything is related. No one system stands alone. Each is a part of the whole and each contributes and interfaces with the total.

Therefore, curricula and programs of study in technology, designed for the purpose of attaining technological literacy, would contain the essential elements of the primary fields of endeavor noted above. Briefly, these essential elements would consist of, but not be limited to, the following categories of *knowing and doing*.

1. The history, evolution, nature, and development of technical means, including knowledge of people, places, and cultures where the means were invented and developed;
2. Knowledge and understanding of the processes of invention and innovation, including experience in the process;
3. Knowledge and understanding of the behavior of adaptive systems and subsystems (physio and bio) such as communication, and transportation and the tools, machines, materials, techniques, and the biological and energy conversion processes associated with these systems; and
4. Knowledge and understanding of the behavior of various technical elements and adaptive systems and the assessment of the impact of these elements and systems in relation to humans, their societies and the natural environment within agreed upon ethical contexts.

This yearbook focuses on one of the three primary systems, transportation. The sections which follow establish the context, content and structure for the study of transportation systems.

Transportation and Society

The Role of Transportation in Society

The critical role and importance of transportation and transportation systems in the evolution of society has often been overlooked.

Yet, movement has always been important to humans whether it contributed to their ability to obtain food as hunters or gatherers, to market their surplus food as agriculturists or to obtain materials for their complex technical systems. President Dwight D. Eisenhower, in a message to the U.S. Congress on February 22, 1955, spoke of the critical role of transportation.

> "Our unity as a nation is sustained by free communication of thought and by easy transportation of people and goods . . . Together, the uniting

> forces of our communication and transportation systems are dynamic elements in the very name we bear—United States. Without them, we would be a mere alliance of many separate parts."

The unity of the United States and its economic vitality has been a result of the development of specialized forms of transportation that have linked farms to markets, oil wells to refineries, factories to consumers, homes to workplaces, and people to academic, cultural and recreational activities. In 1990 the net value of fixed public capital transportation assets in the United States—highways, bridges and roads, aviation and transit facilities and vehicles, inland waterways, and ports and harbors—was approximately $800 billion. Included in these assets were 2.2 million miles of paved highways and roads, 150,000 miles of private railroad track, 26,000 miles of commercially navigable inland and coastal waterways served by 757 commercial ports, 140 million automobiles and 40 million trucks, 5,300 commercial aircraft and 220,000 general aviation aircraft, 20,000 intercity buses and 80,000 local transit service buses, 10,000 subway cars and other commuter transit cars, 1.1 million miles of natural gas pipeline and 205,000 miles of oil pipeline and 4 active launch pads for government and commercial spacecraft.

In 1988 the Federal Highway Administration reported that motor vehicle travel in the United States exceeded the two trillion mile mark and consumption of motor fuel reached a record 129.9 billion gallons; an indication of the importance of mobility and the reliance of society on transportation systems today.

Movement has always been important to humans. Today, we live in an interdependent world where we take as commonplace intercontinental and even planetary travel. The critical importance of this technical capability seldom surfaces until freedom of movement is restricted by political strife, or the most recent energy supply problems interrupt the flow of oil.

There are few items or activities in our daily lives, including work, that are not affected directly by the availability, reliability and quality of transportation. Yet, it is more often true than not that this important variable in the lives of people is generally omitted from serious consideration when planning is done, whether for communities or for national defense. Yet, significant changes take place in a society when new forms of transportation are introduced or existing forms of transportation are improved or extended to new areas. Increases in the speed of travel and increased capacity to move goods and provide services economically and efficiently have brought about changes in: (1) the time, space and distance realities of people, (2) the distribution of resources for production and the output of the production process, and perhaps as significant as the first two results, (3) changes in social relationships made possible by increased mobility. Improvement in the quality-of-life is related to improvements in the mobility potential of people and societies.

Changes in the technical means of transportation and communication have brought forth increased interdependence among national economies, enhanced the role of technological innovation in economic growth and provided the means for the rapid expansion of global corporations designed to take advantage of the new technical means we have designated *the transportation corporations*.

It is important to remind ourselves that new potentials in transportation and increased mobility are not without problems. The potential of current systems are tempered by the economics of energy supply and demand as well as environmental, regulatory, economic and land use issues, among others. Thus, the creation and use of transportation and other technological systems are intimately related to human, social and natural environments.

Transportation and Economic Development

The field of transportation is entering a new era, one in which global competitiveness and major changes in the domestic economies will require a rethinking of transportation system design and investment. There are many markets served by the various transportation subsystems. These include: the intercity passenger; intercity freight; and international, urban/suburban, and rural markets. Changes and demands in these markets bring about demands for new enhanced transportation services and products. As the economy changes and incomes increase and there are higher levels of economic activity, there are concurrent needs for more goods to be shipped, and greater demands for travel, both job related and recreational. Increased emphasis and participation in international trade by the United States has increased from $387 billion in 1970 to $985 billion in 1987. This increased activity increased the demand in the transportation sector. The continued industrialization of developing nations throughout the world will increasingly alter the composition of the transportation sector in the next century.

Global Markets. In 1992, the European Community will become a unified economic entity with a larger population than the United States. In addition, nations of the Pacific Rim are becoming increasingly competitive throughout the world. The role of transportation in the expanding global marketplace will require more productive and efficient means of transportation. Transportation is the foundation and key for success in international markets. The cost of a product increases with increasing costs of transportation. Thus, it is critical to address the design and development of more efficient technical means of transportation.

There is a direct relation between investments in the design, development and operation of efficient transportation vehicles and infrastructures and growth in productivity. Enhancing the efficiency of a nation's transportation system enhances the potential for higher and more efficient productivity. Efficient and economical mobility is essential to improving the cost and productivity ratio. It affects not only the cost of the final product directly in higher or lower costs for the raw material but also affects the efficiency of the productive effort in other aspects such as in the operation of a "just in time manufacturing" program.

Transportation Spending. The magnitude of transportation spending is about 18 percent of the yearly gross national product, some $800 billion a year on freight and passenger transportation services. Almost one of every five dollars spent on goods and services is spent on transportation products and services. Passenger transportation expenditures are $500 billion of the total, 80 percent of which are expenditures for private automobiles. Since 1940, intercity passenger travel has increased more than five-fold. Most of this growth was automobile travel, some 1.5 trillion passenger miles in 1986, while air travel increased to over 320 billion passenger miles by 1986.

The Transportation Mix. The population and economic activity of the United States has become increasingly concentrated in metropolitan areas. This urbanization of the country has placed increasing demands on urban transportation systems. Urban traffic loads have increased and travel between suburbs continues to grow in importance. Three quarters of the 250 million trips made each day are made in metropolitan areas. Over 80 percent of these trips are made in private vehicles. Seventy-five percent of the total freight expenditures are for intercity trucking. The transportation systems that were designed for urban/suburban areas have contributed to the increased growth in these areas. Continued growth is now straining the capacity of the systems.

The freight transportation system is largely a private enterprise consisting of railroads, trucking, water carriers, pipelines and airfreight. All of these sectors have become more competitive over the last decade. Most sectors have retained their market share while air freight has grown dramatically, primarily because it is a high-value time-sensitive form of transportation. During the last ten years a number of approaches have been developed by freight carriers to meet a changing economy. They have increased their use of computers and modern cargo-handling equipment, moved to multi-modal carriers that enable door-to-door coordinated freight service, and expanded the use of containers to facilitate multi-modal shipments.

In the international market imports and exports increased 21 percent from 1970 to 1988. In 1988 U.S. Airlines carried 52 percent of the international passenger traffic and 35 percent of the total air freight moving between the United States and other countries. The U.S. maritime fleet carries only 4 percent of the total tonnage moving to or from the United States.

Transportation and Social Development

The relation between the quality of the mobility available to people and the quality of their society is often overlooked. There is a definite link between progress in transportation and progress in other sectors of a society.

Social Goals and Strategic Planning. There is a need to direct the policies of transportation toward addressing social goals and development. These needs focus on the quality of life, economic growth, competitiveness in a global market, national security and protection and enhancement of the environment.

Any strategic planning begins with an analysis of these factors and the related mobility needs. Primary among items to be considered are population projections. In the United States growth in population has slowed and is projected to reach a zero growth by the year 2040. A population increase of 44 million is projected over the next 30 years.

One of the critical elements in the population issue is the demographic factor of age. In the coming decades the median age of the population in the United States will move from 32.1 years today to 40.2 years in 2020. Between 1990 and 2010, the 45–64 age group will grow at a rate four times faster than that of the total population. After 2010, the proportion of the elderly in the population will rise dramatically. The growth in the labor force will be about half the average of the past 25 years. The consequences of these changes in the population are:

- increases in the growth of personal travel and tourism;
- slower growth in the creation of new households;
- reduced growth in expenditures for housing and durable goods, including automobiles;
- increased labor costs for transportation;

- growth in demand for specialized transportation services and improved transportation amenities;
- reduction in the percentage of work-related trips relative to other travel; and
- continued growth in traffic and congestion in the air and on the ground and a possible smoothing of rush-hour peaks.

Transportation Policies. Policies that meet the changing needs of society should address a number of criteria. They should promote transportation systems that satisfy the mobility needs of individuals and businesses; provide sufficient capacity; be reliable, safe and energy efficient; be cost efficient for the user; and be designed to be in harmony with the environment.

The Study of Transportation

To become involved in the study of transportation and transportation systems it is necessary to set the context in a technical, social and natural setting. In the study of transportation and in the design of new or alternative forms of transportation, the way one views the process of transportation influences one's design and problem solving approach. To perceive of transportation as cars, buses, trains, airplanes, bicycles or roller skates limits one's conceptual world to what is and one's perspective of transportation as things—already created things.

Transportation systems are made up of created elements that function in a natural and human created world. The natural elements form the environmental context in which a given transportation system functions, such as the terrestrial environment, the marine environment, the atmospheric environment or the space environment. The nature of each environment influences directly the design of the technical components of transportation systems for a given environment.

The majority of transportation activity is terrestrial. Some 95 percent of the movement of people and goods occurs in the terrestrial environment. There are two types of terrestrial systems, *vehicular* and *stationary*. Automobiles are vehicular and pipelines and conveyors are stationary.

The *marine* environment has been and continues to be a critical transportation environment. Water covers about 70 percent of the Earth's surface. There are two categories of marine transport; inland waterways and maritime. Inland waterways include canals, rivers, domestic lakes and coastal waters. Maritime includes transport in large inland lakes and oceans.

The *atmospheric* environment category includes any transport of people or goods above the surface of the Earth, in, but not beyond, the atmosphere. Atmospheric transportation includes not only vehicles but also support systems such as airports and navigation devices. The vehicles used in atmospheric transportation are classified as heavier than air and lighter than air.

The *space* environment category involves transportation in the environment beyond the gaseous envelope that surrounds the Earth. Vehicles have been designed that are capable of orbiting the Earth, transporting humans and instrumentation from the Earth to the moon and back again and for carrying instruments to the outer reaches of space as well.

Technical Systems—Transportation

Each transportation device or system operating within a given environment is composed of a number of technical systems specifically designed to function efficiently within that environment. Each form of transportation device or system has, in some form, a means for (1) propelling, (2) suspending, (3) guiding, and (4) controlling the vehicle. Each vehicle also has a (5) structural system that is designed to function in a particular terrestrial, marine, atmospheric or space environment.

These five systems, together with appropriate support systems, are common to all modes of transportation. They vary in design and application by the nature of the transportation task in a given environment.

Propulsion Systems. Energy in some form is required to move a vehicle in a given environment. Improvements in propulsion systems have been responsible for major advances in transportation. Propulsion systems provide the means for converting and transmitting energy to move a vehicle in a given environment.

Propulsion systems consist of (1) an energy source that is available to the vehicle, (2) a means of converting the energy to do work, and (3) a system for converting and transmitting the power.

Guidance Systems. These are systems designed to provide information to the operator of a transportation vehicle or, in the case of automated systems, to computers which initiate action to direct the vehicle along a prescribed path. Guidance systems are the means for providing information to human or other control systems for the purpose of directing a vehicle along a prescribed path in a given environment.

Guidance systems are designed for specific purposes. Two factors determine the complexity of the guidance system; the environment in which the vehicle is designed to operate and the nature of the vehicle and its purpose.

Control Systems. Control systems, either fully automated or activated by humans, receive information from the guidance system. Control systems are the means to change, alter or regulate the velocity, direction or attitude of a vehicle within a given environment.

Control systems consist of sensing devices. The human operator or an instrument that measures velocity, attitude or direction provide the sensing. There are also actuators. These can be humans or mechanical, pneumatic, hydraulic and electrical devices which move a throttle to change the thrust which alters velocity, alter a surface to change altitude or attitude, or that activate devices of various designs to arrest motion. Fully automatic systems combine guidance and control systems into a fully integrated system that uses a computer in place of a human.

Suspension Systems. Suspension systems are the means by which a vehicle is related, connected and/or associated with the environment in which it operates. Each type of transportation vehicle is suspended in some way in the environment in which it operates. Terrestrial vehicles use wheels and springs, magnetic levitation, and surface effect; aircraft use airfoils; watercraft use displacement hulls, surface effect and hydrafoils; spacecraft use reaction and gravity.

Structural Systems. Structural systems are systematic arrangements of the components of a vehicle in a configuration that meets the design service and performance requirements for the vehicle in the environment in which it operates. Structural systems are designed to provide for maximum performance in a given environment while protecting the people, goods or instruments being transported.

Support Systems. Support systems are the infrastructure of transportation systems. These systems provide the services required for the systems to function efficiently and reliably. Included are highways, airports and marine terminal facilities; maintenance; food services; training operations; information services such as meteorological, training and operational materials; maps and charts; and emergency medical services.

Curriculum Structure and Content

Those concerned with curriculum development for technology education face a very difficult and complex task. The task is less formidable if a logical, yet flexible, approach to the identification of structure and content is adopted. The basic tool that provides a logical, yet flexible approach, is a taxonomy. Approaching the task using the rules of taxonomy provides a way to classify knowledge and content in the technologies that provides a logical and agreed upon base with agreed upon terminology for curriculum construction. The result is a common base that meets the needs of general education which is concerned with common learnings based upon cultural universals.

In the field of technology education the outcome of the use of a taxonomy for the classification of the content and structure would be the *identification of universal technological endeavors*, together with the fundamental components and their inter and intra relations. This approach provides an accurate and agreed upon perspective of the content reservoir. Without an accurate perspective of the whole, and knowledge of the relation of the component parts, further work in the identification of concepts, principles, processes, models and systems cannot proceed.

A Taxonomy of Transportation

In this section an overview of the structure of the study of transportation is provided. A more detailed taxonomy will be presented in Chapter 2.

An analysis of the creation and evolution of transportation systems reveals that several mutually exclusive but interrelated systems have been a consistent part of transportation development regardless of the level of sophistication or type of transportation involved. Furthermore, the study of this adaptive system is environmentally related, as are other adaptive systems, but in a different way. All transportation problems are related to terrestrial, marine, atmospheric or space environments. These environments set the context and limits within which transportation systems must operate.

The study of the development of civilization and human efforts in creating technical means and adaptive systems indicates clearly that there has been a definite relation between the adaptive systems created by humans and their societies and cultures. These interrelations are the social cultural elements in the study of transportation and are directly related to the technical elements. These interrelations must be recognized and identified in any analysis if the goal is to develop a valid and universal curriculum structure.

An example of the process involved in the derivation of curricular components for the discipline of transportation and for deriving a taxonomy for the basic sub-systems follows. The example which follows is based on the assumption that the *goal is to identify the universals* for the study of transportation and that these include the knowledge structure and the basic concepts, principles, intellectual processes and their functional relations and the social/cultural elements of the transportation systems.

Figure 1 is a relational matrix of the discipline and content structure for transportation and illustrates the interrelations among the primary components.

TECHNICAL SYSTEMS	DISCIPLINE STRUCTURE					
	KNOWLEDGE STRUCUTRE (TAXONOMY)	CONCEPT TAXONOMY	PRINCIPLE TAXONOMY	PROCESS TAXONOMY	FUNCTIONAL RELATIONS	SOCIAL-CULTURAL ELEMENTS
PROPULSION						
STRUCTURE						
GUIDANCE						
CONTROL						
SUSPENSION						
SUPPORT						

Figure 1: Transportation technology: discipline structure and content.

Figure 2 provides an illustration of the relation of the field of transportation to other content areas of technology. The discipline is identified as technology and the basic element categories are technical *and* social/cultural. The adaptive systems are *production, transportation,* and *communication*. The environmental divisions of transportation are categorized as *terrestrial, marine, atmospheric* and *space*.

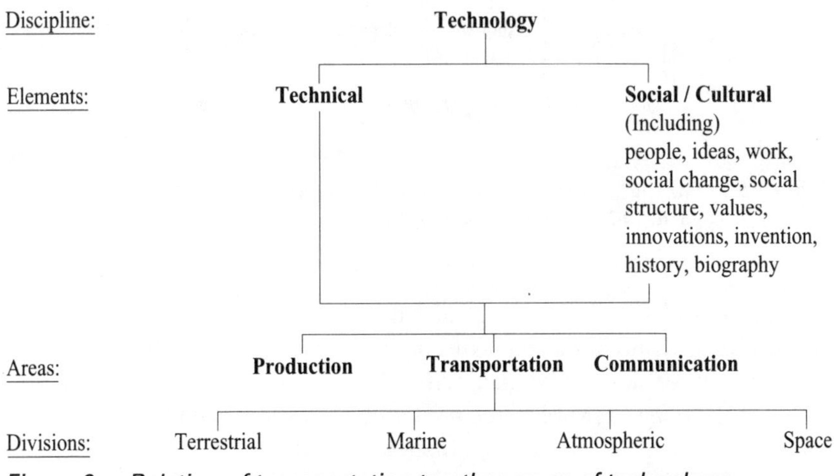

Figure 2: Relation of transportation to other areas of technology.

Figure 3 is a partial taxonomy for transportation illustrating the systems fundamental to all types of transportation regardless of the environmental area, culture, or level of sophistication of the system. Each system can be defined specifically and described functionally. For instance, *control* can be defined as: the actual mechanical procedures used to steer a vehicle along a path, or to maintain its attitude in a specific orientation in space. *Guidance* can be defined as: the information required by a vehicle to follow a prescribed path or fulfill a particular objective. Each system can be defined more specifically by identifying categories and types. In Figure 4 three categories of propulsion systems are identified, together with several types of power or energy.

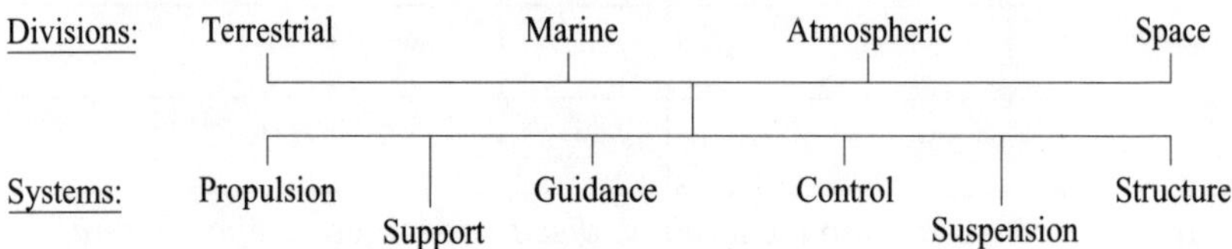

Figure 3: Partial taxonomy illustrating systems fundamental to all types of transportation regardless of environmental division.

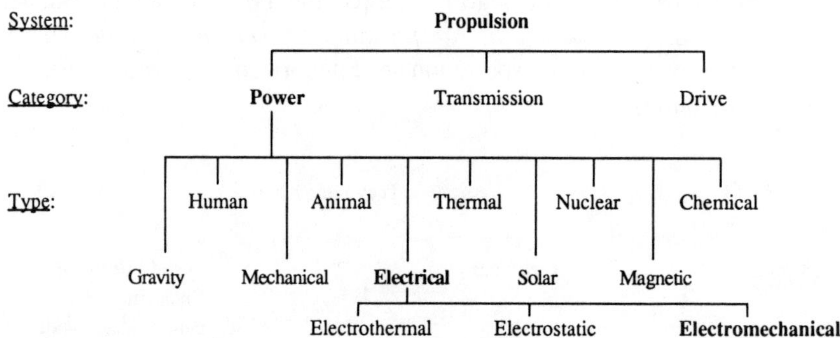

Figure 4: Partial taxonomy illustrating three categories of propulsion and various types of energy and power.

An analysis of *propulsion* indicates that not only are there categories and types of propulsion but also classes and orders as is illustrated in Figures 5 and 6. It is possible to move hierarchically in an analysis of propulsion from the identification of the order (*reciprocating expansible chamber*), to the class (*internal conversion*), to the type (*thermal*), to the category (*power*), to the system (*propulsion*), to the environmental division (*terrestrial*).

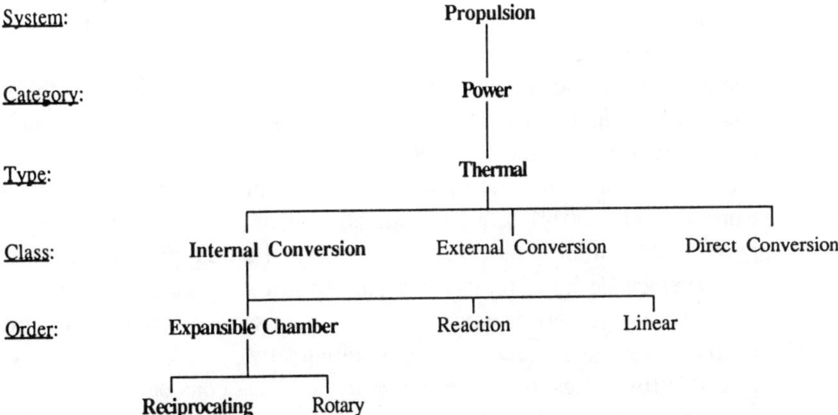

Figure 5: A hierarchical analysis of propulsion from order *(reciprocating expansible chamber), to* class *(internal conversion), to* type *(thermal), to* category *(power), to* system *(propulsion).*

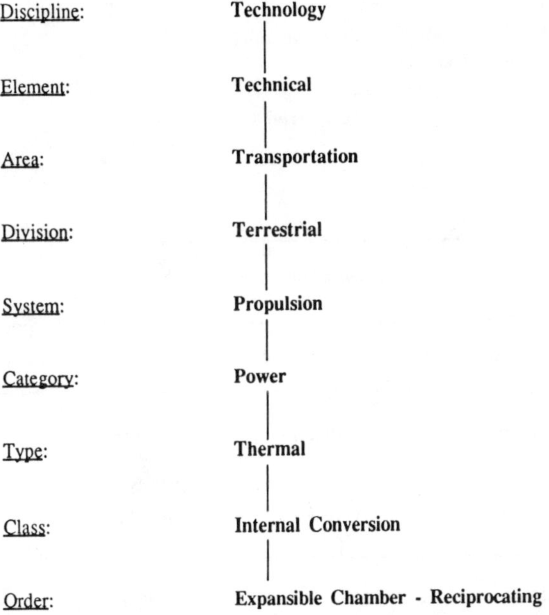

Figure 6: Hierarchical structure of terrestrial propulsion system for transportation focusing on the technical elements in the discipline of technology.

Similar classifications can be determined for the systems *control* and *guidance* as illustrated in Figures 7 and 8. *Control*, as it relates to transportation, involves a static or dynamic situation and utilizes some force to change, alter or regulate the velocity, direction or attitude of a vehicle within a given environment. For instance, a tube-type vehicle, which has one degree of freedom (moves in one direction in one plane only), can be controlled in terms of velocity by altering pressure (type of control) through pneumatic means (class of control) by actuating, arresting or stabilizing directly, remotely or automatically (order of control). Or a vehicle designed for use in an atmospheric environment can be controlled directionally, aerodynamically, by means of surface alteration mechanically, either directly, remotely or automatically.

Whereas control relates to change, *guidance* involves consideration for stability which is concerned with following a prescribed path to fulfill a particular objective. Therefore, guidance is equated with information and interrelates with control by providing information for actuating, arresting, or regulating the velocity, direction or attitude of a vehicle within a given environment. Guidance systems can be categorized three ways, depending upon the type of transporta-

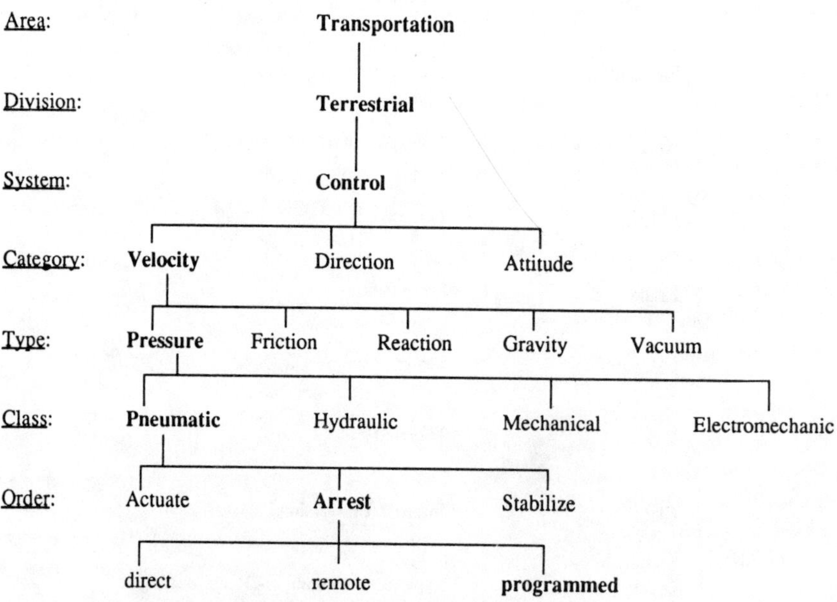

Figure 7: A heirarchical analysis of the system, control, from order *(programmed arrest), to* class *(pneumatics), to* type *(pressure), to* category *(velocity), to* system *(control).*

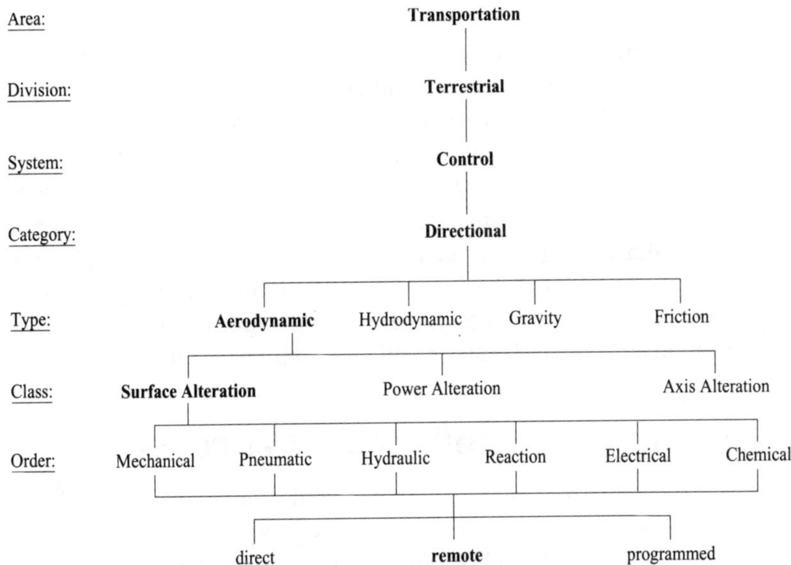

Figure 8: *A heirarchical analysis of the system, control, from* order *(remote hydraulic), to* class *(surface alteration), to* type *(aerodynamics), to* category *(direction), to* system *(control).*

tion device and the environment. These are expressed in degrees of freedom and describe the directional flexibility of a vehicle. The greater the degree of freedom, the more complex the guidance system. A tube-type vehicle has one degree of freedom and can move in one plane in one direction. An automobile has two degrees of freedom and can move in one plane in two directions. A submarine, space vehicle or airplane can move in two planes and in three directions.

Guidance systems are some form of human-machine configuration which relates to a class which describes a guidance function. The order describes the means of sensing, transmitting, displaying or storing information. It is then possible to analyze a guidance system for an automobile as involving the order (optical or acoustical), of the class (sensing), of the type (human to machine), of the category (two degrees of freedom). Each of the elements in the classification hierarchy can be further subdivided into those sub-elements already known, to accommodate new elements or predict probable future elements.

Similar analyses can be made of the *suspension* and *support systems. Suspension* concerns the question of the means of suspending a vehicle in or on a given environment and would consist of categories such as: airfoil, hydrofoil, surface effect, wheels, lubricant, magnetic, and gravity. The *support system* would consist of categories related to life support, operations support, legal support, economic support, and maintenance support.

It should be noted that not only do specific interrelations exist within and between the several systems of transportation but also in a number of specific ways between transportation and communication systems and certain other sub-disciplines in the science of technology. Knowledge development in communication aids directly the development, improvement and understanding of guidance systems. Information theory in the field of communications, such as computers, provides a base for the development of fully automatic transportation systems. Geography, meteorology and astronomy provide knowledge and information about the several transportation environments so vital to the solution of problems related to vehicular design, including propulsion, structure, guidance, control, suspension and support systems.

Concepts and Intellectual Processes

Closely related to the identification of the discipline and knowledge base is the need to identify the concepts, principles, processes and functional inter and intrarelations of the discipline. The processes of a discipline have a distinct function in the teaching-learning situation, inasmuch as they identify what the practitioners of a discipline actually do intellectually as they pursue their discipline.

Parallel and essential to the development of the content base, which identifies the structure of the discipline and the areas of human creative technical endeavor, is the identification of the intellectual processes of the discipline; the modes of thinking, performing and ways of securing, evaluating and using data and information to accumulate knowledge in the advance of the discipline.

Combining a knowledge of the true nature of the discipline, gained through efforts in taxonometric analysis of the content and processes of the discipline, with a knowledge and understanding of proven practices related to the learner, should provide for a combination of content and teaching methodology evidencing a realistic and relevant whole rather than a false dichotomy. The emphasis would be on the *modes of inquiry and ways of thinking in the discipline* which would provide a base for continual learning and adapting to change.

Transportation Systems and the Technological Enterprise

Transportation systems are critical to the proper functioning of any technological enterprise. In the transformation of raw materials to finished products the transportation of raw materials to processing industries begins the essential first step. Various forms of transportation devices are utilized. These include conveyors, trucks, rail cars, pipe lines and specially designed ships. Similar forms of transport are used to move component parts from specialized manufacturing plants to final assembly plants. Manufacturing is particularly dependent on efficient transportation, particularly in operations that have adopted the "just-in-time" mode of manufacturing.

Finally, special forms of transportation are used to move the final product to consumer or consumers.

Communication systems are dependent in various ways on specialized and efficient transportation. On-site video of major news or sporting events is served by all forms of transportation from specially equipped trucks to helicopters. Video tapes, compact disks and film are transported by bicycle, motorcycle, truck, and airplanes often on highly time-sensitive schedules that provide guaranteed one-day service.

Thus, there is an interdependence among the systems of technology. Each system serves the other in some special way.

Research Agendas in Transportation

The Research Environment

Responses to the question of what research about transportation is of most worth tend to vary with changes in the political climate of the nation. These changes alter the focus and direction of the research. Changes in research direction or emphasis are oftentimes detrimental to the attainment of long-term quality solutions required to meet true transportation needs. The unique aspect of the adaptive systems of transportation is that they are of such an order of magnitude that research and development issues related to transportation are in the public realm rather than private. Yet, it is private individual actions that collectively bring about problems requiring research and development in transportation.

Examples of research in the field of transportation linked to individual collective action include: (1) land use and transportation resulting from increasing use of terrestrial means of transportation, (2) pollution in all forms resulting from the manufacture, use and maintenance of transportation vehicles, (3) transportation accidents of all forms and their resulting costs, (4) transportation of hazardous cargo, and (5) energy use and the resulting balance of payment problems faced by many countries.

These and other problems form the base for establishing a research agenda related to a national transportation policy. Basic research is needed to address policy issues related to (1) efficiency and performance of transportation vehicles and systems, (2) economic growth and competitiveness, (3) mobility and accessibility, (4) safety and security, and (5) environmental preservation and energy efficiency.

Research Agendas in Transportation Education

The primary task facing technology education with respect to research agendas is to determine research directions that have meaning and worth for the evolution and development of programs for the study of technology. This should be done not only by practitioners in the field but by practitioners in concert with professionals in the field of transportation. The research record to date is very limited. The research by the technology education community has been done mostly as a requirement for doctoral and masters degrees. This research is seldom continued or built upon. Reviewers of research in technology education have not attempted to evaluate the value of the research in relation to problems in the technological enterprise in general or in relation to teaching/learning issues in technology education. There seems to be no agreed upon research agendas, central themes or critical problems. Nor does there seem to be an on-going identifiable network of researchers pursuing research on specific topics. Perhaps this is because of the general focus of research within the education community. The focus has been on education, schooling, methodology, and the practice of teaching rather than on the discipline content, structure, principles and concepts of technology.

As a result, with few exceptions, the potential of technology education has been greatly limited. The critical research questions related to technology are not being researched. The primary questions that provide a focus and context for the identification of a research agenda for technology education and for the purpose of this discussion, transportation technology, are:

1. *What* to teach and *why*?
2. *Who* to teach it to and *why*?
3. *When* to teach it and *why*?
4. *Where* to teach it and *why*?
5. *How* to teach it and *why*?

For the most part the first four questions are ignored. This may be because the practitioners of the field have generally agreed on the answer to the question, "What learning is of most worth?" Yet, there are few discussions that probe this question in any serious way. In previous sections of this chapter the question was addressed.

This question, "What learning is of most worth?", with respect to technology and specifically transportation education as part of basic or liberal education, is highly relevant and significant. The reason for this is that not only are we on the threshold of transitioning to another technological era brought about by energy and environmental issues which affect directly transportation, but there has been an on-going attempt by technology education to transition and meet the challenges of a continually evolving technological society. The content and context change continually. However, there are some constants, some basic questions from which to formulate a research agenda.

What should all citizens *know about* technical means? What should they be *able to do*? Obviously every citizen cannot know all there is to know about technology or transportation technology. Therefore, the *search must be for the structure of the displine; the central themes, systems, concepts and principles that provide insight into the behavior of technological systems, not only technically but in relation to, and within social-cultural contexts.*

The definition of the discipline technology provides additional clues to research and scholarly activities.

> Technology is the science concerned with the study of the creation, utilization, and behavior of adaptive systems (tools, machines, materials, techniques, physical and biological processes and technical means) and the behavior of these elements and systems in relation to humans, their societies and the life giving and life-sustaining environment.

Studies concerning the creation and evolution of technical means and systems, transportation systems for instance, would provide insight into the relation of these means and systems to human beings and society, thus establishing data for the derivation of concepts and principles concerning their behavior.

Understanding how technical means are created would aid in improving our ability to design and create appropriate technical means for various critical problems associated with energy and environment problems in transportation.

Other research categories implied by the focus on technology as a discipline would be state-of-the-art studies of evolving technical means, and public policy studies concerning the adaption and use of new technical means.

If the discipline base is technology, then the research focus should reflect the central themes, activities and methods of the discipline, including the procedures, problems, objectives and the primary questions of the discipline.

These are the essential elements for addressing the task of establishing a research agenda for technology education and specifically transportation education. The rest is commentary.

REFERENCES

Ayres, Robert U. Technology: wealth of nations. Technological Forecasting and Social Change. 33, 189–201 (1988).

Devore, P. W. (ed). *Introduction to Transportation.* Worcester: Davis Publications, Inc. (1983).

___. Measuring technology literacy: Problems and issues. *Bulletin of Science, Technology & Society.* 6, 202–209 (1986).

___. Technology: An examen. *Journal of Industrial Teacher Education.* 25 No. 3 (1988).

___. *Technology: An Introduction.* Davis Publications, Worcester, MA (1980).

___. Transportation technology: the identification of content and method. *The Journal of Industrial Arts Education.* Vol. XXIX, No. 5. (March–April, 1970).

___. Science and technology: An analysis of meaning. *The Journal of Epsilon Pi Tau.* 13 (1), 2–9. (1987).

Drengson, A. R. *Shifting Paradigms: From Technocrat to Planetary Person.* Lightstar Press, Victoria, B.C. (1983).

Halfin, H. H. *Technology: A Process Approach.* West Virginia University Technology Education Program. Unpublished doctoral dissertation, Morgantown, WV (1973).

Harman, Willis W. The coming transformation. *Futurist* (1977, February).

Jonas, Hans. *The Imperative of Personality: In Search of an Ethic for a Technological Age.* Chicago: The University of Chicago Press (1984).

Schumacher, E. F. *A Guide for the Perplexed.* New York: Harper and Row, (1977).

Slaght, R. L. We can no longer separate the thinkers from the doers in liberal arts. *The Chronical of Higher Education* (1987, February 18).

U.S. Department of Transportation. *Moving America: New Directions, New Opportunities.* Washington, D.C.: U.S. Government Printing Office (1989).

CHAPTER 2

Transportation Technology Education: Rationale, Structure and Content

By Dr. Stanley A. Komacek
(Associate Professor at California University of Pennsylvania)

As a content organizer in technology education, transportation remains relatively undeveloped when compared with communication, construction, and manufacturing. Helsel and Jones (1986) said "of the four systems (Manufacturing, Construction, Transportation and Communication), transportation is probably the least understood and least accepted by teachers in terms of developing and implementing curriculum in their classrooms" (p. 193). The following introductory sections will address the lack of acceptance and understanding of transportation as a content organizer for technology education.

Lack of Acceptance

Evidence of the lack of acceptance can be found by reviewing the data reported since 1980 for the annual surveys conducted by Dugger and others. After his initial survey, which included a sample of 5259 industrial arts courses, Dugger reported finding only eight transportation courses. Those eight courses accounted for less than 2 percent of the total industrial arts offerings in the sample. In the most recent report of the continuing survey, Dugger, French, Peckham and Starkweather (1991) reported transportation course offerings accounting for 14.8 percent of the total; an increase of 740 percent over the 1980 data! However, the 14.8 percent figure for transportation still lags significantly behind communication and manufacturing technology (21.3 percent each) and substantially behind traditional industrial areas of general metals (26.1 percent), drafting (38.1 percent), and woodworking (38.8 percent).

Two additional examples of the lack of acceptance of transportation as a content organizer can be found by reviewing the *Industrial Teacher Education Directory* and the textbooks available for technology education. A quick review of the most recent edition of the *Industrial Teacher Education Directory* (Dennis, 1990–91) reveals only six faculty members, of the 2528 listed, who teach only transportation. Multiple assignments for an additional 18 faculty listed transportation with another course(s), usually energy and/or power. A review of available textbooks is also indicative of the lack of acceptance of transportation as a content organizer. A teacher wishing to implement a new course dedicated to the study of transportation technology need not search long for a textbook. There is only one technology education textbook on the market today devoted exclusively to transportation. There are less than a handful of other texts that cover transportation, energy, and power. By comparison, there are at least six dedicated manufacturing textbooks available today.

Lack of Understanding

The lack of understanding of transportation as a content organizer may stem from the long and somewhat confusing definition of transportation offered by the profession. In the *Jackson's Mill Industrial Arts Curriculum Theory* document, transportation was defined as

> a technical adaptive system designed by the people to efficiently utilize resources to obtain time and place utility and to attain and maintain direct physical contact and exchange among individuals and societal units through the movement of materials/goods and people (Snyder & Hales, 1981, p. 36).

Anyone who studies transportation knows what "obtain time and place utility" and "attain and maintain direct physical contact and exchange" mean. However, with less than 2 percent of the profession offering transportation courses at the time of the Jackson's Mill Symposium, a simpler definition may have lead to better understanding and more implementation.

Contrast the definition of transportation with the comparatively simple and easy-to-understand definition of communication technology offered in the same document: "a technical adaptive system designed by people to efficiently utilize resources to transfer information to extend human potential" (p. 26). It seems logical that the terms "transfer information" are less confusing than those used to define transportation. The increased implementation of communication courses, when compared to transportation, may be due in part to the difference in the simplicity of their definitions.

Complex definitions for transportation are not confined to technology education. Papacostas, in *Fundamentals of Transportation Engineering*, defined transportation as "consisting of the fixed facilities, the flow entities, and the control system that permits people and goods to overcome the friction of geographical space efficiently in order to participate in a timely manner in some desired activity" (1987, p. 1). The complexity of the definition forced Papacostas to provide additional definitions for fixed facilities (e.g., roads, tracks, harbors, airports, etc.), flow entities (e.g., vehicles, container units, railroad cars, etc.), and control systems (e.g., vehicular on-board speed and direction controls and off-board guidance and information systems). Papacostas also poked fun at the complexity of the definition when he suggested that "overcoming the friction of geographical space" was a very awkward way of saying "to move from point A to point B."

Lack of Identifiable Linkages

A final reason suggested for the delay in the development of transportation as a content organizer is the lack of readily identifiable linkages to more traditional industrial arts content organizers (Komacek, 1987). Industrial arts teachers faced with implementing a curriculum based on the study of technology seem to more readily perceive linkages between certain traditional content areas and the systems of technology other than transportation. For example, woodworking and metalworking teachers seem more at ease in converting their programs to manufacturing technology than power technology teachers do in converting to transportation. Partial evidence for this assumption can be found by reviewing the reports of the annual surveys conducted by Dugger et al (1991, 1980), mentioned earlier.

This chapter will attempt to provide teachers interested in understanding and accepting transportation as a content organizer with answers to three questions: (a) why teach transportation?, (b) what should be taught about transportation?, and (c) how should transportation be taught? Asking and answering these questions is a necessary step before the implementation of transportation technology education. The three components of a program of study are addressed with these questions, namely; the philosophy and rationale (why?), course content and curriculum (what?), and instructional activities and teaching strategies (how?).

Why Teach Transportation?

Teachers may be wondering why our students need to study technology, let alone transportation technology. One rationale for the study of technology was established by the International Technology Education Association (ITEA) in *Technology Education: Perspectives on Implementation*:

> the school prepares youths for the world in which they live . . . because the American culture is distinctly characterized as technological, it becomes the function of schools to give every student an insight and understanding of the technological nature of the culture (p. 25).

One basic characteristic of the technological nature of the American culture is transportation. As the U.S. Department of Transportation (US DOT) stated recently, "America is a Nation of prodigious travelers" (1990, p. 5–1). According to the most recent *National Transportation Statistics*, Americans logged about 3.5 trillion passenger miles, or about 11,000 miles of travel per person, in 1987 (US DOT, 1989b). (A passenger mile is one person transported one mile.) Table 1 provides a breakdown of that mileage by mode. (Data for the marine environment is not available.)

On a larger scale, Coyle, Bardi, and Cavinato provided an overview of the impact of transportation on civilized societies:

> Transportation is one of the tools required by civilized [people] to bring order out of chaos. It reaches into every phase and facet of our existence. Viewed in historical, economic, environmental, social, and political terms, it is unquestionably the most important industry in the world. Without transportation, you cannot operate a grocery store or win a war. The more complex life becomes, the more indispensable are the elements of transportation systems (1986, p. 4).

Life in our technological society is very complex. According to Ward (1983), "modern society cannot exist without transportation. . . . It produces neither the food that it requires for survival nor the raw materials that it consumes" (p. 4).

The sections that follow will present information that may be helpful in answering the question "why teach transportation?" Several topics will be discussed, including how transportation changed time and distance perceptions, the economic impact of transportation, the relationship between transportation and energy use, and the biological impacts of transportation on human safety and the natural environment. Also, additional reasons for studying transportation technology, derived from various education philosophies and rationales, will be discussed.

MODES		MILEAGE *
HIGHWAY		
Automobile		2,318,065
Bus		95,000
	TOTAL	2,413,965
AIR		
Commercial		329,215
General Aviation		12,100
	TOTAL	341,315
URBAN PUBLIC TRANSPORT		
Motor Bus		16,833
Commuter Rail		18,142
Trolley		223
Demand Response		72
Ferryboat		177
	TOTAL	35,447
RAIL		
Amtrak		5,361
Other		6,819
	TOTAL	12,180
WATER		NA

** Millions of passenger-miles.*

Table 1: A breakdown of the total U.S. domestic travel miles in 1987 by mode (adapted from U.S. DOT, 1990).

Time and Distance Perceptions

According to DeVore (1983), "increases in speed of travel and increased capacity to move goods economically and efficiently have brought about changes in . . . the time, space and distance realities of people" (p. xix). Consider the time taken for journeys across the United States and the Atlantic Ocean throughout history (see Figure 1). Today, we become anxious when delayed at the airport or stuck in a traffic jam for an hour or two. Less than a lifetime ago, such short delays were not even considered a nuisance. Increasingly sophisticated transportation technologies have altered our perceptions of the distances we can travel and the time we should take to get there. Both time and distance are shortened by transportation. Today, we take for granted a one or two hour airplane trip for business or vacation travel. Only a few short decades ago such a trip would have taken days to complete.

Travel Times Across the United States

YEAR	VEHICLE	TRAVEL TIME
1850	Conestoga Wagon	166 days
1860	Stage Coach	60 days
1870	Steam Locomotive Train	11 days
1923	Early Prop Airplane	26-1/2 hours
1938	DC-3 Prop Airplane	17-1/2 hours
1968	Boeing 707	5 hours
1976	SST Concorde	2 hours
1981	NASA Space Shuttle	9 minutes

Travel Times Across the Atlantic Ocean*

YEAR	VEHICLE	TRAVEL TIME
1001	Viking Longboat	Several months
1620	The "Mayflower"	66 days
1853	Clipper "Dreadnought"	16 days
1909	Steam Ship "Mauretania"	4 days, 10 hours
1936	Airship "Hindenburg"	52 hours
1939	Boeing Prop Clipper	27 hours, 35 min.
1968	Boeing 707	6 hours, 40 min.
1976	SST Concorde	3 hours, 20 min.

**Adapted from Taylor, W. R., (1970)*

Figure 1: Travel times across the United States and the Atlantic Ocean throughout history.

Economic Impact of Transportation

Tomorrow's citizens (today's students) should understand the critical role that transportation plays in shaping the economic future of our society. In economic terms alone, transportation is worthy of study. Nearly all economic activities use transportation directly or indirectly. The US DOT described the relationship between transportation and the economy as "synergistic" when it said, "economic activity generates transportation demand and transportation helps the economy grow" (1990, p. 2–1). Transportation services provide the foundation of our national economy. According to the US DOT, "the food we eat, the clothes we wear, the medicines we take, the books we read, nearly all the essentials of modern life, are delivered over the transportation system" (1990, p. 2–1).

An indication of the importance of transportation to our economy, and to individual citizens, can be found by reviewing the following economic statistics:

1. The transportation system in the United States handles nearly 3.5 trillion passenger miles per year. With those miles come the high costs of owning, operating and/or purchasing the services of various transportation systems. Nearly one of every five dollars spent on goods and services in our economy, approximately 20 percent of America's gross national product, is for transportation products and services. The US DOT estimates annual spending on transportation products and services in the United States at nearly $800 billion (US DOT, 1989a). Table 2, shown on page 40, lists some of America's transportation assets.

2. Household spending on transportation exceeds all other categories, except housing. Americans spend nearly 19 percent of their annual household budget on transportation. In 1987, families with average incomes spent $4500 on transportation products and services (US DOT, 1990).

3. Transportation and transportation-related businesses employ roughly 10 percent (about 10 million in 1988) of the workers in our nation, (US DOT, 1989b).

4. Approximately 15 percent of our federal tax revenues come from transportation (Ward, 1983).

5. Transportation costs account for approximately 30 percent to 75 percent of the final cost of manufactured products (Sule, 1988). In 1987, the United States transported over 3.5 trillion ton-miles (one ton moved one mile) of freight, or about 11,000 ton-miles per citizen (US DOT, 1989b).

LAND TRANSPORTATION	
	2,200,000 miles of paved highways
	1,700,000 miles of unpaved roads
	150,000 miles of railroad track
	140,000,000 automobiles
	40,000,000 trucks
	1,300,000 rail freight cars
	20,000 locomotives
	2,000 rail passenger cars
	20,000 intercity buses
	80,000 local transit service buses
	10,000 subway cars, trolleys, other transit cars
	1,100,000 miles of natural gas pipeline
	205,000 miles of oil pipeline
	Tens of millions of bicycles
MARINE TRANSPORTATION	
	26,000 miles of commercial navigable inland waterways
	40,000 commercial marine vessels
	16,000,000 recreational boats
AIR TRANSPORTATION	
	5,300 airline aircraft
	220,000 general aviation aircraft
	5,700 public airports

Table 2: Some of America's transportation assets (adapted from U.S. DOT, 1989a).

Energy and Transportation

The relationship between transportation and energy use has been well documented in recent years (American Petroleum Institute, 1988; Davis, Shonka, Anderson-Batiste, & Hu, 1989; Greene, Sperling, & McNutt, 1988; U.S. Department of Energy, 1987, 1989; US DOT, 1989a, 1989b, 1990). The future of transportation and worldwide crude oil reserves are closely related. Each reference just listed focused extensively on the importance of petroleum fuels. The various sectors of transportation in the United States are almost totally dependent on petroleum fuels. They account for over 60 percent of all petroleum use (US DOT, 1990). Highway vehicles (automobiles, motorcycles, trucks, and buses) are the dominate petroleum fuel users, consuming over 73 percent of the total used in 1988. Of the other modes, air transportation is the largest and fastest growing sector, consuming nearly 9 percent (Davis, et al, 1989).

The energy problems of the mid-1970's have created a belief that there is a shortage of petroleum reserves. However, according to the US DOT, the energy problem in the 1990's will not be one of running out of energy, but a problem of dependence on imported petroleum. According to US DOT (1990) figures, estimates of proven reserves of crude oil worldwide increased nearly 37 percent between 1977 and 1987. Between 1986 and 1988 the estimates have increased 200 billion barrels, to between 803 and 890 billion barrels. Most of the increases have been in Middle East reserves. While worldwide reserve estimates increased 37 percent in the 10 year period just mentioned, Middle East oil reserves increased 54 percent giving the OPEC member countries hold over 75 percent of the world's proven petroleum reserves. During the same period, proven reserves in the United States declined 15 percent (US DOT, 1990). The U. S. Department of Energy (1987) outlined the problems associated with continued dependence on imported oil, including the negative impact of further increases in fuel costs on the American economy.

Improved Energy Efficiency

Improved energy efficiency is one area pursued in recent years to reduce our dependence on imported petroleum fuels. When gasoline prices increased from 95 cents per gallon (in 1989 dollars) in 1973 to $1.78 in 1981, the transportation sector responded by doubling vehicle energy efficiency from 14 to 28 miles per gallon (Greene, et al, 1988). A combination of various improvements, such as electronic engine control, fuel injection, improved aerodynamics, and reduced vehicle weight, lead to the improvements in miles per gallon without sacrificing performance or passenger comfort. The US DOT (1990) summarized the recent energy efficiency improvements:

> Today's cars have equal interior volume, faster acceleration, and twice the fuel economy of 1974 models. Cars in 1988 averaged 15 percent more horsepower per pound and the fastest acceleration times ever. Between 1975 and 1988, new car [miles per gallon] improved 80 percent, from 15.8 to 28.4 [miles per gallon] (pp. 3-9).

Alternative Fuels

There are hopes that alternative fuels will significantly reduce our dependence on imported petroleum. Four alternative transportation fuels currently being studied for possible large-scale use in the United States are methanol, ethanol, compressed natural gas, and electricity stored in batteries. Other alternative fuel possibilities that are considered to "have problems of technical, economic, and[/or] environmental acceptability" include synthetic fuels from coal and shale, hydrogen, and solar technology (US DOT, 1990, pp. 3–13).

For alternative fuels to be effective, alternative fuel vehicles will be needed. The Alternative Motor Fuels Act of 1988 provides incentives for automobile manufacturers to research and develop alternative fuel vehicles. Manufacturers who produce and sell dual fuel or flexible fuel vehicles will receive up to 1.2 miles per gallon credit in the calculation of corporate average fuel economy (CAFE). According to the US DOT (1990), companies who produce and sell "dedicated alternative fuel vehicles" would receive "unlimited CAFE benefits" (pp. 3–13).

In real terms, the promise of alternative fuels is nothing more than a promise, at this time. There are significant costs associated with their development and

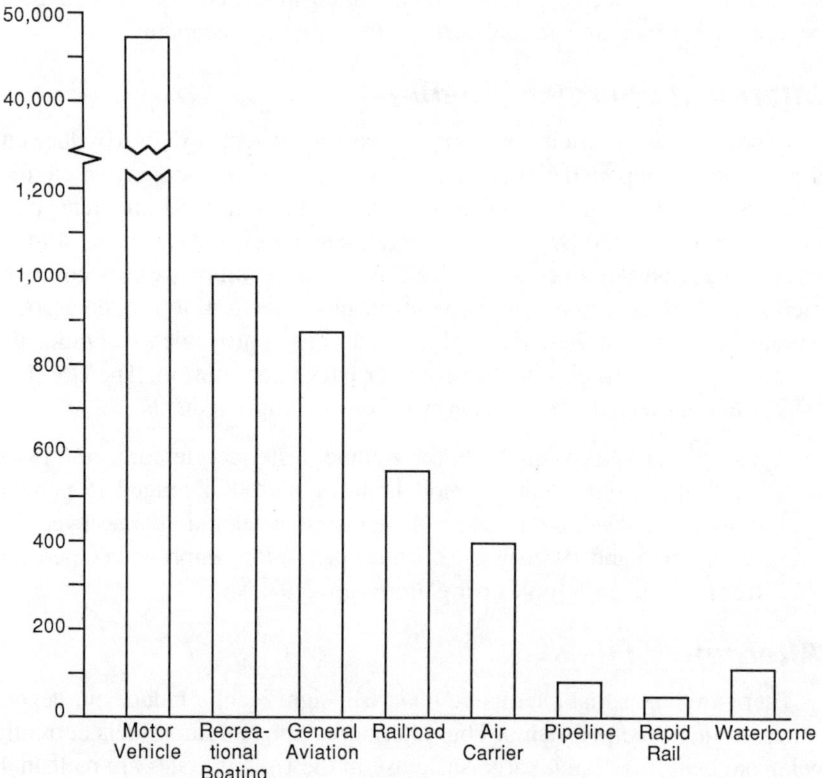

Figure 2: U.S. Transportation fatalities by mode, 1988. (Adapted from US DOT, 1990)

implementation: "the development and investment costs of the new fuels, new engines and vehicles, and new distribution systems could total in the tens of billions" (US DOT, 1990, pp. 3–14).

Transportation Safety

The risk of injury or death in a transportation accident is low. The US DOT (1990) reports the least safe mode of transportation in use today provides passengers with a 99.99 percent probability of completing their trip without an accident. However, the number of accidents and resulting injuries and fatalities is staggering, and unacceptable. Statistics for 1988 show 20.6 million transportation accidents and 49,850 fatalities (US DOT, 1989c). Motor vehicle accidents caused the overwhelming majority of the fatalities (47,093). Fatalities attributable to the other modes of transportation are minor in comparison, Figure 2. The US DOT (1990) suggests one factor that may contribute to reducing the number of transportation accidents and fatalities is changing social attitudes through education.

Environmental Pollution

Transportation is a leading cause of environmental pollution. One important form of environmental pollution due to transportation is air pollution caused by motor vehicle exhaust gases.

Air Pollution

Transportation is a major contributor to air pollution. Four key air pollutants attributable to transportation are carbon monoxide (CO), carbon dioxide (CO_2), nitrogen oxides (NO_x), and hydrocarbons (HC). The following statistics and information from the US DOT and other sources describe the problems, and some improvements, related to each of these pollutants.

Carbon Monoxide. Transportation contributes 70 percent of the carbon monoxide (CO) in the atmosphere. CO is a colorless, tasteless, and odorless gas released into the atmosphere as a product of incomplete combustion, including the combustion of fossil fuels by transportation vehicles. In the human body, CO mixes with hemoglobin, the red-blood cell compounds that carry oxygen. CO has an affinity for hemoglobin 200 times that of oxygen. Nonsmokers normally have a 5 percent concentration of CO in their blood, smokers have less than 10

% of CO CONCENTRATION	SYMPTOMS
<20%	headache, slight shortness of breath
20%–40%	dizziness, impaired judgement, nausea
40%–60%	hallucinations, collapse, possible coma
>60%	usually leads to death

Table 3: Symptoms of CO (carbon monoxide) poisoning at various levels of concentrations.

percent. When CO concentrations reach certain levels, various degrees of CO poisoning occur. Table 3 summarizes CO poisoning symptoms in humans at various concentrations.

In 1970, the average motor vehicle emitted 85 grams of CO per mile. Improvements in emissions control technology reduced that figure to 25 grams per mile in 1988. This decrease occurred despite a 24 percent increase in vehicle travel during the sample period.

Carbon Dioxide. Transportation contributes almost 25 percent of the emissions of carbon dioxide (CO_2), a by-product of burning fossil fuels. CO_2 is a major contributor to the greenhouse effect. The greenhouse effect occurs when solar energy passes through the atmosphere relatively freely and gases in the atmosphere, such as CO_2, methane, and chlorofluorocarbons (CFC's), block heat radiating from the earth. Concentrations of CO_2 in the atmosphere increased from 315 parts per million (ppm) in 1958 to 350 ppm in 1988. CO_2 emissions can only be decreased by reducing fossil fuel use, improving fuel efficiency, or increasing use of alternative fuels.

Nitrogen Oxides. Approximately 50 percent of nitrogen oxide (NO_x) pollution is attributable to transportation. According to estimates by the Environmental Protection Agency, NO_x emissions have been reduced by 15 percent since the 1970's.

NO_x is one contributor to acid rain, a pollution-related phenomenon that affects trees, agricultural crops, and aquatic organisms. In the atmosphere, NO_x mixes with water vapor to form nitric acid. When rain or another form of precipitation falls to earth, it may have a pH of less than 4. (The pH scale ranges from 0 to 14, with lower numbers having greater acidity.) Highly acidic water is toxic to many aquatic organisms and causes a reduction in growth and defoliation of trees and other types of vegetation.

NO_x also contributes to smog. A series of complex petrochemical reactions that involve NO_x, sulfur oxide, oxygen, hydrocarbons and sunlight create smog.

Smog appears as a light brown coloration in the air, which can reduce visibility. It also leads to plant damage, eye irritations, and chest irritations accompanied by cough.

Ozone is a component of smog. This is not the solar ultraviolet radiation-blocking ozone being depleted from the stratosphere by CFC's, but the ozone that is the most irritant gas known. Ozone concentrations as low as 0.12 ppm can cause respiratory problems in healthy people. Concentrations at this level are commonly exceeded in cities where a high density of motor vehicles and meteorologic conditions that produce stagnant air combine to create smog.

Hydrocarbons. Thirty-three (33) percent of the hydrocarbons (HC) in the atmosphere are attributable to transportation. Unburned or partially burned fuels due to insufficient oxygen during the combustion process produce hydrocarbon emissions. As mentioned previously, hydrocarbons are part of the petrochemical reactions that lead to smog.

Hydrocarbon emissions have been reduced by 36 percent since the 1970's. Technologies that improve the efficiency of the combustion process (e.g., air injection reactors (AIR), exhaust gas recirculators (EGR), fuel injection, leaner air-to-fuel mixtures, and higher compression ratios) contributed to these reductions.

Other Forms of Environmental Pollution

Air pollution caused by motor vehicle emissions is not the only form of environmental pollution attributable to transportation. Other important forms include: (a) water pollution due to oil spills caused by tanker accidents, (b) noise pollution around airports and highway systems, (c) air and ground pollution due to spills of hazardous materials transported by truck or rail, (d) air pollution from CFC's used in air conditioning units and the production of certain interior and electronic components for vehicles, and (e) water pollution caused by marine vessel-generated garbage. Transportation technology education can help young people analyze the environmental impacts of transportation and understand the delicate balance between nature and technology.

Other Reasons to Teach Transportation

Additional answers to the question "why teach transportation?" can be found in the education literature. Four examples will be reviewed here; the idea that transportation is a basic technology, the integration of technological systems, the importance of participatory democracy, and the technology/mathematics/science interface.

Transportation is Basic

In 1970, DeVore identified the purpose for including transportation as part of technology education:

> An historical analysis indicates that the three major determiners of technology, throughout the history of [humankind], have been: (1) the area of production, . . . (2) the area of transportation, and (3) the area of communication (p. 20).

All societies are technological, to some degree. DeVore recognized that the "basic" technologies found in all societies include production, communication, *and* transportation. The *Jackson's Mill Industrial Arts Curriculum Theory Document* (Snyder & Hales, 1981) expanded on DeVore's idea of basic technologies while describing production in terms of construction and manufacturing:

> Each of these systems [communication, construction, manufacturing, and transportation] has been in existence at some level of development throughout the history of civilization. Each has a central theme, is universal in all societies, has unique questions and problems, and contributes in some way to the survival and potential of human beings (p. 3).

Studying the behavior of each basic technological system helps students gain insight and understanding of the technological nature of any society.

Systems Integration

The hypothesis proposed by DeVore and the Jackson's Mill Symposium participants that all technological societies have communication, production (construction and manufacturing), and transportation technologies suggests the study of the integration and interdependence of these systems. Impacts between transportation and the other basic technologies are common.

Transportation impacts on production by improving resource utility and providing expanded economic markets. Before the development of sophisticated transportation systems, resource utilization and economic markets were localized. Today resources and goods can be shipped anywhere in a matter of hours or days. Fresh fruits and vegetables produced in California or Florida are available year-round in local grocery stores across the United States. Lumber and other building products produced hundreds of miles away are also available just down the street. In southwestern Pennsylvania, battered steel producers are surviving possible economic collapse by shipping their product to foreign markets. Also, Pennsylvania coal hauled to Maryland and Canada helps generate electricity there. Transportation technologies make possible this resource utility, which aids in economic survival.

The integration between transportation and communication is less obvious at first, but several examples do exist. We are all familiar with the impact of the railroad on the development of the western United States. What role did this play in the development of telecommunication? Without the westward expansion, innovations in telegraphy and telephony may have been delayed. Transportation also made possible the implementation of cables for the first trans-Atlantic telephone conversations. Today, satellites make telecommunication by cable obsolete. Finally, satellites would never get off the ground without sophisticated transportation technologies. Communication systems, from the pony express to worldwide satellite services, are dependent upon transportation.

Transportation made developments possible in other technologies. Consider the following medical and military technologies: organ transplant surgery, mobile emergency medical teams, intercontinental ballistic missiles, and the proposed star wars technology; all are dependent upon transportation.

Participatory Democracy

Maley provided another justification for the study of technology, namely; the need for informed citizens who can participate in our democratic society:

> the purpose of any education . . . must be linked or integrally tied with the functions of the citizen in this democratic society, since a democracy depends upon an informed citizenry. The role of technology, as well as the obvious need for technological "fixes" to societal problems, in the future will demand levels of technological understanding greater than ever before if the citizenry are to share in the decision-making process (1985, p. 5).

The need for decision-making in our society related to transportation exists today. Should the government continue the space exploration program, increase the speed limit to 65 miles per hour, impose national automobile safety belt laws, or fund the high-speed Orient Express? On a local level, what should be done about the need for improved highways, our deteriorating bridges, or the shipping of hazardous materials through our towns and cities? For our students to participate in decisions related to similar problems, they must have a basic understanding of how transportation works and interacts with other technological systems, our societal institutions, and the natural environment.

Technology/Mathematics/Science Interface

As an area of study, transportation is rich with excellent opportunities for teachers to interface technology with mathematics and science. Physical science concepts, such as friction, lift, thrust, drag, gravity, velocity, acceleration, fluid flow, etc., are easily integrated with the study of moving vehicles. In addition, calculating miles per hour, kilometers per hour, fuel efficiencies, coefficients of lift and drag, and cargo payload-to-fuel consumption ratios are just a few of the math problems possible in transportation. Also, transportation teachers can reinforce general technology concepts, such as designing systems, making trade-offs, improving efficiency, and utilizing resources wisely, while providing students with opportunities to integrate the technological systems and participate in a range of activities from producing scale models to operating real-life systems.

Project 2061

A final piece of evidence of the importance placed on studying transportation by the education community comes from Project 2061 organized by the American Association for the Advancement of Science (AAAS). In the final report of Project 2061, entitled *Science for All Americans*, a call was made for scientific literacy, "which embraces science, mathematics, and technology" (AAAS, 1989, p. 3). One part of Project 2061 included a report from the technology panel. In the technology panel report, eleven technologies were identified, including transportation, which the panel "believed to be important for the graduating high school senior to know" (Johnson, 1989, p. 13).

Rouch (1989) provided a summary for why we should teach about transportation:

> Unless all people from every walk of life are informed about the role of transportation in their lives, wrong decisions will be made. There will continue to be inefficient use of our national resources, increased time expenditure for our transportation needs, and higher costs for transporting cargo and people to the desired destination. Therefore, transportation is an essential element of the public school curriculum and is a fundamental need for all students (p. 6).

Transportation Technology: What Should be Taught?

What should be taught in a course on transportation technology? To help answer this question, a review of the following will be conducted: the evolution of transportation curriculum, a taxonomy of transportation technology, the application of the universal systems model to transportation, and various transportation technology education curriculum guides.

The Evolution of Transportation Curriculum

Recently, Rouch (1989) conducted a review of the evolution of transportation curricula in technology education. He cited the following quote from Schubert (1985) as justification for a historical study of transportation curriculum:

> Educational innovators need to be able to use the successes and failures of the past to renew their own contributions. . . . To be ahistorical, devoid of perspective of one's past, is indefensible. If people have thought and worked in one's area of concern, one must take responsibility to learn about what has gone on before (p. 9).

The following brief review of the evolution of transportation curriculum, summarized from Rouch (1989), provides a valuable historical perspective.

Rouch traced the history of transportation curricula back to the *Ecole des Ponts et Chuassees* in 1747, a higher technical school in Paris where engineers trained in road and bridge building. Other significant steps in the evolution of transportation curriculum in technology education cited by Rouch included the following:

1. The 1926 curriculum of Janesville, Wisconsin Junior/ Senior High School, which included shop mechanics and auto mechanics classes.
2. *A Prospectus for Industrial Arts in Ohio* by Warner in 1934, which philosophically recommended the study of transportation as a content organizer because of its important role in economics and society. Unfortunately, according to Rouch, the transportation organizer never translated into practice and the continuation of auto mechanics in the public schools resulted.
3. *A Curriculum to Reflect Technology* by Warner in 1947, which continued to view transportation as a major content organizer because of its socio-economic importance.
4. The Oswego, New York transportation curriculum implementing in 1947 by Kleintjes, a student of Warner's. According to Rouch, the Oswego curriculum was the first teacher education program to use transportation as a content organizer.
5. Master's theses under the direction of Warner at The Ohio State University by Kleintjes in 1947, Tierney and Belton in 1949, and Aman in 1951, which focused on teaching transportation by producing vehicles (often models), studying the impacts of transportation on society, and analyzing transportation vehicle operations.

6. Olson's book, *Industrial Arts and Technology*, in 1963, which envisioned the study of transportation to "include both the manufacture of the equipment and the operation of the transportation systems" (Olson, 1963, p. 137).

7. The American Industry Project by Face and Flug at Wisconsin-Stout State University in the mid-1960's, which identified transportation as one of 13 major concepts students should study to understand American industry.

8. The Industrial Arts Curriculum Project (IACP) by Towers, Lux, and Ray in the mid-1960's at The Ohio State University, which Rouch characterized as a "major ideological setback . . . to the transportation organizer" (1989, p. 29). According to Rouch, the IACP curriculum viewed transportation "as just a support to industry and not significant to the point of including it as a major area of study" (p. 29).

9. A 1970 article by DeVore in the *Journal of Industrial Arts Education*, which supported the use of a taxonomic analysis of transportation systems.

10. Bender's 1973 chapter in a textbook edited by DeVore, which provided a comprehensive review of the taxonomy of transportation technology presented by DeVore in 1970.

11. A doctoral dissertation by Fales in 1975, which involved developing and testing an activity-based transportation course focusing on management and production concepts. According to Rouch, "Fale's work was an innovative shift from transportation curricula which was focused on the automobile and the other hardware of transportation systems" (p. 30).

12. Only five doctoral dissertations listed in the *Dissertation Abstracts International* that focused on the research and development of curricula for transportation technology education (Kleintjes, 1953; Allen, 1963; Bender, 1973; Fales, 1975; and Peterson, 1980). According to Rouch, this small number of dissertations is further evidence of the lack of acceptance of transportation.

13. The *Jackson's Mill Industrial Arts Curriculum Theory* document mentioned previously, which identified transportation, communication, construction, and manufacturing as major technical adaptive systems. The Jackson's Mill document followed Fale's lead by focusing on the productive and managerial aspects of transportation.

Theory-Practice Gap

Although the Jackson's Mill Symposium was to serve as a national consensus building effort, Rouch stated that "most states have adapted the theory to meet their particular philosophy" (p. 32). Colelli (1989) used the term "theory-practice gap" to describe the discrepancy between classroom practices of inservice teachers and contemporary curriculum theory in technology education. Rouch briefly described the curriculum structure in five states; Ohio, Minnesota, Illinois, Indiana, and Utah, as evidence of the theory-practice gap in transportation curricula. He found the Ohio curriculum model uses energy/power as a major content organizer, while Minnesota and Illinois have separate curriculum guides for transportation and energy/power. Indiana and Utah combine transportation and energy/power into one content organizer.

Studies of the status of the field provide further evidence of the theory-practice gap in transportation. In 1962-63 Schmitt and Pelley (1966) surveyed 18,882 schools with industrial arts programs. They identified just over 3.9 million students enrolled in industrial arts courses in grades 7 through 12. Only 3,091 male students, less than one-tenth of one percent of the 3.9 million, were enrolled in the 152 transportation courses they found. Content descriptions for the 152 transportation courses revealed an emphasis on, among other things, power mechanics (44.7%), electricity/electronics (30.9%), metalworking (19.8%), and drafting (1.4%), which suggests a theory-practice gap within many of the transportation courses.

The surveys conducted by Dugger and others (1980, 1991) mentioned earlier, described a very slow increase in transportation course offerings. The 1980 report found transportation accounted for less than 2 percent of the total industrial arts course offerings. In 1991 the figure jumped to 14.8 percent, which still lagged significantly behind the number of course offerings in other technology systems and traditional content areas.

A Taxonomy of Transportation

A taxonomy is a means of classifying the knowledge and content in a particular field of study into basic components and illustrating the relationships among those components. There are many ways the knowledge and content in transportation can be classified or organized. Papacostas (1987) said, "transportation systems can be categorized in several ways . . . they may be classified according to the types of technology they employ, according to the function or type of service they provide, according to who owns or is responsible for their implementation and operation, and so forth" (p. 4). The classification system used in this chapter follows the taxonomy first presented by DeVore (1970).

Technology education focuses on the technical, societal, and biological components of various technologies. Although DeVore first proposed a taxonomy of transportation technology in 1970, the societal and biological components of the taxonomy are not well developed. On the other hand, the technical component is well developed and was revised and presented by Bender (1983), Colelli (1989), Komacek (1988), Snyder and Hales (1981), and Wright and Sterry (1983), among others. A simplified version of the taxonomy appears in Figure 3.

A taxonomy is not a course outline or curriculum guide, but a classification of the field. Also, a taxonomy is an arbitrary classification system that follows certain criteria or rules established by the person who developed the taxonomy. The taxonomy presented here may differ from those presented by others because of individual preferences, but the purpose is the same; to provide a logical, organized way to view the basic components of the field of transportation technology for the purposes of selecting content and developing curricula. With a taxonomy teachers can begin to identify logical content and concepts for a course in transportation technology. On the taxonomy there are three levels of classification: environmental mediums, modes, and universal concepts. DeVore provided an in-depth analysis of certain parts of the taxonomy in Chapter 1. In this chapter, an overview of the entire taxonomy, and its use in selecting course content, will be provided.

Environmental Mediums

On the first level of classification are the environments in which transportation takes place: terrestrial, marine, atmospheric, and space. In each environment there are two divisions of transportation systems. Land-based (terrestrial) systems are either vehicular (a vehicle that moves, such as a bicycle or automobile) or stationary (a fixed structure on which, or in which, people or freight are transported, such as pipelines or conveyor belts). Water-based (marine) systems travel on inland waters (rivers and lakes) or oceanic waters (seas and open oceans). Air-based (atmospheric) systems are lighter-than-air (hot air or gas-filled balloons) or heavier-than-air (fixed or rotary wing aircraft). Space-based systems are unstaffed (no people aboard) or staffed (people aboard). Obviously, there are vastly different design considerations and performance characteristics for each environment and subdivision.

Modes

The second level of the taxonomy identifies the modes, or types of systems found in each environment. There are two basic categories of modes: freight

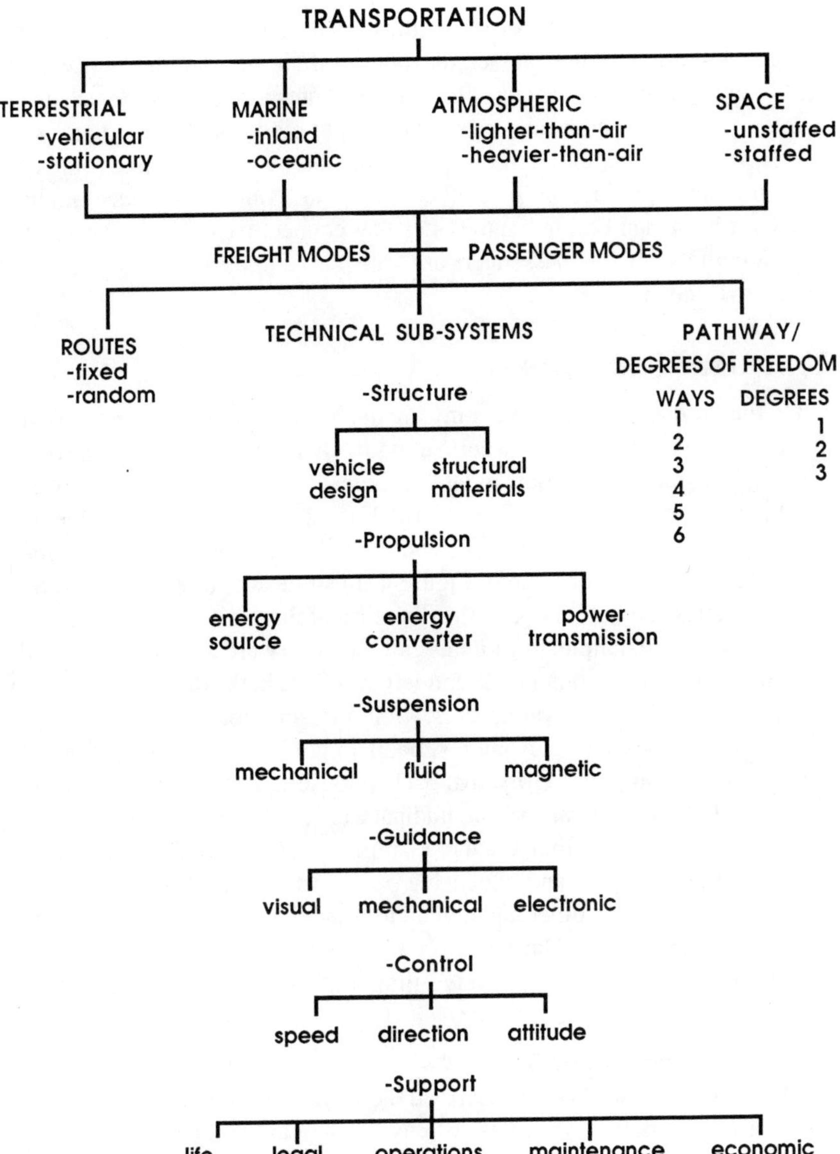

Figure 3: A taxonomy of transportation.

and passenger. Passenger modes are those that carry people, e.g., bicycles, motorcycles, automobiles, passenger trains and airlines, and the space shuttle. Freight is a generic term used for all other transported objects, such as resources, materials, goods, and products. Freight modes include, among other things, liquids in pipelines, granular materials in bucket conveyors, subassemblies on a production line belt conveyor, and finished products shipped to market in trucks. Following the lines that connect the environments to the modes, both freight and passengers are transported in the land, water, air, and space environments.

Universal Concepts

On the third level of the taxonomy are the basic operational characteristics that can be studied in any environment with any mode. These include routes, pathways/degrees of freedom, and the technical subsystems. Routes are either fixed (rigid and inflexible, i.e., escalators) or random (free and flexible, i.e., motorboats). Pathways/degrees of freedom deals with the axes of movement possible for a vehicle or system. Figure 4 illustrates the three axes of movement. Vehicles can only move in the direction of these axes in a limited number of ways. For example, most boats can travel forward and backward in the direction of the longitudinal axis, and left and right in the direction of the lateral axis. Boats do not travel up or down in the direction of the vertical axis. Based on these possible movements, boats might be categorized as vehicles that can travel four ways (forward, backward, left, and right) and have two degrees of freedom (lateral and longitudinal axes). Vehicles that travel only one or two ways, (e.g., elevators, escalators, pipelines, railed vehicles) usually require the most complex and expensive pathways, but have the simplest onboard controls. On the other hand, vehicles that travel five or six ways, (e.g., helicopters, submarines, Harrier jump jet) usually require the most complex on-board control systems, but have the simplest pathways (usually open airspace or water).

Technical Subsystems. The final set of universal concepts are the technical subsystems, or as DeVore described them "the systems fundamental to all types of transportation regardless of environmental area, culture or level of sophistication" (1970, p. 20). There are six technical subsystems in any transportation vehicle; structure, propulsion, suspension, guidance, control, and support.

Again, a boat can be used as an example to describe these constant technical subsystems. The *structure* is the framework and outer shell that make up the body of the boat. The *propulsion* system includes the energy source (fuel), energy converter (internal combustion engine), and power transmission (prop).

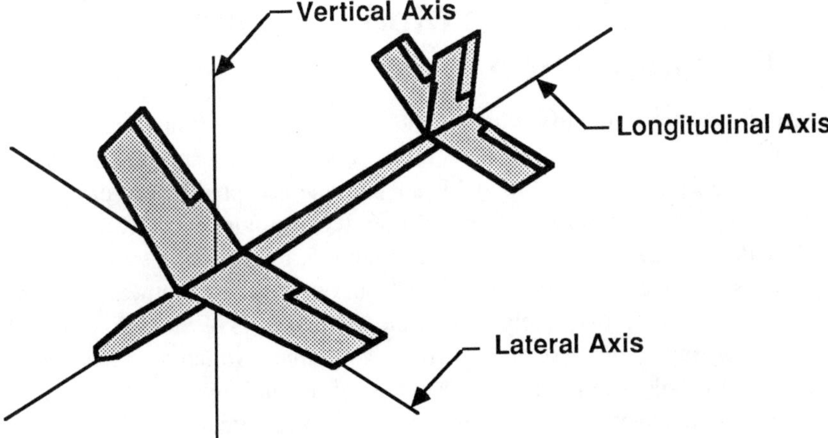

Figure 4: Three axes of movement (degrees of freedom).

Water is the fluid *suspension* medium for a boat. Suspension is the technical system used to associate a vehicle with the environment in which it operates. Guidance systems provide information to the operator of a vehicle. Marine *guidance* systems include visual buoys, channel markers, and possibly electronic sonar equipment. On a boat, we can *control* the speed and direction of travel with the throttle and rudder. *Support* systems include life preservers, coast guard regulations, docking and fueling terminals, and the economic factors that come into play.

An understanding of the technical subsystems provides students with a powerful learning methodology. Any vehicle, from a tricycle to the space shuttle, can be studied and analyzed from the standpoint of its technical subsystems.

Using the Taxonomy for Content Selection

Using the taxonomy, teachers can begin to identify the important technical components for the study of transportation technology. A comprehensive transportation course would involve students in studying various modes in each environment. The universal concepts of routes, ways, degrees of freedom, and most importantly, the six common technical subsystems can be reviewed and related to each mode in each environment.

A well balanced transportation course would give each topic on the taxonomy fair and appropriate, if not equal, treatment and coverage. Such a balance eliminates the justification of power technology or energy/power/ transportation courses, which focus too heavily on only the propulsion aspects of transportation.

Universal Systems Model Applied to Transportation

Another way to identify what should be taught about transportation is to examine how the universal systems model applies to transportation systems (see Figure 5). The systems model is a technique accepted by our profession for helping young people understand how technologies work (Snyder and Hales, 1981; ITEA, 1985). Referring to Figure 5, the *goal* of a transportation system is to move freight or passengers from one place to another. The *criteria* is to make the move safely and efficiently, in terms of the time of travel, location of travel, and economic factors. The *inputs*, which are constant for all technological systems, are the resources of technology; sometimes called elements. The transportation *processes* relate to the technical subsystems identified earlier in the taxonomy. Notice that each process ends with an "ing," identifying them as action verbs. Humans control and manipulate the inputs (resources or elements) of technology using these processes to create transportation systems that will achieve the goal while meeting the criteria specified. Transportation *outputs* include moved freight and/or people and the resulting impacts. *Feedback* mechanisms provide the means of monitoring progress, comparing results with the goal and criteria, and making adjustments to the goal, criteria, inputs, and/or processes when necessary.

Teachers can use the systems model as a guide for the identification of course content. A review of state curriculum guides for transportation in the next section of this chapter will site several examples. Also, students can be taught to apply the systems model to various transportation systems to help them understand "how things work."

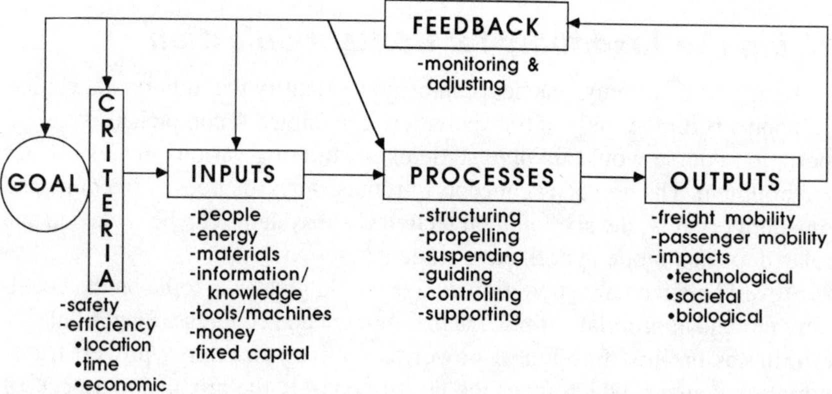

Figure 5: Universal systems model applied to transportation systems.

TRANSPORTATION PROCESSES	
PRODUCTIVE	**MANAGERIAL**
Receiving Holding/Storing Loading Transporting/Moving Unloading Delivering	Planning Organizing Directing Controlling

Table 4: Productive and managerial processes for transportation identified in the Jackson's Mill Industrial Arts Curriculum Theory *(Snyder & Hales, 1981).*

Productive and Managerial Processes

The Jackson's Mill document, as mentioned earlier, identified several productive and managerial processes for transportation (see Table 4). Transportation is a service technology that moves people and freight from one place to another, it does not "produce" in the same way that construction and manufacturing produce structures and products. It seems transportation was forced into the structure used at the Jackson's Mill Symposium to organize the other systems of technology. The productive processes of receiving, loading, etc., have not been well received by transportation curriculum writers. Several of the state curriculum guides reviewed later in this chapter do not even include these productive processes in their taxonomies or content outlines.

The transportation processes described earlier in this chapter with the universal systems model (i.e., propulsion, suspension, guidance, control, structure, and support), were identified in the Jackson's Mill document as subsystems to the productive process of transporting. Propulsion, structure, suspension, guidance, control, and support are universal concepts that can be found in any transportation system. Also, they seem to have more widespread acceptance than the productive processes of receiving, loading, etc. The review of transportation technology curriculum guides that follows will provide evidence for this assumption.

Impacts of Transportation

One key feature of technology education is a focus on the impacts that result from technological systems interacting with other systems of technology, societal institutions, and living things. As mentioned earlier, this area has not been well developed by curriculum designers in technology education. Some basic considerations are presented here as starting points for the derivation of

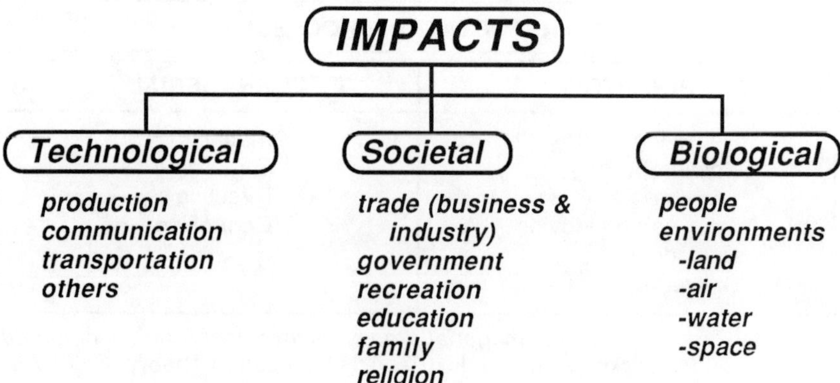

Figure 6: Three categories of technological impacts.

content related to the impacts of transportation. There are three categories of impacts: technological, societal, and biological (see Figure 6). Technological impacts are the "spin-offs" from one field of technology to another. For example, there have been hundreds of spin-offs from NASA's space transportation program to communication, manufacturing, construction, energy utilization, medicine, and military technologies.

Technology also impacts on the various institutions that comprise our society, namely: trade (including business and industry), government (local, national, and international), recreation (sports and the arts), education, family relationships, and religion. By the same token, our societal institutions impact on the development of technology by identifying needs and setting agendas for research and development activities. As an example, one purpose of technology education is to educate citizens who will direct government and trade for the development of responsible, appropriate technologies.

Biological impacts include the affects of technology on people and the air, water, plants and animals in each environment. Wet lands endangered by transportation development, traveling stress, the loss of human life in accidents, and the availability of donor organs for transplant surgery are just four examples of biological impacts from transportation technology. The environmental impacts discussed earlier in this chapter are other examples.

Although the impacts of technology are not well defined or classified there is a basic structure that can be used to generate discussion of the trade-offs associated with impacts (see Figure 7). The chart in Figure 7 can be used to discuss the relative worth of various technologies. As an example, where would you place the impacts of the automobile in Table 5 on the chart in Figure 7? Discussion topics more relevant to their life style, can easily be identified by students.

IMPACTS

	POSITIVE	NEGATIVE
EXPECTED		
UNEXPECTED		

Figure 7: Technological impacts analysis chart.

IMPACTS OF THE AUTOMOBILE	
air pollution	personalized transportation
traffic-related deaths	energy consumption
road and bridge maintenance with tax dollars	auto insurance
	auto maintenance costs
manufacturing of automobiles	traffic jams
roadside billboards	suburban development

Table 5: A partial list of impacts of the automobile.

Curriculum Guides for Transportation Technology

This section will review several dedicated transportation curriculum guides from various sources. The intent is not to recommend one method of organizing content or a curriculum guide from one state or agency, but to examine the relationship between the curriculum guides and the taxonomy of transportation and the universal systems model just described. Such a review will help provide further answers to the question "what should be taught about transportation?"

Industry and Technology Education

The *Industry and Technology Education* curriculum guide, funded by the Technical Foundation of America and directed by Wright and Sterry (1983), provided four transportation course outlines: (a) Transportation Systems, (b) Technical Elements of Transportation, (c) Planning and Designing Transportation Systems, and (d) Human and Product Transporting Systems. Included in the appendix was a taxonomy of transportation (Figure 8). The *Industry and Technology Education* guide was an attempt to provide curriculum that supported the philosophy developed at Jackson's Mill. Figure 8 shows the taxonomy organized by the basic elements of the universal systems model (inputs, processes, outputs), the environmental mediums (terrestrial, marine, atmospheric, and space), and the productive and managerial processes (called the acts of transporting and the acts of managing).

Illinois and Minnesota State Curriculum Guides

The Illinois *Transportation Technology Curriculum Guide* (Illinois State Board of Education, 1984) and the Minnesota *Transportation Technology* (Minnesota Department of Education, 1986) curriculum guide are very similar in structure and content. Figure 9 shows a taxonomy adapted from the Illinois guide. Notice how the modified systems model includes resources, technical

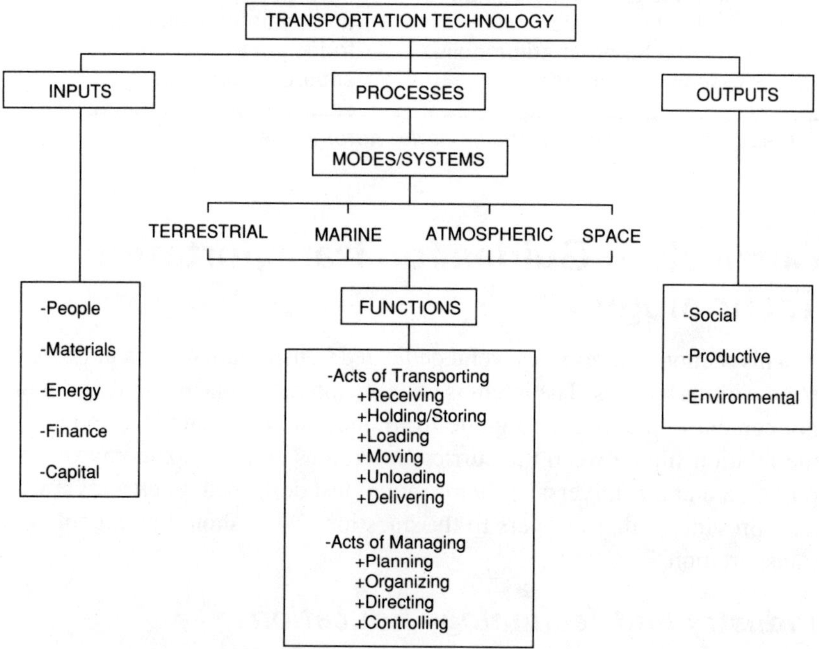

Figure 8: Taxonomy of transportation adapted from Industry and Technology Education *(Wright & Sterry, 1983).*

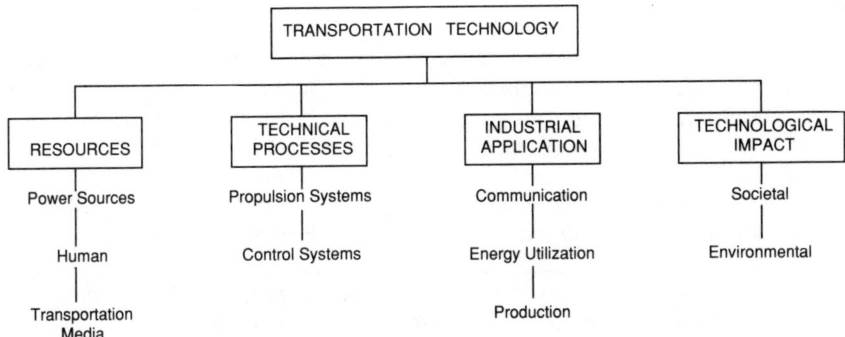

Figure 9: Taxonomy of transportation adapted from the Illinois state curriculum guide.

processes, industrial applications, and technological impacts. A further review shows the resources limited to power sources, humans, and transportation media (environments). The only technical processes listed are propulsion and control systems. The industrial application provides examples of integration between transportation and communication, energy utilization, and production. Societal and environmental are the two categories of technological impacts on the taxonomy.

The left column of Table 6 lists the units of instruction for the Illinois and Minnesota guides. In the right column are common elements found in units II through VI. The relationship between the taxonomy and the common elements in each unit provide an interesting example of revisiting universal concepts or themes.

Curriculum guides that have units of study organized around the environmental mediums and include common elements, such as modes, technical subsystems, and impacts include the following:

1. *Transportation Systems* from the New York State Education Department (Barrow & Jambro, 1987).
2. *Technical Elements of Transportation* (1988a) and *Transportation Systems* (1988b) from the North Carolina State Department of Public Instruction.
3. *Transportation Systems* from the Texas Education Agency (Hughes & Towler, 1983).
4. *Transportation* from the West Virginia Department of Education (Bolyard, 1986).

The guide from West Virginia provides precise detailing of the technical subsystems in each environmental medium that closely matches the taxonomy

UNITS OF INSTRUCTION	COMMON ELEMENTS
I. Introduction to Transportation	A. Types
II. Material Handling Conveyors	B. Propulsion System
III. Terrestrial Transportation	C. Control Systems
IV. Space Transportation	D. Applications/Uses
V. Atmospheric Transportation	E. Impacts
VI. Marine Transportation	F. Career Awareness

Table 6: Units of instruction and common elements in the Illinois and Minnesota state transportation curriculum guides.

presented in Figure 3. Also included in each unit is a review of important historical and possible future developments and extensive examples of enabling objectives and learning activities for students.

One unique curriculum is *Design and Evaluation of Transportation Systems* from the North Carolina State Department of Public Instruction (1988c). The content of the course addresses resources, technical subsystems, impacts, etc., organized around the following modules:

1. Analyzing Transportation Systems,
2. The Design and Evaluation Process,
3. Solving a Transportation Problem, and
4. Presenting Solutions.

The modules seem well suited for a research and development-type transportation course in upper high school grades.

This section did not provide "the" curriculum guide or content structure for transportation technology education. Instead, several good models were reviewed to help the reader answer the question "what should be taught about transportation?" The question "how should transportation be taught?" is examined in the next section.

How Should Transportation be Taught?

Much has been written about how technology education should be taught. The 37th yearbook of the Council on Technology Teacher Education, *Instructional Strategies for Technology Education* (Kemp & Schwaller, 1988), included chapters that described how the following approaches and delivery systems could be used in technology education:

1. Conceptual learning approach.
2. Interdisciplinary approach.
3. Social/cultural approach.
4. Problem solving approach.
5. Integrating the systems of technology approach.
6. Interpretation of industry approach.
7. Formal presentations and demonstrations.
8. Cooperative group interaction techniques.
9. Discovery, inquiry, and experimentation.
10. Games and simulations.

This chapter does not provide an extensive review of these strategies. Chapters that follow focus on teaching transportation technology education at the elementary, middle school, high school, and teacher education levels. Each chapter addresses instructional strategies and student learning activities. In this chapter, one relatively new model for technology teaching and learning, the technological method, will be reviewed and applied to transportation technology education.

The Technological Method

In the September/October, 1990 issue of *The Technology Teacher*, Savage and Sterry presented the technological method (Figure 10). While the model appears complex, the key element is right in the middle; technological processes. Savage and Sterry identified three components to technological processes; (a) analyzing, (b) realizing, and (c) testing. They defined analyzing as:

> the development of a design brief which describes what the solution to the problem should do and what constraints are being imposed to keep the process on track. It also includes the action of information gathering and the generation of alternative solutions (p. 10).

In simple terms, it seems that analyzing is designing or identifying and describing a problem and creating ideas for possible solutions. Realizing was defined as "those actions necessary to turn an idea into reality" (p. 11), or selecting the best solution and making a prototype. Finally, testing was defined as determining if the solution worked, which would include an element of evaluation.

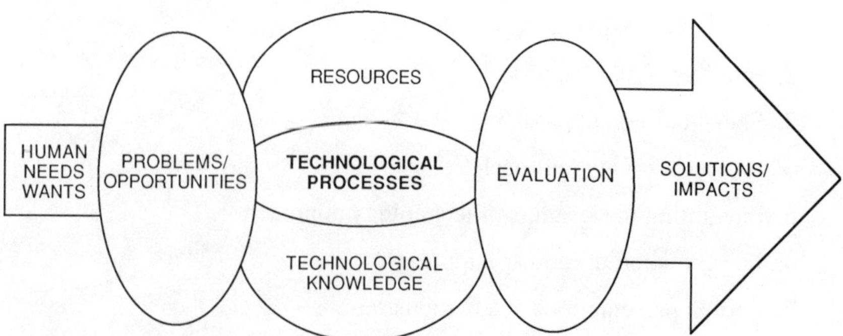

Figure 10: The technological method (Savage & Sterry, 1990).

Modified Technological Processes

Figure 11 presents a modified version of the technological processes component of the technological method. For the sake of simplicity, analyzing was changed to designing, while realizing was changed to producing. In the modified model, analyzing describes the evaluation component following testing. These modifications were made because of the problem described earlier related to a complex definition of transportation. Simple terms can be better, if for no other reason than ease of understanding, which may lead to easier acceptance.

The four processes (designing, producing, testing, and analyzing) seem to be at the heart of the answer to the question "how should transportation be taught (or studied)?". Probably, a comprehensive course in transportation technology education would involve students in designing, producing, testing, and analyzing transportation systems. As the model shows, students would be free to move among the four processes during learning activities.

However, every student learning activity may not include each technological process. At various times throughout the course, one or more of the technological processes may be emphasized to facilitate the attainment of specific concepts. For example, Car Builder(c), a popular low-cost simulation software program, used by some transportation technology teachers involves students in designing an automobile on computer, testing the aerodynamic and

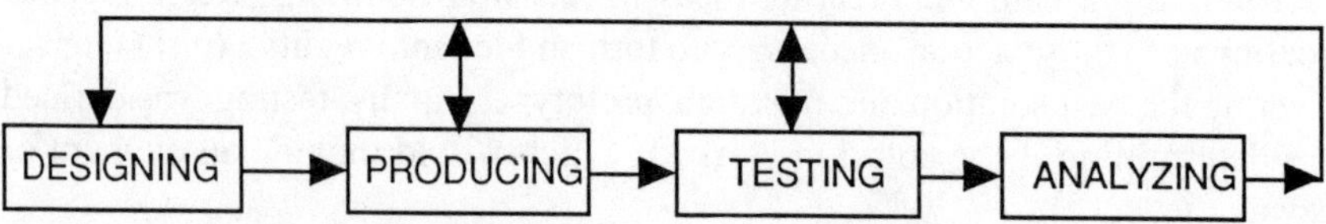

Figure 11: Modified version of technological processes.

track performance on computer, and analyzing the results. Often, students do not produce three dimensional prototypes of the vehicles they design. The main objectives of the activity are to help students understand the concepts of computer-aided drawing, design, and engineering, computer modeling and simulation, and the transportation technical subsystems of propulsion, structure, suspension, and control.

The modified model of technological processes could be applied to other technological systems. Also, it seems logical that an answer to the question of "what is technological literacy?" would include a description of competence in designing, producing, testing, and analyzing various technological systems.

Summary

Transportation is an important part of our technological society and integrally linked to our production and communication systems. Decisions made regarding transportation have long term impacts on people, society, and the environment. This chapter identified just a few points for teachers to consider when they ask the question, "why teach transportation?" as a part of technology education.

This chapter also focused on "what should be taught about transportation?" in technology education. The evolution of transportation curricula, a taxonomy of transportation, the universal systems model (including impacts), and various transportation technology education curriculum guides were reviewed to help teachers identify basic content, concepts, and principles of transportation systems.

The real question for inservice teachers is "how should transportation be taught?" Appropriate hands-on instructional activities are necessary for acceptance by students, parents, and administrators. Four technological processes; designing, producing, testing, and analyzing, were presented as a model for how technology education (including transportation) might be taught and studied. Other chapters in this yearbook focus on how transportation technology education might be taught at various grade levels.

REFERENCES

Allen, W. A. (1963). A study of present practices and trends in industrial arts teacher education undergraduate laboratory courses in transportation, power, and power mechanics, (Doctoral dissertation, Indiana University, 1963). *Dissertation Abstracts International. 24*, 3216A.

American Academy for the Advancement of Science. (1989). *Project 2061: Science for All Americans*. Washington, DC: American Academy for the Advancement of Science.

American Petroleum Institute. (1988). *Energy security white paper: U.S. decision and global trends*. Washington, DC: American Petroleum Institute.

Barrow, T., & Jambro, D. (1987). *Technology education transportation systems: Grades 9–12 systems block course*. Albany, NY: The University of the State of New York, The State Education Department, Division of Occupational Programs.

Bender, M. (1973). Alternative energy systems for the automobile: Implications for content derivation for teaching transportation technology, (Doctoral dissertation, West Virginia University, 1973). *Dissertation Abstracts International. 34*, 3940A.

Bender, M. (1983). Transportation systems: Environmental and technical. In DeVore, P. W. (Ed.). *Introduction to transportation*. (pp 23–50). Worcester, MA: Davis Publications.

Bolyard, G. (1986). *West Virginia industrial arts/technology education curriculum: Transportation*. Charleston, WV: Bureau of Vocational, Technical, and Adult Education.

Colelli, L. A. (1989). *Technology education: A primer*. Reston, VA: International Technology Education Association.

Coyle, J. J., Bardi, E. J., & Cavinato, J. L. (1986). *Transportation*. St. Paul, MN: West Publishing Company.

Davis, S. C., Shonka, D. B., Anderson-Batiste, G. J., & Hu, P. S. (1989). *Transportation energy data book*. Oak Ridge, TN: Oak Ridge National Laboratory.

Dennis, E. A. (Ed.). (1990–91). *Industrial teacher education directory*. South Holland, IL: Goodheart-Willcox Co., Inc.

DeVore, P. W. (Ed.) (1983). *Introduction to transportation*. Worcester, MA: Davis Publications.

DeVore, P. W. (1970). Transportation technology: The identification of content and method. *The Journal of Industrial Arts Education. 29*(6), 18–22.

Dugger, W. E. (1980). *Standards for industrial arts education programs project.* (Department of Health, Education, and Welfare-funded project). Virginia Polytechnic Institute and State University.

Dugger, W. E., French, B. J., Peckham, S., & Starkweather, K. N. (1991). Sixth annual survey of the field shows changes and challenges. *School Shop/Tech Directions. 50*(7), 21–23.

Fales, J. F. (1975). Development and pilot test of a curriculum for transportation in Louisiana. (Doctoral dissertation, Texas A&M University). *Dissertation Abstracts International. 36*, 2686A.

Greene, D. L., Sperling, D., & McNutt, B. (1988). Transportation energy to the year 2000. In Transportation Research Board. *A look ahead: Year 2020.* Washington, DC: Transportation Research Board.

Helsel, L. D., & Jones, R. E. (1986). Undergraduate technology education: The technical sequence. In Jones, R. E., & Wright, J. R., (Eds). *Implementing technology education: 35th Yearbook of the American Council on Industrial Arts Teacher Education.* (pp 171–200). Encino, CA: Glencoe Publishing Co.

Hughes, L. R., & Towler, A. L. (1983). *Transportation systems.* Austin, TX: Center for Occupational Curriculum Development, Division of Continuing Education, The University of Texas at Austin.

Illinois State Board of Education. (1984). *Transportation technology curriculum guide: A guide for developing contemporary transportation technology curricula for 9th–10th grade industrial education programs.* Springfield, IL: Illinois State Board of Education; Bureau of Adult, Vocational, and Technical Education.

International Technology Education Association. (1985). *Technology education: A perspective on implementation.* Reston, VA: ITEA.

Johnson, J. R. (1989). *Technology: Report of the Project 2061 phase I technology panel.* Washington, DC: American Association for the Advancement of Science.

Kemp, W. H., & Schwaller, A. E. (Eds.). (1988). *Instructional strategies for technology education: 37th yearbook of the Council on Technology Teacher Education.* Mission Hills, CA: Glencoe Publishing Co.

Kleintjes, P. L. (1953). Industrial arts transportation: The evaluation, selection and organization of activities, problems and information on the secondary level, unpublished doctoral dissertation, Pennsylvania State College.

Komacek, S. A. (1987). Consider transportation technology! *TEAP Journal. 35* (4), 5–9.

Komacek, S. A. (1988). Transportation technology education: What should be taught? *TEAP Journal. 36*(1), 19–22.

Maley, D. (1985). Keynote address: Issues and trends in technology education. In Andre, N. & Lucy, J. (Eds.). *Proceedings of technology education symposium VII: Technology education: Issues and trends.* (pp. 3–14). California, PA: California University of PA.

Minnesota Department of Education. (1986). *Transportation technology.* White Bear Lake, MN: Minnesota Curriculum Services Center.

North Carolina State Department of Public Instruction. (1988a). *Technical elements in transportation, Grades 11–12, Technology education course guide.* Raleigh, NC: North Carolina State Department of Public Instruction, Division of Vocational Education.

North Carolina State Department of Public Instruction. (1988b). *Transportation systems, Grades 9–10, Technology education course guide.* Raleigh, NC: North Carolina State Department of Public Instruction, Division of Vocational Education.

North Carolina State Department of Public Instruction. (1988c). *Design and evaluation of transportation systems, Grades 11–12, Technology education course guide.* Raleigh, NC: North Carolina State Department of Public Instruction, Division of Vocational Education.

Olson, D. (1963). *Industrial arts and technology.* New Jersey: Prentice-Hall.

Papacostas, C. S. (1987). *Fundamentals of transportation engineering.* Englewood Cliffs, NJ: Prentice-Hall, Inc.

Peterson, R. E. (1980). The identification of key technical concepts germane to the study of transportation technology during the future years 1980–2000, (Doctoral dissertation, West Virginia University, 1979). *Dissertation Abstracts International. 40*, 4449A.

Rouch, D. L. (1989). The rating of curricular learning outcomes by a select group of transportation professionals for transportation technology teacher education, unpublished doctoral dissertation, The Ohio State University.

Savage, E., & Sterry, L. (1990). A conceptual framework for technology education. *The Technology Teacher. 50*(1), 6–11.

Schmitt, M. & Pelley, A. (1966). *Report on nature of programs, teachers, and students in industrial arts.* (Department of Health, Education, and Welfare-funded project). Washington, DC: Department of Education.

Snyder, J. F. & Hales, J. A. (Eds.) (1981). *Jackson's Mill industrial arts curriculum theory.* Charleston, WV: West Virginia Department of Education.

Sule, D. R. (1988). *Manufacturing facilities, location, planning, and design.* New York: McGraw-Hill Book Co.

Taylor, J. W. (1987). *The lore of flight.* New York: Crescent Books.

U.S. Department of Energy. (1987). *Energy security: A report to the President of the United States.* Washington, DC: U.S. Department of Energy.

U.S. Department of Energy. (1988). *Assessment of costs and benefits of flexible and alternative fuel use in the U.S. transportation sector.* Washington, DC: U.S. Department of Energy.

U.S. Department of Energy. (1989). *Annual energy review 1988.* Washington, DC: U.S. Government Printing Office.

U.S. Department of Transportation. (1989a). *Moving America: New directions, new opportunities.* Washington, DC: U.S. Government Printing Office.

U.S. Department of Transportation. (1989b). *National Transportation Statistics.* Washington, DC: U.S. Government Printing Office.

U.S. Department of Transportation. (1989c). *Transportation safety information report, 1988 annual summary.* Washington, DC: U.S. Government Printing Office.

U.S. Department of Transportation. (1990). *National transportation strategic planning study.* Washington, DC: U.S. Government Printing Office.

Ward, R. E. (1983). Societal impacts of transportation. In DeVore, P. W. (Ed.). *Introduction to transportation.* (pp. 1–21). Worcester, MA: Davis Publications.

Warner, W. E. (1934). *A prospectus for industrial arts in Ohio.* Columbus, OH: State Department of Education and Ohio Education Association.

Wright, T. & Sterry, L. (Eds). (1983). *Industry and technology education: A guide for curriculum designers, implementors, and teachers.* Lansing, IL: Technical Foundation of America.

CHAPTER 3

Transportation Technology, Present Development

By Dr. Anthony E. Schwaller
(Professor and Chairperson at St. Cloud State University)

Introduction

Need for Studying Technical Aspects of Transportation

The study of transportation technology is very broad. As part of this study, various technical and technological aspects are important. Understanding the concepts, developments, state-of-the-art technology, provides the opportunity to observe the total picture of transportation technology. Understanding the technical and technological aspects of transportation technology helps to correctly view transportation, its related industries, career areas, integrativeness with other technologies, and complexity.

Technological Direction and Goals for Transportation Industries

Within the transportation industry many changes are constantly taking place within technology. Various influences cause these changes to take place. Some influences include economic, political, social, and environmental concerns by our society. During the past 15 years technological development and innovation has occurred to make all transportation vehicles:

- more *economically* attractive
- more *environmentally* sound
- *safer* for passengers in route

- more economically *fuel* efficient
- more *comfortable* for passengers

The two most important changes in the past few years have been that of increasing fuel economy as well as to make transportation vehicles more environmentally efficient. For example, in terms of the environment, manufacturers have added various pollution control devices during the 1970's and, today, pollution is controlled rather effectively by on-board computers. In addition, computers have had a significant effect on improved fuel economy of almost all vehicles used to transport both people and goods throughout our society. Diesel vehicles, for example, have improved their fuel mileage significantly and reduced pollution by computerizing the fuel injection systems.

In the United States, people use transportation systems in different ways than in other countries. Essentially, we have a very wasteful system for transportation of goods and people throughout the country. For example, today we use the automobile for 80–83 percent of our transportation needs while the average miles per gallon per person (mpg times average number of people in vehicle) is between 20–35. We use bus transportation for 2–5% of our transportation needs, yet the bus gets more than 113 miles/gallon per person. Essentially this is because of our society's strong desire for convenience in daily life styles. This obviously increases the need for more oil.

Added to this is an increased use of recreational vehicles. Today, there are numerous vehicles used to make leisure activities more enjoyable. From boats and wave runners to four wheelers, our society constantly is increasing its demand for oil needed within the transportation sector of society. Because of these demands, the transportation industry is constantly trying to decrease fuel consumption by making propulsion systems more efficient and reducing vehicle weight. In addition, many programs and projects are designed to change our society's values to use more mass transportation systems rather than use inefficient vehicles.

State-of-the-Art Technology in Transportation Systems

Introduction

Technology is growing at a very rapid pace. Many scientists, engineers, and technologists suggest that technology is doubling every 4–5 years. This is also true in the area of transportation technology. Each day, new and innovative designs are being built and tested for feasibility. This section is about several state-of-the-art and future technologies in the area of transportation technology. This section also addresses how these technologies add to the goals of change in the industry and suggest some possible alternatives in transportation technology.

When studying transportation, certain changes have occurred in the past. These changes in all probability will continue to occur in the future. Some of the major changes for the future include:

- Reduction in Friction—All transportation technology will continue to change by reducing friction. Developments will include low friction bearings, lower coefficient of drag on vehicles, less internal friction in engines, etc. For example, a simple vortex design is being tested for cars and airplanes. Small vortex generators are being tested above the rear window of cars. The vortex has a tendency to keep the air flow over the car close to its surface. Small fins placed on the roof help to direct the air flow more efficiently. This will in turn, reduce the air drag from the vehicle, thus, improving fuel mileage.

- Improved Engine Efficiency—Engines used for propulsion systems will continue to become more efficient. Engines of the future will continue to be controlled by computers with more control and power. Engines will also use lighter materials so that better fuel mileage can be achieved. Eventually, it is predicted that engines will have efficiencies in the range of 50–70%. For companies, typical engines in the 1980's and 1990's were only 25–30% efficient.

- Lighter Materials—There are continuous developments in new synthetic and composite materials. Synthetic and composite means artificial and multiple materials mixed together to produce a certain structural characteristic. These materials will offer less weight, be stronger, have better thermal shielding and greater usability than those presently available. These materials will be applied to engines, bearings, structures, and other transportation vehicle parts. For example, tires designed by computers have been produced to reduce rolling resistance and producing better fuel mileage.

- Improved Computer Control—In all areas, the use of computer controls will continue to increase. Eventually, many of the human controls now used on transportation vehicles will be transferred to the computer.

- Suspension of vehicles will become more controlled by computers. The result will be to offer extremely comfortable and safer rides for passengers.

- Four wheel steering will become more developed for automobiles. This will improve control and movability of vehicles.
- Marine applications will continue to use improved propeller design. The propeller design will improve efficiency and performance.
- Wing shapes on airplanes will be developed to improve fuel efficiency and performance.
- Hull design on power, sailboats, and other marine transportation will be more efficient with less fractional losses. Today, hulls can be accurately designed by computers. In fact, a computer program generated the hull design for one type of sailboat used in the America's Cup. This computer program is able to apply stresses to check for stability in water.
- Active suspension system will be developed on vehicles. These systems, controlled by the on-board computer will keep the vehicle level throughout all operation.

Propulsion Technology

Electronic Controls. Most propulsion systems are now using computers to monitor and control the amount of fuel added to the air intake of the engine. Figure 1 shows an example of various inputs and outputs on a computer placed in a vehicle. Many variables change the air/fuel ratio. These are considered the inputs to the computer. The inputs to the computer and the variables that may cause the air/fuel ratio to change include engine rpm, engine temperature, load, air temperature, vehicle speed, volume of air into the engine, and exhaust oxygen. Based upon these variables, (identified as electronic signals), the computer controls both the ignition timing and the fuel injection, injecting the exact amount of fuel to each cylinder. Electronic fuel injection improves fuel economy at the same time reducing emissions.

Synthetic Engines. Today and in the future, engine parts and eventually the entire engine, will be made of synthetic materials. The object of using synthetic materials is to be able to increase the internal temperatures of the engine, at the same time reducing its weight. The higher the internal temperatures, the less need for a cooling system. This means that less heat will be lost and higher engine efficiency will result. Frictional horsepower losses will also lessen. Problems still arise concerning the ability of materials to resist warping and still maintain the needed strength.

Presently several manufacturers are designing synthetic engine parts. Eventually the entire engine will be made of synthetic materials. Another advantage

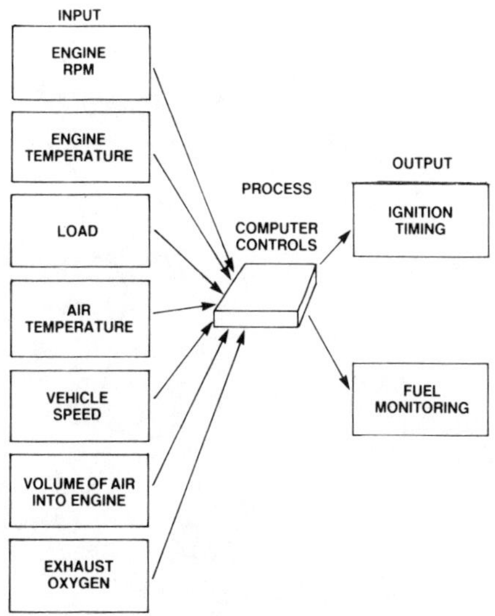

Figure 1: Electronic controls are used extensively in most propulsion systems today. This particular system shows a small computer utilizing various inputs to control both the ignition timing and fuel monitoring functions.

of using synthetic materials is that of weight. Lighter engines will be made with more horsepower and improved efficiency. Some experts suggest that the standard 30% engine efficiency could be raised as high as 60% using synthetic material.

Solar Powered Vehicles. One area that is receiving much attention is propulsion of a vehicle (automobiles, planes or boats) by solar power. Several manufacturers and universities have designed solar vehicles and solar airplanes in competitive contests. A great deal of applied research has come from these contests. Solar cells are being developed with greater efficiency. In addition, battery technology is constantly improving. With these two technologies forging forward, solar power vehicles may become a reality. A great deal of research must still be done on solar cells. In addition, friction of the vehicle must be held to a minimum. Some companies believe that in the future, many vehicles will be able to run efficiently and reliably on solar cells.

One of the big advantages of using a solar power vehicle is the reduction of pollution. If vehicles could be powered by solar cells, the amount of carbon monoxide, nitrogen oxides, and hydrocarbons would be greatly reduced. This could have a significant and positive impact on the environment within our society.

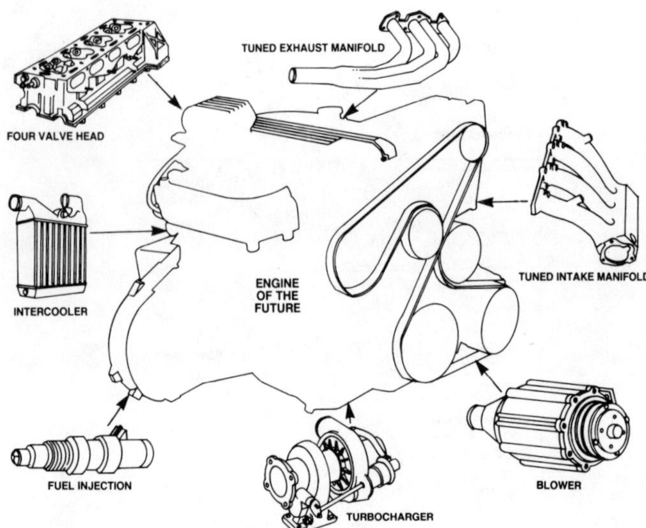

Figure 2: Today's propulsion systems utilize various components to improve its operation. These components are generally used to increase output power while manufacturing smaller engines.

Higher Performance Engines. Engines of the future will be using various components as standard equipment. The transportation manufacturers are designing small-displacement, high horsepower engines. Figure 2 shows some of these components which include:

- The use of turbochargers to extract the heat of the exhaust to turn a turbine. The turbocharger is one method used to supercharge an engine. The result is additional air forced into the engine.
- Blowers that are driven by belts are also used to supercharge an engine. Blowers increase the amount of air being sent into the engine. When more fuel is added, increased performance is the result. Note however, that a blower increases the amount of frictional horsepower produced in the engine.
- Intercoolers used to cool the input air after being compressed by a turbocharger or blower. When the air is cooled, the air becomes more dense. The result is that more air can be forced into the engine.
- Fuel injection controlled by computers. Fuel injection used in most cars today, will be improved. The computer will be able to inject more precise amounts based upon more computer signals so that accurate air/fuel ratios can be produced.

- Tuned intake manifolds used to improve air intake. In a tuned manifold, high frequency air pulses are set up by the opening and closing of the intake valves. By designing the pulses to occur at the right time, additional air can be forced into the cylinder.
- Four valve cylinder heads used to increase the ease at which air and fuel can enter the engine. Volumetric (eased air flow through the engine) efficiency is thus improved.
- Tuned exhaust manifolds used to increase exhaust scavenging. In tuned exhaust manifolds, the exhaust pulses from one cylinder empty into the manifold between the pulses of the other cylinders. This has a tendency to better clean the exhaust gases from the cylinder. Thus, more air can be added to the cylinder during intake.

Related Technological Concepts. To help understand Propulsion Technology many technological concepts are used. This section can be used as a guide to a selected number of concepts and definitions. Those included are by no means complete, but may act as a guide to further study.

Types of Air Pollution. The need to reduce pollution by transportation vehicles is certainly a national goal. There are several forms of pollution (among others), which are emitted during the combustion process in most transportation vehicles. These include:

- Carbon Monoxide (CO)
- Nitrogen Oxides (NO_x)
- Hydrocarbons (HC)

Carbon monoxide, a by-product of combustion, is considered a deadly poison gas that is colorless and odorless. When people inhale carbon monoxide in small quantities, it causes headaches and vision difficulties. In larger quantities, it causes sleepiness and in many cases, death.

Nitrogen oxides are formed by a chemical union of nitrogen molecules with one or more oxygen molecules. Nitrogen oxides form more freely under extremely high temperature conditions in combustion chambers. When combustion temperatures reach 2,200–2,500 degrees F, increased amounts of nitrogen oxides are produced. Oxides of nitrogen also contribute to the depletion of the ozone layer.

Hydrocarbons, also a by-product of combustion of fossil fuels, are also called organic materials. Hydrocarbons are primarily unburned portions of the fuel. Any fuel that is partially burned contains hydrocarbons. Most hydrocarbons are poisonous at concentrations above several hundred parts per million.

Although they are not dangerous by themselves, they are the main ingredient in the production of photochemical smog. Basically, when HC are mixed with No_x in the presence of sunlight, the result is called photochemical smog. It is the goal of all transportation industries to develop technologies that will in effect reduce these three emissions.

Combustion Theory. All vehicles used today have some sort of propulsion system. This is true in terrestrial, marine, atmospheric, and space transportation. Common systems included the reciprocating piston engine, rotary engine, or reaction engine. Except for electrical motors used for propulsion, most devices use one of these types of engines. All of these engines are designed to convert the chemical energy in fuel to mechanical energy for propulsion. To do this efficiently, combustion process of the fuel must be very exact.

a. Air/Fuel Ratio—Efficient combustion usually occurs when proper amount of air and fuel are ignited within the combustion chamber. The air/fuel ratio is defined at the ratio of air to fuel within the combustion chamber. The most efficient ratio has been defined at 14.7 parts of air to 1 part of fuel. This measurement is calculated by weight. When this occurs, there is the right amount of air molecules surrounding the fuel molecules for most efficient combustion. Generally, when more fuel is added to this ratio, it is considered a "rich" mixture. When more air is added to the ratio it is called a "lean" mixture.

This mixture is constantly changing. In an aircraft for example, as the craft goes faster and gets to higher altitude the volume of air per cubic foot changes. Thus the air/fuel ratio is altered. On-board computers are used to adjust the fuel to get the most optimal air fuel ratio at all speeds and altitude. The air/fuel ratio directly effects the pollution produced from the propulsion source. When the air/fuel mixture is too rich, both carbon monoxide and hydrocarbons are increasingly produced. Also, when a lean mixture is occurring in the combustion chamber, the internal combustion temperatures increase, thus, producing increasing amounts of nitrogen oxides. Figure 3 illustrates the relationship between air/fuel ratio, efficiency, and amounts of pollution.

b. Compression Ratio—In order to get the air and fuel mixed thoroughly, the mixture must be compressed. This is true on all propulsion systems that burn fossil fuels. The ratio at which air and fuel are compressed is called the compression ratio. It is primarily in reference to gasoline and diesel engines. Compression ratio is defined as the ratio of the volume in the cylinder above a piston at the bottom of its stroke as compared to the volume in the cylinder above the piston at its upper most stroke. Compression ratios normally range from 6–1 on small gasoline engines to as high as 25–1 on diesel engines depending upon the application and type of engine.

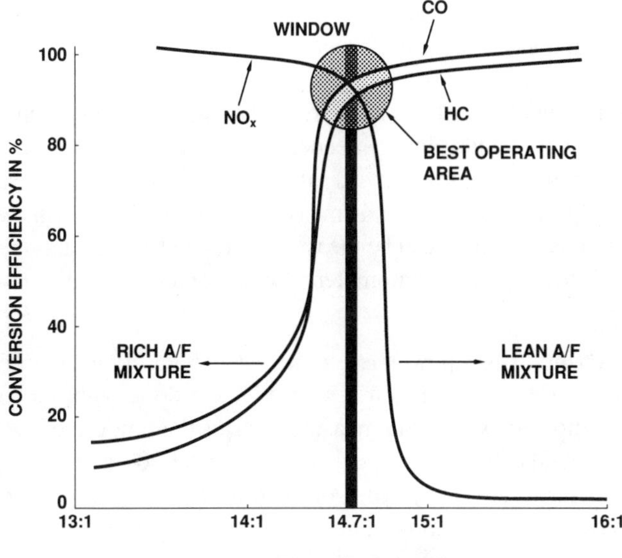

Figure 3: *Any combustion-type propulsion source needs to have an exact air-fuel ratio. The best mixture is exactly 14.7 to 1. Rich ratios produce increased amounts of CO and HC (low conversion efficiencies). Leaner ratios produce increased amounts of NO_x.*

Supercharging. When air and fuel enter any combustion chamber under normal atmospheric pressures it is said to be naturally aspirated. In certain propulsion systems, it is necessary to increase the volume of air and fuel inside the combustion chamber. For example, many diesel propulsion systems need increased amounts of air and fuel, especially if they are operated in mountainous or higher terrain conditions. This can be done by supercharging the engine. Supercharging an engine means to deliver a greater volume of air to the engine than being naturally aspirated. When more air is forced into the combustion chamber there must also be a corresponding increase in fuel in order to maintain the 14.7–1 air/fuel ratio. Supercharging can be done either with a blower or a turbocharger. A blower is a mechanical pump that forces more air into the engine. A turbocharger uses the energy of the exhaust gas to pump more air into the engine.

Torque. Torque is one way to measure work. Torque is defined as twisting force on a shaft. For example, a torque wrench produces a twisting force, measured in ft. lbs. Torque is also produced on the output shaft of engines because of the combustion of fuel. Combustion of gases push internal pistons downward or turn turbine blades. This causes a crankshaft or output shaft to rotate producing torque. This force causes objects to rotate. For example, torque is needed to turn transmissions and wheels, turn a boat prop, a propeller in an airplane, etc.

Torque is actually available at the rear of all propulsion systems. Torque is expressed in foot pounds (energy needed to move a certain number of pounds, one foot). For example, an engine is said to have 500 ft. lbs. of torque at a certain speed. Speed on all engines is measured in RPM. This term means *r*evolutions *p*er *m*inute. Torque can be measured directly from a rotating shaft. This is done with the use of dynamometers. Dynamometers are discussed later in this chapter.

Horsepower. Horsepower is a term used to describe the rate at which the output work of a propulsion system is being done within a certain time period. One horsepower is the measurement of the amount of work needed to lift 550 pounds, one foot, in one second, or 33,000 pounds, one foot, in one minute. There are many types of horsepower used in the transportation sector today. The most common include:

1. Brake horsepower-called BPH the actual horsepower measured at the rear of the engine under normal conditions.
2. Road horsepower—the horsepower available at the drive wheels of the vehicle.
3. Indicated horsepower—a theoretical horsepower calculated by the manufacturer, representing the maximum horsepower available from the engine under ideal conditions.
4. Frictional horsepower—the horsepower exerted to overcome internal and external friction and resistance on any vehicle. Examples include rolling resistance, bearing friction, wind resistance, gear resistance, etc. One goal of vehicle manufacturers is to reduce frictional horsepower as much as possible, thus improving fuel economy.

Thrust. Thrust is a term used to describe force in a certain direction. Specifically, thrust is defined as any force tending to produce a motion in a body or alter the motion of that body. Forward thrust is created by the motion of a jet of water being pushed backward, or the forward force on an airplane from the air and fuel energy provided by the engine. Thrust, called reaction can be produced from jet engines as well as rocket engines. Thrust is most often measured in pounds of thrust. For example, thrust generated during lift-off for the space shuttle is about 6,400,000 pounds.

Coefficient of Drag. A term that is commonly used today in reference to terrestrial vehicles is called coefficient of drag. The coefficient of drag is a number that manufacturers use to indicate the ease at which a vehicle cuts through the air. Automobiles, trucks, airplanes, etc., all have a certain coefficient of drag. The number is an indicator as to how much air a typical vehicle must move as the vehicle passes from one point to another. Normally, coefficient of drag numbers are determined in wind tunnels. Lower coefficient of drag numbers mean less frictional resistance and improved fuel mileage. Higher coefficient of drag numbers mean more resistance and poorer fuel mileage. Coefficient of drag numbers typically are in the range from .8 on the high end, to .2 on the low end depending upon the vehicles shape. Manufacturers are designing vehicles to have the lowest coefficient of drag so as to improve fuel economy as much as possible.

Suspension Technology

Magnetic Levitation. In the past few years a great deal of research has been developed to produce superconducting materials. Superconducting materials are those that produce little or no resistance to the flow of electricity. These advancements are leading the way to improved and highly efficient magnets.

These magnets can then be used to levitate or raise vehicles on a magnetic field. Instead of pounding along on tires or rails, the vehicle floats four inches above its guideway on a cushion of magnetism. This will make the vehicle much more efficient.

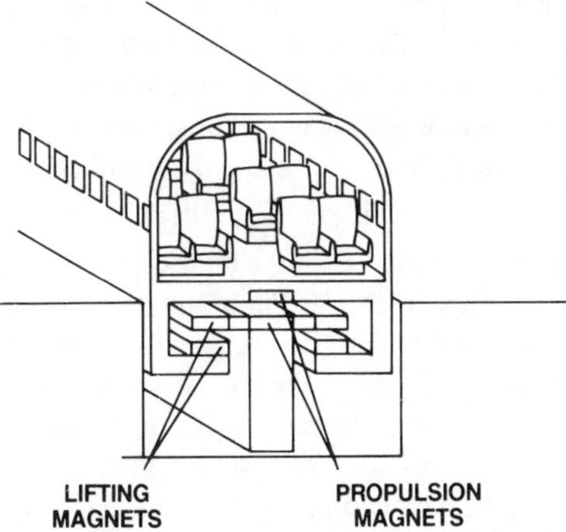

Figure 4: Magnetic levitation is becoming more and more a reality. This schematic shows how a vehicle could be lifted using magnetic levitation. In addition, magnetism is used to propel the vehicle.

One such system is shown in Figure 4. This system is designed for a train. There are a set of lifting magnets. These are used to raise the vehicle up on the magnetic cushion. The propulsion magnets are used to propel the vehicle forward. As the development of superconducting materials improves, magnetic levitation will certainly become popular.

Air-Cushion Vehicle. The air cushion vehicle (ACV) is also being developed as a form of marine transportation mode. This craft maintains altitude just a few feet above the surface of the water. The craft uses large fans that blow downward through the hull. An air cushion is developed between the craft and the water. The vehicle is then propelled forward by stern mounted propellers. Air is drawn in through an intake and then compressed. It is then forced down both sides of the ship and directed inward under the hull. This creates a cushion of air that is able to lift the vehicle off the water. The cushion is maintained by a continuous airflow. In the past, several ACV have been used to ferry passengers across short bodies of water. Although these crafts have been tested and used, research needs to continue before ACV are used to any extent within our society.

Hydrofoils. Hydrofoils (a marine application) operate on much the same principle as the airplane. Hydrofoils have struts attached to the vessel on the outside of the hull. There are commonly two types used. These are the "surface piercing" and the "fully submerged" type. The surface piercing is primarily used on calm waters. The fully submerged is somewhat more stable and can handle rougher waters. These foils generate lift when water flows around them.

Using a hydrofoil eliminates a great deal of hull friction in the water. The result is that the hydrofoil can travel at up to 40 knots without the effect of waves on the craft. Typically hydrofoils can travel about 60%–70% faster than conventional crafts of similar size. There have been several companies that have developed and are now selling hydrofoils. Presently hydrofoils are used in European countries and the Soviet Union. The United States has several in use, however, more testing and research is still needed.

Hull Design. In recent years, shipping hulls especially those of oil tankers, have been improved. This is largely due to the increased need for oil in the world. Newly constructed tankers are built with a double hull to improve strength. This was done in light of the Exxon Valdez oil spill several years ago. In addition, because of the increased size of oil tankers and huge hulls, the single propeller now uses six blades so that the necessary thrust is delivered without overstressing metal in part of the blade. Today, most large ships and tankers also use a bulbous bow. This type of hull is shaped like a bulb in the front or bow of the ship. This design allows or modifies the flow of water at the bow, thus reducing the power requirements of the propulsion source.

Related Technological Concepts. To help understand Suspension Technology many technological concepts are used. This section can be used as a guide to a selected number of concepts and definitions. Those included are by no means complete, but may act as a guide to further study.

Air Foils and Lift. When an aircraft leaves the ground, it is supported by the aerodynamic force of lift. Lift is produced by a device called an airfoil. An aircraft wing is designed as an airfoil to produce lift. Lift on an aircraft can be explained by using Bernoulli's Principle. This principle states that with any airflow, as the speed of the air increases, (velocity increases) pressure decreases. Because of the curvature and shape of an aircraft wing, as the wing cuts through the air, the air speeds up on top of the wing produces a lower pressure. On the bottom of the wing, pressure is greater because of the angle of the wing to the air. The difference in pressure from the top to the bottom of the wing produces lift.

Angle of Attack. A second way to cause lift is by changing the angle of attack. If the angle of attack is increased there is a greater force against the lower surface of the wing. This increased force aids in producing lift. However, most of the lift, about 75%, comes from the difference in pressure between the upper and lower surfaces of the wing. Lift can thus be increased in two ways. One is by increasing the forward speed of the aircraft. A second way is to increase the angle of attack.

Stall. Quite often one hears about the term stall within the aviation industry. Stall is defined as a condition in which there is no more lift on an airfoil. Stall can be produced by continually increasing the angle of attack on the airfoil. As the angle of attack increases, eventually air on the top may start to separate from the wing. When this happens a gurgling or turbulent pattern is produced near the trailing edge of the airfoil. As the angle of attack increases more, this turbulence progresses forward. Eventually, all lift is removed from the airfoil producing a stall.

Buoyancy. The term buoyancy is used to describe how marine vehicles stay afloat. A body partially or completely immersed in water is said to be buoyed up or in a state of buoyancy. It is sustained by a force equal to the weight of the fluid displaced. Cork and wood float because they are lighter than water. Metal however, is denser and will not float unless it is shaped correctly. If a one pound piece of metal is shaped into a bowl, it will float. It is now presenting a larger surface area to the water. When placed on the water it will displace more water, in this case, a pound of water. A force equal to the weight of the displaced water is buoying up the metal bowl. In reality, the buoyed forces work against gravity. The relationship between these two forces helps to stabilize the marine vehicle in the water.

Levitation. The term levitation is associated with several new vehicle designs in which a vehicle, heavier than air, is actually lifted slightly off the ground. To levitate means to raise or float in the air or to cause a body to be buoyant in the air. One reason levitation vehicles are being studied is that frictional horsepower is greatly reduced because there are no tires, wheels, etc. to cause resistance. Several designs are currently being tested with one of the most popular being magnetic levitation. In this case, strong magnetic fields with opposing magnetic poles are placed on the vehicle and on the road bed. The opposing forces between the two, cause the vehicle to rise or levitate above the road bed. Then as the vehicle is propelled forward it actually rides on the magnetic forces, thus reducing friction.

Superconductivity. One of the most promising breakthroughs in electrical power within the transportation sector is called superconductivity. Superconductivity is defined as the lack of all resistance to the flow of electricity in a conductive material. This resistance has limited electrical circuits considerably. Superconductive materials have a large potential for transportation, (magnetic levitation, computer speed, microcircuits, electrical storage and transmission, and instrumentation).

The resistance of most materials increases with increasing temperature. The reverse is also true. As a temperature of a material is reduced, its resistance also is reduced. At or near absolute zero (0°Kelvin = –273°C = –460°F) many materials have no resistance to electricity. A ring of lead (as the conductor) was tested for over a year, and kept at 7.2 degrees Kelvin. Once the current started in the ring, it continued without diminishing. When the temperature increased, the current stopped immediately because of the internal resistance. The advantage of having superconductivity then is less energy needed for electrical systems.

It has been known for a long time that resistance in a conducting material can be reduced by dropping its temperature. For example, there is no resistance in a material when at absolute zero (–273 degrees C or –460 degrees F). In the past few years much has been done to increase the temperature at which superconductivity occurs. This temperature is called the transition temperature. The goal is to develop a material that has no resistance at near atmospheric temperature. When this happens the effects will be dramatic. Electrical circuits will be extremely efficient without losses that occur. Recently materials have been produced that have minimum electrical resistance at –33 degrees C. One such material is a complex oxide called the lanthanum-strontium copper oxide. Other materials are being tested to see if superconductivity can be achieved at even higher temperatures in the future with practical cost to industries.

Guidance Technology

Navigational Systems. Navigational systems are those that provide guidance and control over the vehicles direction, speed, torque, horsepower, etc.

The future holds a great deal of promise in this area. Eventually, automobile navigational system will be able to monitor the vehicle's position aiding in route guidance. A map (local/regional) can be displayed on the computer video screen in the dashboard. Signals from the car computer will be sent to satellites and beamed back to the vehicle. The position of the vehicle will then be shown on the map.

Sonar. Today many water craft utilize sonar for determining the depth of a water body. Although used on all commercial vessels, only in the past 15–20 years has *sonar* been economically available for smaller craft. The word sonar is an abbreviation for the words *s*ound, *n*avigation, and *r*anging. It was developed as a means of tracking enemy submarines during World War II.

In the simplest terms, an electrical impulse is converted into a sound wave and transmitted into the water. When this wave strikes an obstacle it rebounds. Sound, when transmitted through water, travels at approximately 4800 feet per second. Sound when transmitted through air, travels about 1100 feet per second.

Since the speed of sound in water is known, the time between the transmitted signal and the received echo can be measured. This can then give the distance to the obstacle such as the bottom of the lake or water body. Electronic sonar units can both send and receive sound waves, measure and record them as a certain depth.

Smart Highways. In the future, there will be highways with sophisticated communication systems integrated with each driver. These systems, called "Smart Highways" will feature traffic monitoring, navigational equipment, and computer links in an effort to improve safety and reduced travel time. These systems are also identified as (IVHS), Intelligent Vehicle/Highway Systems.

An example of how the system might work follows. When the driver pulls out of the driveway the position of the car is immediately linked into satellite systems. The first effect would be that the location and position of the vehicle would be indicated on the instrument panel video display. In addition, the onboard computer would be connected to a city-wide network of traffic sensors to receive traffic information. A computer voice would be able to give five possible routes to the destination entered into the computer. With the touch of a button the best route is outline in red on the screen. As the vehicle approaches the freeway, the computer alerts the drive of a vehicle accident resulting in a major delay on the most direct route. Thus, a new route on a toll road is planned and displayed on the screen.

As the vehicle approaches the toll gate, the driver holds a coded card against the window for the billing camera to read. Traffic on the toll road is bumper to bumper, but it flows smoothly at 60 mph. Radar braking devices are used to keep all vehicles approximately five feet apart from the vehicle in front. The driver settles down for a ride. Ten minutes into the trip, the computer generated voice warns that congestion ahead has slowed traffic to a crawl. The computer advises the driver to take the next exit. The video display map shows the best route utilizing local streets to the final destination. Presently there are several smart highway systems that are being tested for costs, feasibility, driver use, and effectiveness. The most popular systems include:

1. Road/Communication Systems—This system in Tokyo has data on road conditions and navigation transmitted to a video display map in the vehicle. Approximately ninety sensors and roadside beacons cover a 350 kilometer area. Another similar system is being tested in West Berlin using two hundred forty beacons.
2. Advanced Mobile Traffic Information and Communications—This system, much the same as above, and also in Tokyo, uses a central transmission to communicate with vehicles rather than roadside beacons.
3. TravTek—This system, located in Orlando will be used to equip about one hundred vehicles with display terminals and navigational systems. Both beacons and satellite links will be used. This system is being coordinated by General Motors, the American Automobile Association, and the Federal Highway Administration. Various state agencies are also providing partial funding for this project.

Control Technology

Automatic Braking System. Future automobiles and other passenger vehicles can use a form of radar to monitor the distance between itself and vehicles in the front. The system monitors and detects differences in speed of two vehicles. The radar signals are transmitted to an on-board computer. Based upon the rate of difference between two vehicles, warning lights are flashed to tell the driver about the vehicle in front. Eventually, there will not be a need to warn the driver as the car will automatically slow down.

Anti-Lock Braking Systems. With the computer on-board, the vehicle can incorporate equal braking on each wheel. This eliminates the possibility of skidding, possibly producing an accident. A sensor on each wheel tells the exact RPM (revolutions per minute) to the computer. During braking, when one wheel begins to skid, the computer senses this and immediately releases the brake on that wheel. This causes all wheels to brake evenly, reducing skids and improving safety.

Automatic Leveling. When the vehicle is braking or accelerating, both front end alignment and braking are affected. With the computer on-board the vehicle, sensors can tell the computer which part of the vehicle is tilting to the front or back. Based upon this input, the computer immediately pumps up load leveling shock absorbers to keep the vehicle level.

Constant Velocity Transmissions. Another innovation that is promising is that of the constant velocity transmission (CVT). The CVT is a type of transmission that has no gears for changing torque and speed requirements. Typically there are two variable speed pulleys that change speed ratios as RPM changes. Normally as the drive pulley speeds up, its running diameter gets larger. As the driven pulley increases in speed, its running diameter gets smaller. The combination of these pulleys produces infinite speed ratios between the input and output. The CVT enables the engine to operate at the most efficient RPM for best fuel mileage.

Wing Tip Vortex. As an aircraft is flying there is considerable wake (wind) turbulence generated behind the wings. In effect there are vortices (wing tip vortex) produced at the tip of each wing. Vortices are circular wind channels produced at the end of an aircraft wing. They are caused by a pressure differential between the top and the bottom of the wing during flight. The high pressures on the bottom of the wing have a tendency to slide outward and curl around the wingtips. The vortices produced may have serious effects. For example, the vortices can be very dangerous to smaller aircraft flying behind larger aircraft. These vortices may last for as long as five minutes.

One design that is being incorporated today to help reduce wing vortices is to use winglets. Winglets are small vertical stabilizers placed directly on the end of each wing. These winglets reduce the vortices that are normally produced and also increase the amount of lift on the aircraft.

Related Technological Concepts. To help understand Control Technology many technological concepts are used. This section can be used as a guide to a selected number of concepts and definitions. Those included are by no means complete, but may act as a guide to further study.

Cavitation. Boat and ship propellers or props can be damaged by the process called cavitation. A partial vacuum can be produced in water near a propeller. As the propeller blades cut through the water, vacuum bubbles are formed on the back edge of the blades. As these bubbles explode, they have a tendency to eat away at the nearby metal, causing damage to the metal. This is called cavitation. In some cases, the metal looks like it has been attached by acid. However, the cavitation process has simply eaten away the metal.

Propeller Pitch. The term pitch is used to indicate the angle of the blades of the propeller on a boat or ship. The pitch is a measure of the distance the propeller moves forward during each revolution. The purpose for changing the pitch of a propeller is to gain additional control over the vehicle. For example, a pitch of 17 means the propeller, and thus the boat or ship will move 17 inches forward for each revolution of the propeller. This assumes that there is no slip between the propeller blades and the water. In reality, of course, there will always be some amount of slip. In comparison, a pitch of 19 usually produces higher top end speed on a boat but not as much pulling power. A pitch of 15 produces a lower speed but much more pulling power.

Miles Per Hour Verses Knots. The velocity of a vehicle on water is measured differently than that of land. Marine vehicles use knots. One knot is equal to the speed of 6,080 feet per hour or about 1.15 miles per hour. For example, if a ship is going 30 knots, it is going about 34.5 miles per hour. Or if a boat is going 35 miles per hour, it is going about 30.1 knots. 1 knot equals 1.15 miles per hour and 1 mile per hour equals .896 knots.

Support Technology

All vehicles need some form of support technology. Support technology is defined as systems of technology that are used for processing the vehicle, moving passengers to and from the vehicle, and bringing freight to and from the vehicle, etc. Support technologies may include airports, marinas, launch pads, harbors, gasoline stations, parts dealers, service shops, etc. None of the transportation modes can operate without support technologies. In fact one of the reasons that it is difficult to incorporate new transportation technologies is because the support systems are not yet in place. Take for example the battery powered car. Although a good technology, there was never any support systems such as battery charging stations, service shops, etc. to support its growth. Several support technologies for terrestrial transportation include:

1. Fuel stations—Without fuel stations, cars and trucks would not be able to continue running.

2. Bridges—Bridges allow various highways to be connected over water and other objects such as roads, etc.
3. Highways—Highways give the passenger in the automobile ease of driving especially on interstate systems.
4. Harbor/land connections—Trains bringing freight to boats and tankers.
5. Highway construction systems—There are many companies that build highways. These companies are part of the support systems for land transportation.
6. Bus stops—Without bus stops as a support system, bus passengers would not be able to get on and off of the bus.
7. Control Centers—Control centers (many of which are computerized) are used as a support system to aid in maintaining speeds, controlling input and output of trucks, and maintaining position of vehicles with respect to each other. In addition, control centers are used to help control pipeline products such as natural gas and oil transportation.
8. Parts Distribution Centers—All transportation forms need maintenance and repair of parts to keep operating and running efficiently.
9. Switching Centers—Switching centers are used to switch trains in direction, and to put them on the correct tract to their destination.

Without these systems (almost all of which are computer controlled), support for our transportation networks on land, water, air or space travel would not be usable today.

Computer-Aided Dispatching. Transportation systems are being controlled more and more by computers. In addition to having computers control engine performance (air/fuel ratio) they can also be used to help various service industries with their orders. One example, is a computer-aided centralized natural gas service dispatching center. In operation, service orders will be automatically transmitted to 700 vehicles and 100 portable terminals. This type of computer network improves communication between the central office and the many individual service vehicles. This type of network is also being incorporated by other industries that require close contact between the central office and the dispatch vehicle. The goal of such systems is to improve response time and enhance overall customer satisfaction.

Materials Technology. In today's advanced technological society, many new materials and structures are being used to build transportation components and systems. The most recent goal has been for the structure of many components to be designed lighter with stronger characteristics. Materials technology is being used to make vehicles lighter, more heat resistant, stronger, etc. For example, the materials used in an engine (propulsion technology) are being made lighter and stronger so that efficiency can be improved and temperatures increased. Automobile manufacturers for example are now designing synthetic engines rather than cast iron. Synthetic engines are able to withstand higher internal temperatures. This translates to more fuel economy and improved efficiency.

Vehicle Weight. All vehicles have been reduced in weight by changing the materials used. Engine parts are being manufactured with lighter synthetic materials. The synthetic engine is already being tested for possible use in cars today.

Methods of Testing, Research, and Development in Transportation

The field of transportation technology is changing very rapidly. Many influences have caused these changes to develop. As part of the ever changing scene of transportation technology a sound research, testing and development program in all transportation industries is critical. This section looks at some of the most common systems that are used for testing, research and development in transportation.

Research Testing Centers

Many transportation industries have complete research testing centers. These centers are staffed by personnel from the particular manufacturing company. For example, the automotive manufacturers have huge research centers used to test engines, vehicles, braking systems, computer controls, etc. These systems are tested under many adverse conditions. Conditions may range from super highways to dirt roads, from banked high-speed test tracks, to punishing bumps, from powdery sand to soupy mud, from hairpin curves to seemingly impossible grades.

The purpose of these and other research testing centers is to have the transportation systems and components experience all possible conditions which may exist during normal operation. Based upon the results from many tests, components and systems are refined in their design so as to maintain the highest degree of safety, efficiency, comfort, and reliability of parts being used.

Wind Tunnels

One testing component used today in land and air transportation is that of the wind tunnel. Essentially, a wind tunnel is a device that produces high velocity and high volumes of air within a tunnel or tube shaped device. The size of the wind tunnel is determined by the size of the components being tested. Huge wind tunnels are able to collect and measure by computers such data as the coefficient of drag of cars, trucks, buses, etc. as well as airplane bodies and shapes. In addition wind tunnels are also able to measure lift and shape of airfoils, wing flaps, winglets, etc. The overall result is to produce the most efficient, reliable and safe design. Based upon the results, engineering centers will further design each component being tested.

Dynamometers

Another testing device used in research and testing centers is the dynamometer. In order to measure the output power of any propulsion device, work must be done. This means a load must be applied to the propulsion system while it is operating. Common examples of loading include:

- pulling a trailer up a steep hill
- producing thrust in a reaction engine
- plowing through water in a boat

A dynamometer is a device attached to the back of the engine or propulsion system used to absorb the power being created. When the engine is at idle, it is impossible to determine how much horsepower or torque can be produced. If an engine is run on a dynamometer, it can be loaded to simulate actual working conditions. The dynamometer can be located on the back of the engine on a propeller, on a wheel, etc. The dynamometer is measuring torque at the output shaft of the engine or application.

Note that a dynamometer can only measure the torque being produced at the rear of an engine or at the drive wheels of a vehicle. The dynamometer does not measure horsepower. In order to obtain horsepower readings the following formula is used:

$$\text{Horsepower} = \frac{\text{Torque} \times \text{RPM}}{5252}$$

The number 5252 is a constant and is mathematically related to how torque is measured on a certain size diameter rotating shaft.

Another type of dynamometer can be used to measure road horsepower on over the road vehicles such as automobiles and trucks. It is called a chassis dynamometer. A chassis dynamometer measures the horsepower and torque available at the drive wheels of any vehicle. In this case the tires roll on two rollers. These are called the idle roll and the drive roll. A power absorption unit is used to absorb the energy. This unit acts as the load on the vehicle. Both speed (RPM) and torque are measured by a computer. Based upon the results of different testing sequences, propulsion systems can be completely tested under load before being put in place in the application. Results can be fed back to engineering departments for further research and development if necessary.

Performance Charts

Gasoline, diesel, reaction, and other engines have certain operating characteristics. This means that they have different torque, horsepower and fuel consumption at different RPM. By using a dynamometer, a performance chart (also called characteristic curve) can be developed. Figure 5 shows a standard performance chart.

When the engine is loaded down with a dynamometer, a certain maximum torque and horsepower can be produced at a specific RPM. For example, referring to the figure, this particular engine is capable of producing about 130 ft. lbs. of torque at 1500 RPM. Also, this engine can produce about 65 BHP at 3500 RPM. This chart shows the characteristics of the engine throughout its RPM range. A fuel consumption curve is also shown. This indicates the amount of fuel used in pounds per brake horsepower, per hour. This unit is sometimes referred to as BSFC or (brake specific fuel consumption).

Feedback Systems

All manufacturers of transportation systems need to have some form of feedback from the consumer to the engineering departments. This is commonly done by the manufacturer. Each transportation company has a rather extensive service program. Service is required on most transportation systems. Service is commonly done through service centers and service departments. A great deal of information is available at these service centers which has been generated by the consumer. Each manufacturer then has a service department within its own company structure. Their purpose is to answer many of the field service problems as well as feedback technical information to the manufacturers so as to improve the product. These service departments also may have a "failure analysis" program in house. Failure analysis is the process of actually causing a part or system to fail purposely. Data can then be collected to improve each design as necessary.

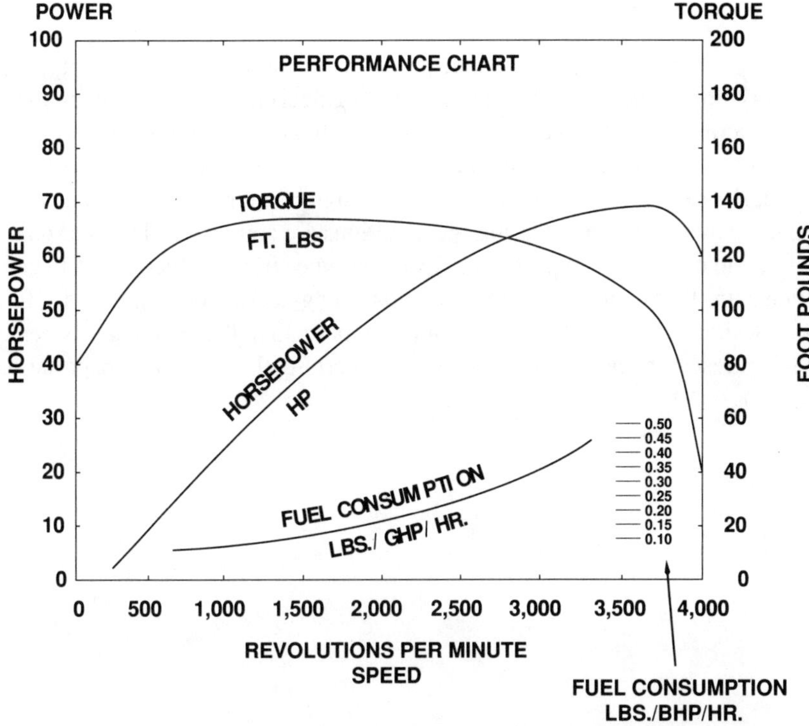

Figure 5: *All propulsion systems have performance charts used to describe the parameters which the vehicle will operate in. One such chart shows the horsepower, torque, fuel consumption, and RPM of the system. The bottom scale shows the RPM of the engine. The left scale shows the torque on the engine. The right scale shows the horsepower or thrust being produced on the engine. Also, note that on the bottom right, a fuel consumption scale is included.*

Computerized Design

Today in many of the transportation industries, most design of parts are done on Computer Aided (Integrated) Drafting, Design, and Manufacturing systems, (CAD, CADD, CAM, CIM). There are many such systems presently being used in the industry. These systems aid the engineering departments in not only drafting parts and systems, but also in testing of systems. Various computer programs are now available to design and test different parts. For example, tires are now designed on computers. They are then tested under varying conditions (within the computer program) to determine tread life, reliability, safety, etc. This process of using computers for design and testing reduces the testing program time considerably.

Prototype Testing

Another process used in the transportation industries is that of prototyping. Prototyping is the process of taking the engineering drawings and actually constructing the first object. The purpose for building a prototype is to see if the theoretical designs can be built with safety, reliability and efficiency in mind. For example, consider when a new design of aircraft is going to be built. First the theoretical engineering specifications are completed. The next phase is to build or construct a prototype. The prototype aircraft is then tested to generate data. This data is then fed back into the engineering departments for further design before the aircraft is built commercially. The end result is better testing, research and development data concerning the specific transportation system.

REFERENCES

Brus, John. (1989). *Perceptions on the Future of Personal Ground Transportation.* Technical Information Department, Volume 24, No. 2. General Motors Research Laboratories, Warren, Michigan.

Brus, John. (1984). *Trends in Engine Design.* Technical Information Department, Volume 19, No. 1. General Motors Research Laboratories, Warren, Michigan.

Caarone, Anthony L. and John Free. (1989). *Tri-Hull Ship*. Popular Science, August 60–62. Times Mirror Magazines, Inc. New York, N.Y.

De Old, Alan R. Everett Sheets, and William Alexander. (1986). *Transportation, The Technology of Moving People and Products.* Davis Publications, Inc. Worcester, Massachusetts.

DeVore, Paul W. (1983). *Introduction to Transportation.* Davis Publications, Inc. Worcester, Massachusetts.

DiChristina, Mariette. (1990). *Hello Satellite, Get Me Central.* Popular Science, April, 96–97. Times Mirror Magazines, Inc. New York, N.Y.

Hor, Shoon, and Frost, Lerinda. (1989). *The Automotive Engine: GM Looks Ahead.* Technical Information Department, General Motors Research Laboratories, Warren, Michigan.

Floyd, Thomas H. Jr. *Personalizing Public Transportation.* The Futurist. Nov./Dec. 1990. World Future Society, Bethesda, Maryland.

Frost, Lerinda. (1989). *Lanelok: Lane-Sensing System Provides First Step In Automated Vehicle Guidance.* Technical Information Department, General Motors Research Laboratories, Warren, Michigan.

Frost, Lerinda. (1988). *Computer Modeling Capability Simulates Safety Restraints.* Technical Information Department, Volume 23, No. 2, General Motors Research Laboratories, Warren, Michigan.

Frost, Lerinda. (1989). *Side-Impact Protection: GM Tackles the Next Safety Frontier.* Technical Information Department, Volume 24, No. 3. General Motors Research Laboratories, Warren, Michigan.

McCosh, Dan. (1990). *Automotive Newsfront.* Popular Science, April, 96–97. 29–39. Times Mirror Magazines, Inc. New York, N.Y.

McCosh, Dan. (1989). *Automotive Newsfront.* Popular Science, January 22–24. 29–39. Times Mirror Magazines, Inc. New York, N.Y.

McCosh, Dan. (1989). *The Any Fuel Engine.* Popular Science, February, 73 and 102. Times Mirror Magazines, Inc. New York, N.Y.

Schwaller, Anthony E. (1988). *Motor Automotives Mechanics.* Delmar Publishers, Albany, N.Y.

Schwaller, Anthony E. (1989). *Transportation, Energy and Power Technology.* Delmar Publishers, Albany, N.Y.

Sheldrick, Michael. (1990). *Driving While Automated.* Scientific American. Scientific American Inc., 415 Madison Ave., New York, N.Y. 10017.

University of Minnesota. (1989). *Center for Transportation Studies, Annual Report.* University of Minnesota. Minneapolis, Minnesota.

CHAPTER 4

Technical, Social, and Biological Impacts of Transportation Technology

By Dr. Robert W. Gubala, P.E.
(Senior Engineer, Connecticut Department of Transportation)

Transportation projects (examples: airports, ports, railroads, and highways) require the application of technology to bring them from concept to physical reality. Because transportation facilities are designed for long service, occupy space for which there is competing societal use, and greatly affect life style by encouraging travel, commerce, and communication, there are environmental impacts associated with every major Transportation project. In order to adequately address Transportation technology education, the technology teacher must be sensitive to environmental aspects, their measurement, their reporting, and how they parallel the technological development of a project.

What is the environmental interface with Transportation? It would be best to begin with a definition of the term "environment."

> Environment: The aggregate of external conditions that influence the life of an individual or population, specifically the life of man.

How best to associate Transportation facility development with the aggregate of external conditions, "Environment" defined above? A process of identifying and assessing environmental impacts has evolved in both scientific and legal frameworks. The key to the process is being able to view a transportation facility development and concurrently pointing out environmental impacts that will occur if the development becomes reality—and if it is not built.

An environmental impact has the connotation of being something adverse. The word "impact" has the sense of hitting, of collision, of force. That is not its meaning in an environmental review process. An environmental impact is a consequence of doing or not doing a project, the project here being a transportation project. An environmental impact may be beneficial or adverse and it can be different things for different people. For example, the development of the transportation project to have coast-to-coast train service was an overall beneficial environmental impact for those who craved mobility and the economic well-being that accompanied it. For those whose livelihood depended on Pony Express and wagon trains for freight hauling the environmental impact of the project's development was adverse indeed.

At this juncture, the reader may be troubled that there may be too much vagueness and subjectivity in the environmental impact process for it to be of any worth in Transportation technology education. Early attempts to address the subject were prone to these criticisms. However, various laws evolved from increased scientific knowledge about our environment. They have shaped how environmental impacts must be reported, measured, assessed and reported. A review of the most important environmental law will be helpful in stressing that environmental impact assessment of transportation facilities is "do-able" in a technology education format and required. That key law is the National Environmental Policy Act of 1969 (known as NEPA).

As with many laws, NEPA had its foundation in public outcry to its elected representatives. There had been oil spills, books such as "Silent Spring" by Rachel Carson that warned of environmental excesses, and public outcries concerning projects which appeared an affront to environmental concerns. All these caused a demand that there be an accounting before projects were undertaken and that it be a public accounting.

The National Environmental Policy Act of 1969 evolved, quickly passed the Congress and became law. Title I of the Act gave its reasons for enactment. It provides in part as follows:

(a) The Congress, recognizing the profound impact of our activity on the interrelations of all components of the natural environment, particularly the profound influences of population growth, high-density urbanization, industrial expansion, resource exploitation, and new and expanding technological advances and recognizing further the critical importance of restoring and maintaining environmental quality to the overall welfare and development of man, declares that it is the continuing policy of the federal government, in cooperation with state and local governments and other concerned public and private organizations, to use all practicable means and measures, including financial and technical assistance, in a manner calculated to foster and promote the general welfare, to create and maintain conditions under which man and nature can exist in productive harmony, and fulfill the social, economic, and other requirements of present and future generations of Americans.

(b) In order to carry out the policy set forth in this chapter, it is the continuing responsibility of the federal government to use all practicable means, consistent with other essential considerations of national policy, to improve and coordinate federal plans, functions, programs, and resources to the end that the nation may—

(1) fulfill the responsibilities of each generation as trustee of the environment for succeeding generations;

(2) assure for all Americans safe, healthful, productive, and aesthetically and culturally pleasing surroundings;

(3) attain the widest range of beneficial uses of the environment without degradation, risk to health or safety, or other undesirable and unintended consequences;

(4) preserve important historic, cultural, and natural aspects of our national heritage, and maintain, wherever possible, an environment which supports diversity and variety of individual choices;

(5) achieve a balance between population and resource use which will permit high standards of living and wide sharing of life's amenities; and

(6) enhance the quality of renewable resources and approach the maximum attainable recycling of depletable resources.

(c) The Congress recognizes that each person has a responsibility to contribute to the preservation and enhancement of the environment.

The National Environmental Policy Act did not stop at stating lofty environmental goals for the country. It also required that environmental impact statements be included in every recommendation or report on proposals for legislation and other major federal actions (including expenditures of federal funds) significantly affecting the quality of the human environment. This detailed statement by a responsible official would include:

1) The environmental impact of the proposed action;

2) Any adverse environmental effects which cannot be avoided if the proposal should be implemented;

3) Alternatives to the proposed action;

4) The relationship between local and short-term uses of man's environment and the maintenance and enhancement of long-term productivity;

5) Any irreversible and irretrievable commitments of resources which would be involved if the proposed action should be implemented.

All of the above translates into an assignment for those involved in Transportation technology to recognize an environmental impact statement is required to move a project from concept to construction.

The first of the environmental impact statements were little more than project endorsements with less than adequate handling of the five environmental impact measures detailed previously. And because the environmental impact statement was a public document and was required to be circulated to interested parties for their comment and criticism, the failings became known quickly. Some groups even challenged environmental impact statement adequacy in court. All this led to an upsurge in improving the quality of environmental impact statements so they would objectively be what lawmakers wanted—a test of environmental reasonableness before funds were spent irreversibly on a project.

The most important requirement of NEPA is to reveal the environmental impact of a proposed action. This results in Transportation technicians giving new attention to studying the effects of doing or not doing projects. This is an expansion of the job duties of technical people involved in a project. They cannot only concern themselves with the technical "hows" to design and build a project but also the accompanying environmental ramifications.

This NEPA requirement has been in force for twenty years. The detailing of environmental impacts has improved in their technical content over the years. And what began as a vague assignment has evolved into a procedure that most technology trained people can feel comfortable in and competent to accomplish.

The Description of Environmental Impacts

The writers of an environmental impact statement usually begin the detailing of environmental impacts with the technical aspects of the project. It makes sense to do it this way because the reader first must become acquainted with what the project is and why it is being proposed. A technical description of the proposed does that and sets the stage for further writing about environmental impacts.

The technical description of the project (here a transportation project) should include the following:

1. What the project is (a new highway on new location, a reconstruction of an existing highway, expansion of an airport, the dredging of a

harbor to open up a port to commerce, a light rail to connect suburbs to the central city etc., etc.).

2. The project status—The history of the project, who is in charge of its development, actions which are pending (government permits for instance, or legal challenges), what the cost is, who's responsible for the cost, time schedules set forth for the development.
3. The Transportation purpose for the project—How does the project fit the adopted Transportation plans of a region? Is it a missing last piece of the beginning of a new system? What is the forecasted traffic that will use the project if built? Is it new traffic or traffic diverted from another overtaxed facility? How will the project mesh with other transportation links such as mass transit or access to airports?
4. The transportation benefits for the project—Will the proposed project address a known safety hazard? Will the type of project change the type of frequency of accidents? Will the project increase the capacity of the transportation in the region? Will traffic improve in level of service (for instance from grid lock to free flow)?
5. Alternatives—All reasonable alternatives have to be detailed for the reader's study. This includes describing the "null" alternative or "do nothing" alternative; in other words, what would happen if the project is not constructed.

The transportation system management alternative also has to be described. This is the alternative where traffic movement and safety is improved using the existing transportation facility and improving operations on it by traffic engineering techniques (new traffic signals, parking management, selective pavement additions).

In the case of a highway transportation project, the mass transit alternative requires exploration. Will reasonable and feasible transit (buses, car and van pools, rail, water ferry service) take the place of the proposed highway project or lessen its impacts?

Reasonable alternatives are dependent on the type of transportation facility being studied in the environmental impact statement. With highways, reasonable alternatives would be different alignments and types of highway (freeways, parkways, one-way streets) which could serve the same traffic purpose. With airports, different locations for the airport or the arrangement of flight paths would be the reasonable alternatives studied. Rail lines are similar to highways where different alignments are the alternates.

This technical description of the proposal and reasonable/feasible alternatives require maps and other visual aids to orient the reader who many times does not have the familiarization with the project. It is important that this initial part of the environmental impact statement be written well and be easily understood using visual aides, because all the rest of the environmental impact description depends on this foundation.

The writers of environmental impact statements tend to next describe economic impacts of a proposal after need for the project, the matters of financial impact logically follow. The economic subject matters explored include:

1. Effects of the transportation project on businesses which are multifaceted. One of the most quantitative are the direct and induced expenditures on labor and materials involved in actually building the project. There are many examples when transportation or other civil engineering projects were used to put people back to work during hard economic times. Over time, certain relationships have been found to be reliable. For highway projects, the distribution of costs are: wages 25%; equipment overhead and profit 35%; aggregates 12%; Portland cement 5%; bitumens 3%; steel 10%; and other materials 10%. Knowing the cost of a project and what it is composed of, direct expenditures for the categories above can be reported. However, there is a spill over effect that also must be included. For every dollar put into the economy, it becomes income for someone else to spend. Taxes whittle away at each cycle of spending so the amount that can be respent eventually reaches zero. History supports that for each dollar generated by building a project, the impact is the same as if $2.50 were added to the region's economy. In environmental impact statements, this economic impact is provided and expressed as jobs and dollars circulating in the region.
2. The effect on business due to constructing a project are not as definable but must be reported nevertheless because the effects are real. When intercontinental railroads were laid out, communities bypassed whithered and became ghost towns. Others which became railheads flourished with business growth. The job of the environmental impact statement writer is to objectively as possible catalog "who wins" and "who loses" economically if a project gets built. There are case studies of other transportation projects which can be used as predictors of what will happen if a project is built. The writer should also report if the changes are in concert with adopted economic plans for a region. If a region has determined through a planning process that it should retain mining as a primary industry, a rail project that would induce a rush to change mining acres into manufacturing and housing acres is an impact project decision makers need to weigh.

3. There are special business impacts that also require research effort. One is the effect of a project on agriculture. Once an acre of farmland becomes subdivided into housing lots or is cut through by a highway, its use to feed the nation is denied. Transportation projects have as their nature the ability to change accessibility. This can be a two-edged sword when considering impacts on agriculture. Better accessibility for farm products afforded by a better highway or rail can also allow suburban housing to sprawl to consume farm acres. The environmental impact statement writer has to make judgements about the effect the new transportation link will have. He/she does this by identifying the production characteristics of farms and comparing those to the market/supply characteristics of the consumers. This comparison will give insights whether new transportation facilities will diminish or enhance the preservation of agriculture.

4. Another special business impact is tourism. Improved accessibility, a usual by-product of transportation projects, can stimulate growth and therefore jobs. The environmental writer must be careful to not overestimate this economic impact. There are just so many leisure hours and there are competitors for tourism dollars. The writer may find it difficult to quantify this effect but it should be included in the impact statement because it is a consequence of a project.

5. An economic impact that has social impact ramifications as well, is the residential impact of constructing a project. There is the obvious very cost definable portion, the number of homes that have to be demolished to build the transportation project. More subtle but as real a consequence are the changes in residential activity that comes with building a project and the effect on property taxes which are the mainstay of the economy in many regions. This subject is so intertwined with other factors such as planning, political structure, parallel employment capability, that impact analysis and reporting is crude. A way of approaching this untenable but real consequence of building a project is to review what residential growth (expressed in percent of additional units per year) in the region has been for the previous ten years without the project. Then the writer should implant the project and make a value judgment of its percentage additive to that base line growth. This should be done for each reasonable alternative. The "no build" alternative will support the average growth for the ten year period before the new highway project was contemplated. An alternative for traffic engineering improvements to an existing road will support more growth but not near as much as a

new freeway alternative. Based on known taxing patterns, the increased housing can be equated to new income and based on known community resources, the cost of new school or fire service to support the new residential units can be assessed. The results are reported in a comparison way for the eventual decision maker to weigh along with all the other economic impacts to a transportation proposal.

6. Although not thought of in pure economic terms communication, military preparedness and medical accessibility are vitally affected by building *and* not building a transportation project and need to be addressed in the environmental impact statement. With the shift in the county to service type employment, good communications is important. With so many regions dependent on military contracts, military preparedness carries an economic impact as well as a strategic consequence. With health costs rising faster than other societal costs, medical accessibility can be weighted in economic terms. All of the above have a common measure—time, not distance. The environmental impact statement writer has the obligation to show time durations from population centers needing medical accessibility to available or planned medical facilities for all the reasonable alternatives plus the proposed transportation project. Likewise the time comparison must be made for military preparedness both for troop movements and materials coming from manufacturing areas to military storage depots. For communication, the time comparison of travel along the various alternatives is the measure recognizing that not all communication must be face to face (fax, closed circuit television, being other ways).

In depicting economic impacts and later social and physical impacts, the environmental impact statement writer, the transportation technology education student, must endeavor to not fall into the trap early writers addressing NEPA did, that is, reporting only the negatives of the project and then writing a defensive document. All projects have impacts and they can be good or bad depending on a reader's point of view or vision of the future. The environmental impact statement writer's job is not to orchestrate opinion but to report impacts as accurately as available technology will allow, provide alternative comparisons where hard number technology is absent, in order to let other decision makers make an informed judgment about a project.

Closely allied with economic impacts of transportation projects are social impacts. One cannot adjust the economic and land use elements without affecting social fabric. But unlike economic impacts which attempt to equate impacts in terms of dollars and cents, social impacts analysis delves into how people interact and gauge their quality of life. Social impact analysis and reporting is more subjective than many environmental impacts that are included in environmental impact statements. That does not mean they are considered less important, or are weighed less in decision making, or should be avoided by technically oriented writers.

Breaking down the spectrum of social impacts to understandable elements will make the impact assessment tenable. One of the most productive ways to weigh the social impacts of a transportation project is to ask and answer (for the proposal and its alternatives) the question "What is the effect on Community Cohesion?"

Community Cohesion is a basic descriptor of community, and community is the preferred way most people choose to live. Community is a set of behavior patterns individuals and groups hold in common and cohesion is the degree of attractions. Local facilities, local organizations, neighborhoods become the physical manifestations of these shared perceptions and attitudes and therefore disruption, adjustment and enhancement become important environmental impacts to research and report.

A transportation technician charged with reporting community cohesion impacts of building a new subway system in Los Angeles may feel he/she has been given an impossible mission. There are methods that can be employed.

The first is to bring in community resource people and ask them to outline neighborhoods, areas of high social importance (parks, religious sites). Another is to look at discontinuities where dramatic changes in topography or man-made features cause social interaction to differ markedly on either side and display those boundaries on mapping. A third way is for the technical writer to collaborate with sociologists who are developing mathematical and/or pictorial models to defining communities.

All of the above information is best handled by superimposing it on maps of the area. Neighborhoods can be highlighted, discontinuities like rivers or zoned industrial areas can be shown. Then superimposed on top of all that is the transportation project (highway, airport, harbor improvement, etc.). The environmental impact statement writer then asks himself/herself many hard questions:

> Will the proposed or any of its alternatives displace homes or businesses?
>
> Will the proposal or any of its alternatives cleave established neighborhoods?
>
> Will the traffic improvement help local mobility or just serve through traffic?

> Will the proposal or any of its alternatives precipitate land use (parks, school districts, fire response policy and emergency access, government services proximity to neighborhoods) changes and if so, will they benefit or detract from community cohesion as it exists?

The answers are many times judgement calls, but by listing them in chart form with community characteristics (such as family size, income level, school district, park access, employment centers, hospital access) across the top and the transportation project and its alternatives vertical on the side, the chart boxes can then be filled in positive, neutral, or negative signs and comments. Decision makers will then have a framework to assess the social impact effects of community cohesion.

Though the chart can be used to address the social impacts of displacement of people and accessibility to services, these many times command their own space in the environmental impact statement. It is not enough to list the number of homes which will have to be razed to build the transportation project. Age, physical handicap, racial and ethnic background, length of residence in an area, distance to replacement housing and adequacy of compensation all require addressing. During the writing of an environmental impact statement, this information is derived from census data and other public records such as assessor maps, town service area mapping and site walks with local planning officials and community leaders. The alternatives are charted against the proposed project as to the number of and type of displacement of people.

Accessibility to facilities and service (schools, religious, employment centers, parks and recreational facilities, other transportation hubs, public utilities, major shopping areas) are the communication and interactive settings that keep community cohesion vibrant. The transportation project by its nature to serve the movement of people and goods, will affect the order of the accessibility. It is the environmental impact statement writer's job to best assess what accessibilities will be enhanced or diminished by building a proposed project or any of the alternatives or by staying with the status quo.

In the usual order of writing, an environmental impact statement, the describing of biological impacts follow economic and social impact discussions. Biological impacts have direct health effects on humans and therefore have been researched to a greater extent than socioeconomic effects. There is more quantification of effects possible and therefore for those in the transportation technology field, the reporting of air, noise, and water impacts of a transportation project become a natural extension of the engineering process. Many technicians in the civil engineering field have made the transition to being environmental specialists in air, noise and water impact analysis.

Air quality impacts are normally found in environmental impact statements concerned with transportation projects. The transportation facilities do not cause air pollution but the modal vehicles (especially cars and trucks on highways projects) do. In the impact statement, the writer must take the environmental responsibility for that traffic and reports its impact.

The place of beginning an air quality analysis is the estimate of traffic for the proposed facility and its alternates. Planners have forecasting computer models that accomplish this. Indeed, it should have been done prior to the layout of the project because transportation facilities are designed for multi-decade use. With the forecasted traffic, there are traffic capacity and fluidity models, that can superimpose that traffic on alternates of different types and predict how efficiently the traffic will move in any given year. With this information, the connection can be made between the ease or difficulty traffic moves and amounts of pollutants emitted per vehicle. What are those pollutants? For highway projects, carbon monoxide (CO), hydrocarbons (HC) and nitrogen oxide (NO_x) are of the most interest because they have health effects and there are standards set which cannot be exceeded. Carbon monoxide (CO) can cause symptoms from headaches to death depending on concentration. Hydrocarbons and nitrogen oxides combine with sunlight and create photochemical oxidants (more commonly called "smog"). Smog can cause respiratory ill effects.

The environmental impact statement writer has to take the forecasted traffic, state how free flowing or congested it is, state how many new vehicles with good pollution controls versus older vehicles out of tune with malfunctioning pollutant controls are in the traffic mix, know how much of each type of pollutant is emitted per mile or hour, and express the answer in terms of whether air quality standards are violated by the project. It is a herculean task; however, computer programs have been developed to do the calculations and the adjustment for speeds and vehicle ages.

The computer programs allow comparisons to be made between alternatives in air quality terms. As described earlier under the social impact discussion, charts can be drawn up with pollutant loads (expressed in kg/day for example) for each pollutant of interest across the left side of the chart and the project alternatives arrayed horizontally. Each box in the chart would be the kg/day of a pollutant for an alternative. Comparisons can be then made between alternatives which would give a cleaner atmosphere. An example of such a chart is shown on page 108.

Along with kilograms per day air pollutant data (called mesoscale analysis), the environmental writer has to be concerned about microscale concerns. These are predominantly vehicle carbon monoxide pollution emissions. Because carbon monoxide has definite health effects, standards have been set for one hour and eight hour exposures. There are computer programs which can translate vehicles flows for different alternatives into projected one hour and eight hour concentrations. These can be compared to the standards. The environmental writer must report the concentrations and this will allow air pollution authorities and the general public to judge whether the project should move ahead or be modified or even recommended to cancellation.

The air quality report in an environmental impact statement is very technical because it deals with pollutants, their chemical nature, the effect of wind and sunlight, the mix of cars and trucks and their particular generation of pollutants. It is an area that technology students have gravitated to because it is an extension of chemistry, math, physics and engineering course work.

Another biological impact that has an important place in environmental impact statements and has drawn technology students is noise quality. Transportation vehicles make noise. Although much has been done to quiet exhausts,

MESOSCALE ANALYSIS
TOTAL EMISSIONS (Kg/Day)

	No-Build	Widen Rt 7	Expressway Alternatives A	B	C	D	Combination Alternatives A/7	B/7	C/7	D/7
1995 Daily Vehicle Miles of Travel (x 1000)	3749	3749	4196	4196	4196	4196	4196	4196	4196	4196
Non-Methane Hydrocarbons	4404	4404	4736	4736	4736	4736	4736	4736	4736	4736
Oxides of Nitrogen	7568	7568	8382	8382	8382	8382	8382	8382	8382	8382
Carbon Monoxide	47831	47831	46804	46804	46804	46804	46804	46804	46804	46804
2010 Daily Vehicle Miles of Travel (x 1000)	4496	3749	4196	4196	4196	4196	4196	4196	4196	4196
Non-Methane Hydrocarbons	4570	4570	4426	4426	4426	4426	4426	4426	4426	4426
Oxides of Nitrogen	8131	8131	8103	8103	8103	8103	8103	8103	8103	8103
Carbon Monoxide	53736	53736	49227	49227	49227	49227	49227	49227	49227	49227

Temperature: NMHC, NOX 75 (F); CO 20 (F)

engine noise, tire whine, the problem of traffic noise and its effects on abutters to the transportation facility draws the attention of environmental impact statement readers.

To deal with traffic noise, the technical writer must have an understanding of what constitutes a noise impact. Heavy metal music can be noise to one person or a coveted concert ticket to someone else. For some people, the sound of silence can be the most intrusive. So sound and noise (defined as unwanted sound) can be very subjective.

For transportation facility impact assessment, the objective measure of noise is noise's inference to communication. The technical measure of noise is the decibel, a measure of sound pressure on the human ear. Standards for allowable decibel levels have been established and these become the measures of comparison of noise between the alternatives. The noise impact part of the environmental impact statement involves taking and reporting existing noise levels near affected neighborhoods and predicting what future noise levels will be when the transportation facility is built. This gives the technical writer/preparer of the impact statement a field data collection duty and a mathematical noise prediction task to do. There are excellent user friendly noise meters available for doing the field work and computer programs and/or nomographs (pictorial solving of mathematical noise equations) for doing the noise prediction of future traffic. As with other environmental impacts, the writer discusses existing and predicted future noise levels of the various alternatives and their impact on the neighboring people being able to enjoy their property and being able to communicate thereon.

There are mitigations to noise impacts apart from the government requiring quieter vehicles that the environmental impact writer should address. Noise abatement walls can be built between the traffic and people receptors of noise (in parks, their backyards, etc.) and if the predicted noise will be intense, the technical writer shows how much sound will be cut by constructing such a noise wall. There are design methods to cut down noise as well. A road or railroad track can be put in cut or have high berms placed on either side of the travelway. Both design methods will intercept noise and cause it to be less intense. The roadway surface can be designed to dampen certain tire noise. Vegetation, if can be provided deep and dense enough, can be used to dampen noise. A designer in conjunction with landscape architects can affect noise reduction by contouring the land and plantings.

The noise chapter of an environmental impact statement is one where very good technical field data and predictive computer models can accurately describe a biological impact, noise, and what can be done about it to reduce its impact. Noise assessment is a field that technology education students can apply their skills learned in a mathematics and science based curriculum.

The broadest biological impact subject matter in an environmental impact statement are the effects of a project on terrestrial and aquatic ecosystems. From the complexity of the words, one might assume that this area of analysis must be left to specialists. The conclusions of complex land-water-fish-animal interaction are the province of professionals highly trained in this area. However, there are many activities that can be readily accomplished by technology trained individuals to aid the impact analysis process. In order to indicate what these areas are, an outlining of what occurs in an analysis is in order. And before outlining methodology, a statement of the goal of the analysis is appropriate.

The study of the impacts of a transportation project on the terrestrial and aquatic ecosystem (the interrelationships of living things to each other and to their environment) is the identification of the physical impacts of the transportation project on the physical base and natural life systems impacted by the project.

This search for knowledge in a very complex area begins with knowing what is out there in the environs of the transportation project. With the land that means knowing the geology and soils in the area. With water, that means knowing the surface and groundwater characteristics. With the natural life system, that means knowing the plant and animal life that lives (and hopefully thrives) from the soils and water base.

Once a knowledge base is gained of the terrestrial and aquatic conditions, the ecologically trained professional can then impose the transportation project onto that land/water area and assess what changes will occur, beneficial or adverse. The place for the transportation technology trained professional in all of this is to assist the ecological assessment leader in gathering data and doing assistance tasks at his/her direction.

This work can be directly related to skills acquired in a technology education curriculum. These would involve surveying skills, geology knowledge, ability to read maps and reports, taking water samples, taking plant material samples, aiding in animal counts and assessment of their living zones.

The determination of what a transportation project will or will not do to the balance of land-water-plant-animal ecosystems is subjective and depends on the skill of the ecological impact professional assessor. The assessor will look at plant/animal communities and how the vegetation development will be interrupted or enhanced by the building of the transportation facility. The assessor will also look at the diversity and stability of life forms and whether the transportation facility will cause disruption or enhancement. The transportation technician's job in all of this is to give what assistance in data collection, computer analysis, and field work as is directed by the ecological professional during this analysis.

Relative to aquatic (water) impacts, there are additional impact assessments to be pursued. Water and wetlands have been considered so important that special legislation has been enacted for their protection. This then requires additional permit applications following specific procedures and reporting. The role of the transportation technologist is to aid in the preparation of the permit applications and to be at attendance at subsequent meetings and hearings with permit issuing agencies. The permit procedures for water and wetland impacts require detailed knowledge of the transportation facility design. Runoff, hydraulics, drainage piping, flooding, erosion all become factors in wetland and water impact analysis. The technologist has a definite role in working with the impact assessor by knowing the features of the design and being able to translate them into calculations for the movement of water on and adjacent to the project.

The assessment of terrestrial and aquatic impacts of a transportation project are very important in the total acceptance of the project being constructed. Transportation projects take up a great deal of space and by their construction affect water flows and wetlands. The determination of the impacts, beneficial and adverse are the province of ecological specialists. The technical technologist has roles throughout the assessment to aid the ecological specialist by using his/her knowledge of the design of the project and doing field and office reviews and computations in support of the ecologist's impact assessment.

As can be inferred from the description of what goes into an impact statement, the document can become voluminous and very technical in nature. The National Environmental Policy Act requires that the writing and eventual decision making not be done in a vacuum but in fact be subject to public scrutiny and comment.

Apart from his/her role in helping to prepare the impact assessment, the technologist has the administrative duty to seek comment from appropriate government agencies and the public. This means mailings and public notices and inclusions of comments and responses to them in the final document provided to decision makers for their administrative decision on whether the transportation project can go forward and be constructed.

Because transportation projects are so long lasting, occupy land that many times has to be acquired from private owners and have direct influence on people's lives and employment, public hearings are required before they can be constructed. At the public hearings, the entire project, its reason for being proposed, its design and environmental impacts have to be presented to the public by its sponsors for their questions and pro and con opinion whether the project should be built, modified, or abandoned.

The transportation-trained technologist has an important role in this process. He/she best knows the project having lived with it from its conception.

At the public hearing, he/she must be available to answer the public's questions and respond to other's testimony. English, public speaking, and humanity courses in a technology education curriculum come into play here, with the ability of the technologist being able to put into written and oral expression being as important as the technical courses attended which led to the design features. Through public hearings, the technologist becomes the technical extension of the sponsor/developer for the project. The project's very construction may turn on his/her ability to take technical knowledge and make it understood by the public to draw their support.

The writing of an environmental statement and all the field and technical work that accompanies it may seem an overwhelming task. It is time-consuming and costly, no doubt about that. However, the requirement is the law of the land and if conducted with the right attitude, the eventual project will be a better project because of the process. How can this be? What is the conclusion of the environmental impact statement writing process? These are fair questions and asked frequently by technology students who become involved in the data collection or the myriad of staff tasks that go into an environmental report.

The environmental impact report does not become a stale document resigned to a dusty shelf. By policy and regulation, the report must be prepared in a full public disclosure way. That means there can be no secret reports which are seen only by a chosen few. Anybody has the right to inspect any part of an environmental report. They may question the methods of field study, make suggestions, even submit studies of their own for consideration. When the environmental writers get to the point where they believe they've identified the social, economical and environmental impacts of a proposed project, those findings must be held up for public disclosure, scrutiny and criticism. It is not unlike preparing a term paper and presenting it for a grade. In this situation, there is not one teacher giving the grade. It is the public and depending on their perceptions of what they read, the grade can be "A" to "F." Responsible criticisms have to be addressed in final environmental impact statements. The technical writer must address each substantive comment received on the draft environmental statement which was circulated for comments or received at public meetings and hearings and include his/her answers to them within the covers of the final environmental statement.

Where does the statement which could be rather voluminous go from this point? To the decision maker. And who is that individual? It is a high governmental official which has the federal responsibility for the program under which the proposed project will seek funds in order to be built. Most transportation projects, highways, airports, harbor improvements, new buses, subways, rail lines, depend on federal tax dollars for their viability because they provide for *public* transportation. A new building project or the introduction of a new model car can be solely a private funds matter because their success or failure is a matter of their acceptance by the public in a competitive market place.

So the environmental impact statement, its data base, record of comments received and subsequent answers, is delivered to the decision maker's office for review and approval/disapproval. The decision maker may have a staff which will review the documents and advise him/her. In the final analysis, it is he or she that must render the decision whether the project can proceed, be sent back for modification, or flat out rejected as too harmful to the environment to be built. This decision maker will also require information which came out of the impact statement research to become parts of the project. He/she could require noise walls, stream crossings, neighborhood park creation, moving of historical buildings (etc.) to be made parts of the transportation project. These would not have happened if it weren't for an environmental impact process. These are tremendous responsibilities and ones that are not taken lightly by top administrators who by their office are entrusted with these decision making responsibilities. It all comes down to these decisions which are based on hundreds, perhaps thousands, of technical inputs that comprise in their totality an environmental impact statement. The prime authors of the document are technology-trained individuals.

Although most transportation projects go through the environmental impact assessment process, public disclosure, public hearings and permit process and eventually are constructed for the benefit of the public, there are some projects which become very controversial. Sometimes the federal decision makers finding is challenged as being incorrect. Eventually, the controversy ends up in court, state and/or federal with plaintiffs, defendants, lawyers, judges and witnesses. The role of the technologist will most likely be that of a witness. Here his/her technical knowledge coupled with his/her ability to express that knowledge in terms that can be readily understood by judges and/or juries becomes very important. Courts have final jurisdiction whether a controversial project is constructed and their decision can very well turn on the expert testimony from a technologist.

Summary

When one embarks on a technology career in transportation, the need to jointly assess environmental impacts is married to the technical application of skills obtained during formal training. The technology teacher in preparing students for careers in transportation must recognize that physical, natural, and social sciences have as great a bearing on a successful professional career as attainment of skills in (for example) structural design or survey or strength of materials. Further written and oral skills development in order to properly put environmental assessments to public scrutiny have an important place in the technology's students curriculum because if he/she cannot express technical work in written or oral expression, the graduate in the work place is at a severe disadvantage.

The environmental assessment component in transportation project development is critical to whether they ever get built or remain on the shelf, a useless roll of plans. The complete technology education curriculum embodying the sciences, social sciences, humanities, communication and written skills are in their total basic to the technology student being able to function and excel in the environmental assessment component. And therefore, the totally prepared technology student is key to whether the transportation project dream becomes a functioning reality.

REFERENCES

Gubala, Robert W. "The Processing of Environmental Impact Assessment and Reporting With Transportation Project Development." Ph.D. dissertation University of Connecticut, 1978.

National Environmental Policy Act of 1969. 42 United States Code (U.S.C.) 4321 et. seq.

U.S. Department of Transportation. *Environmental Assessment Notebook Series* by Skidmore, Owings and Merril, Washington, D.C.: Government Printing Office, 1975.

U.S. Department of Transportation. Federal Highway Administration *Guidance for Preparing and Processing Environmental and Section 4 (f) Documents*, FHWA Technical Advisory T 6640. 8A, October 30, 1987.

CHAPTER 5

Transportation Technology Education in the Elementary School

By Dr. William R. Cupples
(Assistant Professor at Western Illinois University)

Philosophical Basis

The primary goal of education is to nurture the process of lifelong learning in a technological world. The program is extremely complex and must provide citizens with historical, sociological, technological and scientific knowledges that will educate decision makers for the future. Because technological knowledge is an integral part of the entire knowledge base, it should logically follow that experiences that include an integration of technology should be included in the elementary school curriculum. Peterson (1986) states, "The elementary school is where the development of an understanding should begin. Technology constitutes a universal element within all cultures and provides an important requisite for cultural survival" (p.47).

Elementary school children are constantly exposed to technology each day of their lives. However, they, as most adults, do not understand the underlying principles and concepts that cause the technological dominance in their world. When considering the technology associated with transportation, young people may be cognizant of personal, private and public transportation modes, but they may not understand the key foundational technological ideas that comprised the development, nor would they have been exposed to the social and cultural consequences of the technology. DeVore (1980) states,

> The primary reason for inquiry into the nature of technology is because of the significance of the relationship of technology, humankind and society. Of all the creations of the human mind, those concerned with tools,

> machines, techniques and technical systems have the greatest impact on altering reality. The cultural and social structures of entire societies, the relationships of humankind to the natural environment, and of individuals to society and to each other have been altered by the new technologies. . . . The new environment, created by humankind is a technological environment. . . . There is a new awareness about technology, ranging from deep uncertainty and anxiety about humankind's ability to control and use technology for human fulfillment rather than destruction. Life today depends on a technology that most people do not understand, one that operates within a social structure they are unable to control (p. 215).

The elementary school classroom is an appropriate environment to study technology including those key foundational principles and concepts of transportation. Students enrolled in elementary programs will become future decision makers of our technological society. With the power of their voices, actions and votes, they will be able to determine the solutions to complex technological questions that may determine new directions and consequences for the society. These young people must be provided with the foundational knowledge to make them a technologically literate electorate in the future.

Transportation Technology Content at the Elementary School Level

Technological questions and problems related to transportation technology can be effectively studied at the elementary school level. Topics selected should be relevant and should be easily integrated with other academic areas rather than teaching units separately.

Each of the state plans surveyed have included insights of the nature of transportation technology at the elementary and middle school levels. The "West Virginia Plan for Technology Education" (1987) provides for an awareness level, integrated technology to be included in the K–4 level and an exploration of transportation at the 5–8 level. No specific goals are presented for the elementary/middle school levels. The Missouri Industrial Technology Education Guide (1987) also recommends the "awareness" of technology and the integration of activities into the on-going program for grades K–5. Ohio's model (1989) presents the study of technology at the awareness level in the primary grades as the means for illustrating the interrelatedness of the curriculum that includes the sciences, math, language, social studies, etc. The program continues exploration and integration at the middle grades. "The Technology Education in Pennsylvania Program Guide" also recommends the integration of activities for an understanding of "how people transport." In addition, Pennsylvania includes laboratory experiences in power/transportation.

Instructional Strategies

The student should be an active participant in the teaching/learning situation. Activities should serve to reinforce formal learning so students may retain the principles and concepts presented in the unit. Students will then have the opportunity to apply the knowledge gained in many subject areas to the activity. Kieft (1989) states that activity based instruction is a recommended approach to achieve this goal. Through manipulative, or learn-by-doing experiences, children acquire understandings that they are more apt to integrate and retain (p. 36).

Since studies in transportation technology shall be structured to reinforce and integrate the existing formal curriculum, it is suggested that teachers use current text materials to determine appropriate activities that will demonstrate transportation concepts. Activities can then be designed by establishing appropriate goals and objectives that might be related to the study of transportation technology. Activities should be realistic, challenging, and interesting so that students will have a desire to continue the learning process on an individual basis and will have the incentive to participate in another activity based experience.

Instructional strategies will depend upon the age-level, skills and other characteristics of the students, size of the class, availability of published materials, availability of museums and commercial expositions and examples related to transportation technology; the availability of tools and materials that may be safely used by the students, the classroom setting and the abilities of the teacher. The teacher needs to consider the students' special characteristics, needs and interests when preparing both the content and the method of instruction (Kieft, p. 41).

Selecting Learning Activities

Typical learning activities may include: role-playing, design and construction of simulations or models, design of games, field trips, problem solving exercises, use of toys that demonstrate technological concepts, planning exercises using maps and other visuals, computer programs and kits.

Appropriate activity or activities must be determined by the teacher and support goals, purposes and objectives of the unit. First, the objectives must be defined. These must include any science, math, language, history/social studies and other subject area objectives that are to be accomplished. Second, objectives related to the study of transportation must be defined. These objectives must be integrated with those listed above. Finally, student behaviors (behavioral objectives) must be defined. Student behaviors must consider age level, psychomotor development and safety factors that will ensure successful completion of the unit. All levels of objectives must reflect appropriate guidelines for general education.

Activities, materials, delivery, management strategies and evaluation can be determined from listed objectives. Activities may be designed to achieve immediate feedback or they may be defined to last several days.

For example, a short primary level teaching/learning unit may be designed that uses terrestrial transportation to integrate math and language concepts. The language component may include a letter written by the class to government agencies to ask for materials related to the lesson. The same unit may include a construction activity. Students might reinforce mathematics concepts by counting parts, measuring or naming geometric shapes of components that will be used to construct simple models. In addition, the students might develop psychomotor skills by gluing and painting the same models.

A sixth grade class may use terrestrial transportation activities to integrate a greater number of subject areas and issues. For example, the activities may include the integration of reading to investigate a specific topic, writing and spelling to synthesize and report findings, science and math to explain physical changes, history to determine key foundational developments and social studies to define social and cultural consequences. In addition, students might construct working models and products that involve the use of tools, processes and unique materials. Finally, students may have the opportunity to become involved in the study of several careers.

The unit may last several weeks at the sixth grade level and only a few hours at the primary level. But, students should have indefinite opportunity to learn, develop critical thinking skills and to synthesize knowledge at each level.

As teachers become more sophisticated in using interdisciplinary units to teach concepts, the problem solving approach may be used to present the unit. Typically, five steps are used in problem solving:

1. define the problem
2. brainstorm

3. select solutions
4. implement solutions
5. evaluate

The approach is derived from the scientific community and lends itself well to the solution of technological problems. Peterson (1986) states that, "Students enjoy this method of learning and find it challenging. Problem solving and subsequent exploration and discovery affords them opportunities to consolidate their knowledge in unique ways through application to the solution of a real problem" (p.60).

Students may repeat steps as often as is needed to arrive at an appropriate solution or, the approach allows for several solutions to be affected simultaneously. However problem solving may be used, students will have the opportunity to be creative in the use of knowledge, tools, materials and techniques in their solutions. Problem solving encourages students to be responsible for evaluating their own progress, because it is clearly evident when a workable solution has been developed (Peterson, 1986, p. 60).

Several problem solving programs have been developed to promote the problem solving capabilities of youth and young adults. Two such programs are "Invent America" and "Olympics of the Mind". These two programs encourage the use of problem solving techniques. The process used in each of these programs could be adapted for use in teacher designed teaching/learning units. In addition, science fairs are held annually in most regions of the country. Students have the opportunity to enter solutions to problems that involve each of the formal subject learning areas with transportation technology.

Many industries and technical societies have entered into partnerships with schools. These organizations sponsor contests, provide technical assistance and resource persons to lecture/demonstrate in the classroom environment. Teachers, administrators and students can develop resource networks that will identify organizations and industries in their local area that are willing to develop partnerships with the school.

Sample Transportation Technology Units

Two examples of transportation technology units are offered to demonstrate how technological concepts can be implemented into elementary school programs. The units are designed to be examples only and may require modification to be appropriate for individual classroom implementation.

Title of unit: Transportation—An Introduction
Student population: Kindergarten
Time: 1–3 days

Goals:

1. Students will identify different modes of transportation.
2. Students will become aware of the four environments for transportation: land, marine, atmospheric and space.
3. Integrated activities will provide motivation to students to continue the learning process.

Lesson Objectives:

General:

1. Understand how and why people use transportation to move themselves and goods (social studies).
2. Apply concepts of measurement in the construction of models depicting different modes of transportation (math).
3. Use music and poetry to provide an understanding of transportation (fine arts).
4. Write letters requesting information related to transportation (language arts).

Transportation:

1. Understanding the meaning of transportation.
2. Identify types of transportation.

Behaviors to be Demonstrated:

1. Copy or clip examples of transportation from magazines.
2. Define the word "transportation" and give example modes of transportation.
3. Copy an example letter requesting information on transportation examples.
4. Construct models of transportation vehicles.
5. Construct a background scene for the transportation vehicles using poster paints.
6. Sing music and repeat poetry related to transportation.

Sequence of Instruction:

1. Introduce basic concepts of transportation by having students name several means of transportation.

2. Have students draw or cut several examples named previously from magazines and have them make a collage.
3. Have students request materials from a local transportation company. The teacher and students will compose the letter on the chalk board. The students will copy the letter.
4. Have students build wooden models of different modes of transportation. (Materials will be precut. Students assemble and paint the models.)
5. Permit the students to complete a background for the completed model to be displayed.
6. Select music, poetry or a short story related to transportation and involve the students in presenting the activity.
7. Complete an evaluation/wrap-up session to review unit and student outcomes.

Title of Unit: Space Transportation
Student Population: 5th or 6th grade
Time: 2–4 weeks

Goals:

1. Students will become aware of the integration of science, mathematics, technology and other areas when people and goods are transported into space.
2. Students will identify types and characteristics of space vehicles.
3. Students will be provided with a challenging experience that will provide motivation for continued learning experiences.

Lesson Objectives:
General:

1. Write letters to a regional NASA resource center requesting information on space flight (language arts).
2. Research space travel and complete reports on their findings (language arts).
3. Complete a lineage study of space research (history/social studies).

4. Calculate altitudes of launched rockets (math).
5. Identify, list and describe components of rocket fuels for model rocket engines (science).

Transportation:

1. Identify list and describe materials used in space vehicles.
2. Identify, list and describe propulsion systems used in space vehicles.
3. Identify list and describe the integration of technologies required to achieve space flight.
4. Describe a basic guidance system used in space vehicles.
5. Describe the support system associated with space travel that maintains life and assures safe travel to and from destinations.

Behaviors to be Demonstrated:

1. Complete a lineage study that identifies key technical developments in space travel.
2. Design and build and launch a single or multi-stage rocket.
3. Research, design and build a tracking device that will aid in determining altitudes traveled by the rocket.
4. Write letters to NASA requesting materials related to space travel.
5. Write a technical report on one technical development related to a system used in space travel.
6. Design and build a display that relates to space travel.

Sequence of Instruction:

1. Introduce space transportation by discussing some of the key ideas, principles and concepts that are unique to space transportation.
2. Assign readings that will enhance the students' perspectives about space travel.
3. Assign the rocket design problem. Have students use the problem solving approach to complete appropriate solutions to the problem.
4. Include writing exercises—reports, information requests, worksheets and others—that will allow

students opportunities to express themselves and achieve depth in understanding of knowledge presented.

5. Assign other technical problems as needed. These may include: launchers, tracking devices, recovery devices, etc.
6. Schedule launch day. Invite guests, including the news media to witness the students' efforts.
7. Complete an evaluation/wrap-up session with the students to review unit and student outcomes.

Evaluation

Teachers need to evaluate the effectiveness of each activity to determine the effectiveness in terms of the students' expectations and objectives having been met. Each unit should be revised or rewritten based upon the evaluations. The following items should be considered when evaluating the unit.

1. Student learning outcomes.
   Did the student actually learn what was defined in the objectives? Should objectives be rewritten to more carefully define what was expected?
2. Concepts and content.
   Was the unit appropriate for the age level and experience of the student?
3. Manipulative skills.
   Were the students able to complete the required tasks in a manner that ensured success? What additional planning would be required to make the lab experience run more smoothly?
4. Interdisciplinary outcomes.
   Were objectives met? Were new relationships discovered that should be included in future units? Were students made aware of the interdisciplinary nature of the activity?

Laboratory Facilities

Experiences in transportation technology can be incorporated into most classroom environments with little modification. Successful activities probably depend as much on attention to good planning and implementation strategies as they do on quality laboratory facilities. Doyle (1989) discusses four models that can be included within the classroom or can be separate:

> Learning Centers. "A learning center is usually a small area within the classroom that can accommodate a small number of students (1–5) at any one time . . . A learning center could be organized for simple laboratory experiments or for constructional activities" (p. 46).
>
> Work Areas. "A work area is a special section of the classroom that is set aside for experiments and manipulative activities. It should be located away from students that are doing academic activities. This space does not have the same characteristics as a learning center in that it is usually not a permanent spot nor is it separated from other areas of the classroom. Tools, equipment and materials are usually moved into the area and remain there until a selected activity is completed" (p. 47).
>
> Multipurpose Room. "A multipurpose room is a separate room...used for a variety of special activities. Tools, equipment and materials can be moved into the multipurpose room and used by students to work on large projects" (p. 47).
>
> General, Comprehensive Laboratory. The ideal comprehensive laboratory is designed and built specifically to house a technology program. The comprehensive laboratory includes office space, storage space and a laboratory or work area that includes the tools, equipment and furniture appropriate for teaching young learners about technology" (pp. 47–48).

Each facility has definite advantages for the teacher and the learner. Activities associated with kindergarten and primary grade level students work well in learning centers or work areas. Older students who work on more complex projects and materials require more of the advantages of the multipurpose room or general laboratory.

Many activities associated with the study of transportation technology require some specialized equipment. For example, experiments associated with aerodynamics may require the use of a small wind tunnel or other inquiry with marine transportation may require water testing. These and other specialized kinds of equipment require special design for storage. Teachers should consider modeling specialized to scale so that space requirements do not dominate physical facilities.

In addition, activities requiring more than one day require storage while work is in process. Teachers need to plan for storage when designing both facilities and activities.

Tools and Supplies

Teachers need to select quality tools that are designed to accommodate the dexterity of the students. Doyle (1989) suggests that the type and quantity of tools will vary according to the type of program and activities planned (p. 48). General purpose tools for measuring, fastening, sawing, marking, clamping and forming should be kept in good repair. Programs on limited budgets and kindergarten through grade three level programs may wish to consider using portable tool carts that contain a basic cadre of tools. Specialized tools can be purchased to accommodate specific activities.

Doyle (1989) recommends a basic set of tools for technology activities (p. 49). These include:

Awl
Auger bit set
Expansion bit
Bit brace
C clamps, 4"
Bar clamps
Spring clamps
Countersink
Wing dividers
Hand drill
Drill points 1/16–11/64
Twist drills, high speed
Files, all purpose 8"
Surform shaver
Woodworker's vise (soft face), clamp on
Bench rule, wood, 12"
File card
Plane, block 1-5/8" × 6"
Pliers, side cutting, 6"
Tape, steel, metric and English 2/4" × 3m
Surform replacement blade, flat fine cut; round; pocket type
Yardstick, maple brass strips
Back saw, 12", 12 point
Crosscut saw, 16", 14 point
Saw angle guide
Hack saw, 12"
Coping saw
Saw horses
Screwdriver set
Snips
Combination square, English and metric
Try square
Homeowner's square 24" with tables and conversion information
Surform tool, file type, regular cut
Surform tool, round
Rasp and file, 4" in-hand, 8"
Hammer, curved claw, 13 oz, 10 oz, 7 oz
Utility knife, 6" retractable
Utility knife replacement blades
Plane, bench 1-3/4" × 9-1/4"
Plane, trimming, 2" × 3-1/2"
Nail set, 3 per set, 1/32", 1/16", 3/32"
Coping saw blade, 6-1/2" pin end, 15 teeth per inch

Safety items, paper products, fasteners, lumber and other general art supplies can be accommodated when placing an annual order for general supplies. Materials unique to specific transportation related activities may be purchased as needed by the school or by the students.

Student Displays

As students complete assigned activities, space should be provided to publicly display their achievements. Areas may be set aside in the classroom or school for the purpose of displaying completed work. In addition, arrangements may be made with municipal authorities or private business to display completed activities. Public displays provide recognition to students and help teachers to promote an awareness of the importance of technology education.

Summary

Transportation technology education in the elementary school provides opportunities to integrate learning experiences for young people. Such studies are important elements in the life-long educational experiences of citizens who will be decision makers in a technological world. Many activities will provide brief visits and comprehensions of that world, while other activities will provide more in-depth experiences. All integrated activities will provide opportunities for students to develop skills and knowledge that may have been difficult or impossible with traditional teaching/learning activities. Activities that show interrelationships of subjects will provide challenging and rewarding learning experiences that should encourage students to actively and enthusiastically continue the learning process.

REFERENCES

Bolyard, G. (1986). *Transportation: A West Virginia Industrial Arts/Technology Education Curriculum.* Charleston, WV: The West Virginia Board of Education: Bureau of Vocational, Technical and Adult Education.

Calder, C. R. (1989). Safety Practices in Teaching Technology. In M. A. Doyle & C. R. Calder, Jr. (Eds.) *Technology Education for the Elementary School* (pp. 41–45). TECC Monograph 15.

Colelli, L. A. (1989). The World of Technology. In M. A. Doyle & C. R. Calder, Jr. (Eds.) *Technology Education for the Elementary School* (pp. 11–29). TECC Monograph 15.

DeVore, P. W. (1980). *Technology: An Introduction.* Worcester: Davis Publications, Inc.

Doyle, M. A. (1989). The Learning Environment. In M. A. Doyle & C. R. Calder, Jr. (Eds.) *Technology Education for the Elementary School* (pp. 46–52). TECC Monograph 15.

Kieft, L. D. (1989). Activities for Teaching Technology Education. In M. A. Doyle & C. R. Calder, Jr. (Ed.) *Technology Education for the Elementary School* (pp. 53–68). TECC Monograph 15.

Kieft, L. D. (1989). Strategies for Implementation. In M. A. Doyle & C. R. Carter, Jr. (Eds.) *Technology Education for the Elementary School* (pp. 30–40). TECC Monograph 15.

Nanny, R. W. (1989). A Rationale for Studying Technology Education in the K–6 Curriculum. In M. A. Doyle & C. R. Calder, Jr. (Eds.) *Technology Education for the Elementary School* (pp. 3–10). TECC Monograph 15.

Peterson, R. E. (1986). Elementary School Technology Education Programs. In R. E. Jones & J. R. Wright (Eds.) *Implementing Technology Education* Encino: Glencoe Publishing Company.

West Virginia Industrial Arts/Technology Education Curriculum Guide (Transportation) (1986). Charleston: The West Virginia Board of Education, Bureau of Vocational, Technical and Adult Education.

SOURCES OF LEARNING ACTIVITIES

Bame, E. A. & Cummings, P. *Exploring Technology.* Worcester, MA: Davis Publications, Inc., 1980.

The package of text, activity manual and teacher's guide provide information and suggested activities in transportation.

Los Angeles Unified School District—Elementary Industrial Technology Office, 632 N. Madison Avenue, Los Angeles, CA 90004.

An interdisciplinary teaching/learning "heads-on/hands-on" strategy designed to provide experiences in aerospace technology.

National Aeronautics and Space Administration, Goddard Space Flight Center, Greenbelt, MD 20771.

Nine NASA research centers throughout the country provide NASA publications, video tapes, 35 mm slides, audio-cassettes, filmstrips, lesson plans, reference materials and computer software for mathematics, science and technology education teachers that may be incorporated into their classroom lessons.

CHAPTER 6

Transportation Technology Education in the Middle School

By Mr. William E. Tracey, Jr.
(Assistant Professor at Central Connecticut State University)

Evolution of the Middle School

The Junior High School was a product of the many education reform movements that occurred during the late 19th century and early years of the 20th century. Various factors, including a new understanding of adolescent psychology, increased student population, demands for vocational education, studies of student dropouts, criticism of the eight-year elementary school, and increased funding for education have enabled and supported the growth of junior high schools. Ideally, these changes over the past century should provide educational objectives for the junior high school that reflect contemporary society and prepare students to be successful and contributing members.

Not all junior high school teachers and administrators believe that the stated educational objectives for the junior high school have changed to best meet societal or students' needs. Many educators have criticized the junior high school as being too imitative of the senior high school. Critics claim the four-year sequence of college entrance requirements inhibits creative curriculum development in the three-year junior high school. A major emphasis of junior high school becomes starting college bound students off on an educational track. Students not on this track are placed in generalized classes and pass on to more general education or vocational education in high school. These factors, among others, including the earlier onset of puberty among children, have contributed to the establishment of middle schools containing grades 5 or 6 through 8.

Proponents regard the emergence of the middle school not as a rearrangement of the junior high school but a new educational program that identifies and meets the individual needs and interests of students. Eichhorn (1966) suggests that the middle school address psychological, physical and socio-cultural aspects of student development. Students must work on the developmental tasks associated to transitional stages of life. The hallmark of a middle school is that learning is student centered not subject centered.

Definition and Characteristics of Middle Schools

The definition of a middle school best suited to the purposes of this chapter was identified by Cuff (1967). He found that middle school includes grades seven and eight in its organization and does not extend below grades four or above grade eight. Additional research indicates that the vast majority of middle schools typically provide education in grades six through eight.

Georgiady, Riegle, and Romano (1973, pp. 74–85) presented a variety of characteristics that provide a framework for middle schools. These conclusions were reached following a review of the literature, discussions with educators in the field, and observations. The technology educator should find these characteristics helpful in evaluating an existing middle school, establishing a new one or developing middle school programs and curriculum:

- Continuous progress non-graded organization that allows students to progress at their own individual rate regardless of chronological age
- Multi-material approach
- Flexible schedules
- Social experiences appropriate for transient youth
- Team teaching
- Exploratory and enrichment studies
- Independent study
- Basic skill repair and extension
- Creative experiences
- Security factor that meets students needs for a security group
- Evaluation that is personal, positive, nonthreatening and individualized
- Community relations program that is two-way
- Auxiliary staffing to provide individual help

The Middle School Student

Many psychologists have identified the onset of adolescence as a critical period of biological and psychological change for the individual (Bloom, 1976; Elkind, 1974; Rogers, 1969). Puberty is one of the most far-reaching and stressful biological events in the life span. For many young adolescents, the timing of puberty also involves drastic changes in their social environment, foremost among them the transition from elementary to secondary school. These years are highly formative for behavior patterns that impact students' future education, health and have significance throughout adulthood. Adolescence is typically characterized by exploratory behavior, much of which is developmentally appropriate and socially adaptive for most young people.

There is a crucial need to help adolescents at this early age to acquire lasting self-esteem, a flexible and inquiring intellect, reliable relatively close and enduring human relationships, a sense of belonging and contributing to a valued group, and a sense of usefulness in some way beyond the self. They need to find constructive outlet for their inherent curiosity and exploratory energy; and they need a basis for making informed, deliberate decisions, especially on matters that have large consequences, such as future educational choices.

The Middle School Curriculum

Middle school curriculum has been defined by Moss (1976) as all the activities that are carried on under the auspices of the school, including skills, academic subjects, art, music, industrial arts, health, recreation, physical education, outdoor education, clubs and activities. Moss also identified a four area approach for middle school curriculum. Although not all middle schools have this organization most are similar in that the curriculum is separated into areas with a need for integration among the areas to serve the goals of the middle school.

Area I teaches the skills of reading, spelling, writing, computation, typing, library and listening. Area I skills are grouped together because they will be developed on an individual basis, whereas social and athletic skills and the like are developed through and individual instruction within the appropriate subject.

Area II includes the academics, english, social studies, science, mathematics and foreign language. Elementary school teachers are usually certified to teach all these subjects, while other levels allow only certification in individual subjects. The recent trend in teacher education of dual certification is particularly important for middle schools who need teachers that can cross over academic disciplines. Certification in technology education and an academic area such as science or math will allow the technology teacher to share teaching responsibilities or experiment with new and exciting courses.

Area III contains the general education programs, health, recreation and physical education. The subjects included in Area III, have frequently been grouped together. While personal health and sex education may be included in the science curriculum, these and related topics can also be included in technology education as part of bio-related systems.

Area IV consists of art, music, drama and industrial arts which have often been classified together under the heading "the arts." Moss stated "industrial arts with its recent emphasis on technology, could be grouped in Area II, but for reasons of emphasis as well as because of the appellation arts in its title, it is included in Area IV" (p. 46). The fact that one word in the title of the discipline of industrial arts caused as important and broad a subject to be seen in such a limited fashion brings yet another example of the importance of the change to technology education. Technology education has forever removed the "arts" from its title and what is taught in the discipline. This change has in fact moved not only closer to Area II (academics) but technology education can now become a focal point for integrated studies in the middle school. Figure 1 provides a model for the middle school technology education program that is in agreement with Moss but sees technology education as central in the curriculum in the middle school. Transportation technology education curriculum that is well designed, integrated, implemented and offers a broad range of learning opportunities can become a powerful and effective part of the interdisciplinary model through the natural linkages with mathematics and science and all human endeavors.

Transportation Technology

An early attempt was made in 1947 to develop a course of study for transportation as a part of William E. Warner's *A Curriculum to Reflect Technology*. The suggested content was arranged in three categories, land transportation, air transportation, and sea transportation. Although far reaching for the time, this outline was heavily oriented to vehicles and the mechanics of the vehicle.

DeVore (1970) suggested a taxonomy for transportation as one area of the discipline of technology. His taxonomy is divided into systems, type of transportation, class, and order.

Asper (1973) used a matrix to describe his concept of transportation technology. He identified management practices, transportive practices, and trans-

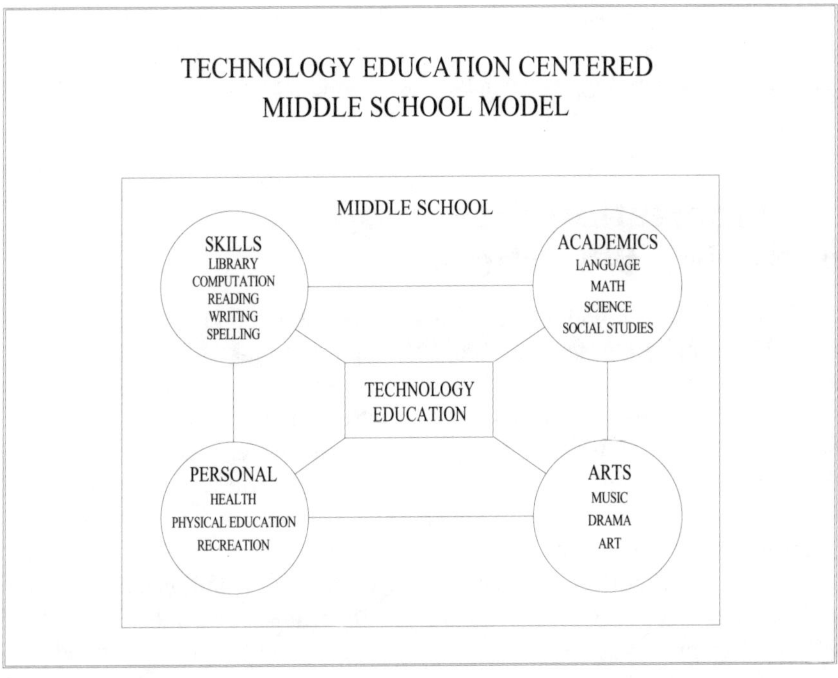

Figure 1

portive installations as his major focus. The subcategories of land, sea and space were included in the matrix.

In 1975, the program of *Transportation in Louisiana* (1974) was published by the combined efforts of the Louisiana State University and the Louisiana State Department of Education. This model was based on a matrix with the moving of cargo and people as one axes and the planning organizing and controlling transportation as another.

Bender (1980) identifies the study of transportation as a system within the context of ideological, sociological, and technological concerns of people.

Several states including Virginia (Power and Transportation, 1977), Tennessee (Tennessee Industrial Arts Curriculum Model, 1977), have identified transportation as a major area of study as well as outlining subject matter content. Fales & Kuetemeyer (1982) noted that most of these descriptions of transportation "leads one to surmise that industrial arts people view the subject from one frame of reference—the 'nuts-and-bolts' of engines" (p. 2).

The definition that is most appropriate to describe transportation technology education in the middle school was offered by Bolyard and Komacek. They state that transportation technology education is "the study of how people use the elements of technology (resources) to design and produce technical systems for the purposes of moving freight and passengers, safely and efficiently, in land, water, air, and space environments, and the impacts these systems have on technological, societal, and biological systems" (1990, p.4).

Transportation Technology in the Middle School

The International Technology Education Association (1985) recommends that all students in the middle school be required to take technology education. Their suggested course sequence calls for a required course, one semester in length for grades 6–7, focusing on an introduction to industrial and technological systems. After completing the required course students should have the opportunity to select elective courses a semester in length studying the technological systems of Communication, Construction, Manufacturing or Transportation. The goal of this curriculum structure is to provide students an orientation to technology and a chance to explore, with additional depth, in an area or areas they find of interest. This type of vertically integrated curriculum is typical of public junior high schools. Although educationally sound and steeped in tradition, middle school proponents would argue that it misses out on the spirit and unique aims of middle school curriculum development.

The ideal structure for middle school technology education must satisfy the philosophical ideals presented by both middle school and technology education proponents. Figure 2 identifies a middle school structure which allows both vertical and horizontal curriculum development. Traditional junior high school technology education programs use the vertical structure in advancing the depth of study in technological systems and complexity of concepts. Middle schools require vertical structure too, but of more importance is a horizontal structure to allow a total integration of technology education and all endeavors and activities within the school. This model, by providing both horizontal and vertical structures will work for all technology education programs whether transitioned from industrial arts in a traditional junior high school or middle school, a non traditional program such as Science Technology and Society (STS), or integration of technology education with other academic areas in schools without specific technology education "programs."

The scope and sequence of technology education in the middle school is influenced by many factors. One of these factors is what kind of technology education program is available in the elementary school. Although technology education is not a traditional elementary school subject, a great deal of curriculum development has been done recently related to elementary school

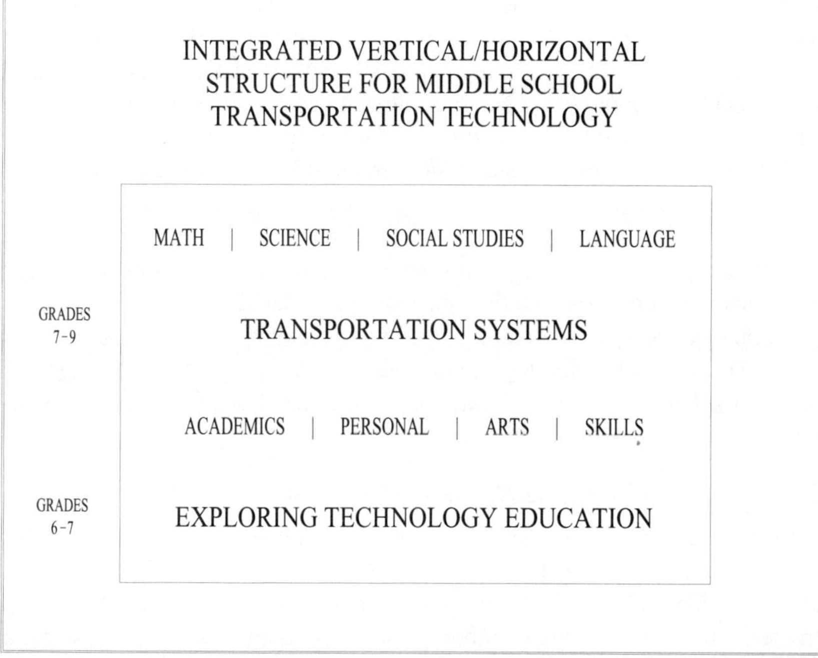

Figure 2

programming. Particular attention has been given to the area of transportation in that NASA, the Challenger Center and the Elementary Aerospace Program in Los Angeles County, among others have developed teaching materials that will provide a "fun" experience while participating in integrated and hands on activities related to transportation and transportation systems. If a technology education program exists in the lower grades, similar but enriched experiences may be developed in the middle school. An elementary program that introduces students to new technologies, tool use, construction of class related projects to further study mathematics, science and social studies, and introduces the systems and impact of technology will provide a middle school with the opportunity for an outstanding program with able and willing students. On the other hand, if there has been minimal or no introduction to technology in grades K–4 or K–5, the program in middle school is well suited to provide the introduction to technology.

High school program offerings in technology education will also influence a middle school curriculum. Students who are excited and interested by middle school transportation technology education will have the opportunity to enroll in additional technology education courses when they transition to high school. High school programs should offer more advanced orientation courses to the technological systems in grades 9 and 10 and technical content specific courses in the higher grades. Some students as a result of their experience in middle school programs may look favorably at the option of a vocational course of study in high school or seek admission to a vocational high school. Middle school can be a place to recruit students for further studies but it must be remembered that technology education in the middle school is not vocational, should have a horizontal as well as vertical structure and it is separate from high school.

A transportation technology program suited to the purposes of the middle school should emphasize four major areas: 1) correlated construction activities with other subjects, 2) awareness of technology and its impact on the students world, 3) a study of technology jointly planned and taught by science, social studies, mathematics and the technology teacher, and 4) development of simple tool skills and awareness.

Correlated Construction Activities

Correlated construction activities with other subjects encompasses a wide variety of projects primarily in core technology and academic classes. For example, a science class may be studying a unit on the solar system. To develop greater perception and understanding the students may want to construct a scale model. The technology education teacher, acting as a consultant, can assist the science teacher and class in designing and constructing the model. This may be undertaken in a technology education class or in the science class or by combining two classes for the purpose of completing the project.

A mathematics class studying concepts that can be illustrated by technology based examples could take advantage of correlated construction activities. Students could build models of gear systems, pulley systems, and simple machines to study ratios, equations and perform calculations related to power transmission. The technology teacher can serve as a consultant sharing with the math class knowledge of model building, materials processing and mechanical power transmission. Technology education core class students could bring their bicycles to school and calculate gear ratios and efficiency while learning to perform simple maintenance. Mathematics teachers could work as consultants to technology education teachers and develop units around this type activity and make mathematics less abstract.

Another example of the correlated construction activity is for a social studies class studying geography or world economics to work on a unit in mass transportation, and with the aid of the technology teacher, plan a facility and construct a model that would move goods, people or both. The joint cooperation of the core teacher and technology education teacher may help students develop a better understanding of technology, the complexity of transportation systems and economic impacts of world trade. Activities of this nature have been carried out in many elementary and junior high schools, but they have frequently been done in isolation, either by technology education teachers alone or by academic teachers. Because an understanding of our economic system has been an important part of the social studies program, and an understanding of the systems of human endeavor has long been a rationale for technology education, there should be closer cooperation between these two curricular areas.

In order to fulfil this area of the middle school technology education program, the technology education teachers should serve as consultants. At least two technology education teacher-consultants should be required in a middle school of 1200 pupils. The technology teachers share responsibility for teaching all four technology systems classes as well as the introduction program in order that one teacher can be available to meet with other subject teachers in planning sessions.

Awareness of Technology

The previous example of a correlated activity on mass transportation leads to perhaps the most important phase of the technology education curriculum. Technology is a complex system of many related fields of study concerned with the human endeavors. Included are scientific invention, engineering design and construction, economics, environmental and social impact. Because technology profoundly affects people's lives, history and sociology are related areas. Rapid scientific and engineering advances leads to new industrial processes and products ranging from the silicone chip to banks of computers controlling an airport. Further application of automation results in temporary technological unemployment of unskilled workers, while creating a demand for skilled technicians. The future will witness even greater scientific/engineering/industrial/economic/sociological changes. If we are to prepare today's youth adequately for life in the future we must include a study of technology in the curriculum.

Jointly Planned and Taught Technology Education

A teaching team composed of science, social studies, mathematics and technology education teachers is recommended in order to plan and teach this complex area effectively. The science teacher should be "generalists" in the branches of science. One of the social studies teachers should have a background in economics, and the other should have a background in sociology and history. The technology instructors must have a thorough understanding of the technological systems, the mathematics teacher should have strength in geometry and trigonometry. This six-teacher team should stress a technology program that is: 1) based on the growth characteristics of middle school youth, 2) part of a system wide K–12 sequence, and 3) related to the other subject matter areas.

The technology units may be divided so that in science class new inventions are studied as applications of scientific principles. For a core, the students study the economic and social effects of automation, while in math classes the same children learn elements of problem solving. The technology teachers illustrate industrial application of computer-based automation through classes in the technology laboratory and through field trips to industries.

Another approach to the study of technology would be to pool the times set aside for core technology, science and mathematics classes. The technology, science and math classes can be grouped on the basis of ability, heterogeneously grouped or part of a special program such as gifted and talented. The groups can be rotated in team taught social studies, science, mathematics and technology classes for an integrated curriculum.

The technology team plans and meets together in order to allocate teaching and project responsibilities and to evaluate progress. Other arrangements, taking into account the previous work of students in technology and industrial processes, can be devised by the team. Because the middle school schedule is flexible, the possibilities for this interdisciplinary approach to technology are almost limitless.

Tool Use Skills

In the area of tool use and simple manipulative activities it is critical to pay attention for conflicts between the students of different sexes. Ten to twelve year old boys may feel antagonism toward girls. The girls may be insecure in using tools and care must be taken so they are not embarrassed to make mistakes in front of the boys. Because of the accident-prone nature of early adolescents and the danger of personal injury, class size should be limited.

If the proper use and care of hand tools was not taught in elementary school, a unit of this nature should be introduced early in the middle school technology education program. The correct way to handle saws, hammers, screwdrivers, wrenches, chisels, and drills should be taught in functional situations.

The tools can function as a bridge for the students to explore areas of technology related to transportation. In the traditional area of power when taught as a subsystem of transportation the understanding of home wiring, fuse boxes, short circuits and other electrical phenomena will provide students with a conceptual knowledge of electricity, transmission of electricity and how tools extend human capability. A unit of this nature might be correlated with the science program or taught exclusively by the technology education teacher. In any event, communication channels should be kept open between these areas of the curriculum in order to avoid duplication of effort.

The ultimate objectives of a transportation technology education program in the middle school is that by studying the human adaptive system of transportation the student can:

- Experience practical application of science principles.
- Experience practical application of mathematical principles.
- Become aware of the career opportunities created by technology.
- Develop possible solutions to technology related problems.
- Work as a group member on tasks related to technological endeavors.
- Identify how technology effects humans and their social systems.
- Identify how technology effects the environment.

Special Needs Students

Two groups of students who will benefit from transportation technology programs in the middle school are the gifted and talented and the special needs populations.

Special needs students can benefit from taking part in middle school transportation technology programs. Some concerns have been expressed about serving both low-incidence handicapped students (e.g. visual, hearing, and orthopedically impaired) and the high-incidence categories of "educable mentally retarded" and/or "learning disabled" in technology education. These groups of students, commonly referred to as "mildly handicapped", comprise the majority of handicapped students who are main-streamed into required technology education orientation classes or elective technological systems exploration classes.

Learning styles that are not commonly needed or used in other so-called "academically-oriented" subjects come into play through involvement in technology education activities (Scott 1985, p.5). Mildly handicapped students can achieve a degree of success in the variety of activities that a transportation program offers. Educational success improves self-concept, helps students feel an interrelatedness with other students and develops an attitude that may improve future school performance, often for the first time in their school careers.

In addition, all students, including the handicapped, will eventually live in a technologically oriented society. With middle school technology education and its integrated curriculum philosophy, mildly handicapped students can receive even greater educational benefits in terms of "academic" knowledge and "technological literacy."

The gifted and talented, and special education philosophies are similar to the middle school philosophy in that the technology teacher uses individualized instruction that allows all students to progress at their own rate. Technology teachers who use the "project method" (individual or group projects) are using individualized instruction. It has been claimed that in fact, technology teachers probably have more experience at individualized instruction than teachers in other subject areas. Both of these groups of students will benefit from transportation technology and activities that are interdisciplinary, of personal interest, and allow students to progress at a pace that is comfortable to them.

Student Learning Activities

Activities that interest students, and enable and reinforce learning are central to the middle school curriculum. Student centered learning requires that teachers use a great many types of activities and allow students to choose, evaluate, and try several different activities.

The activity model presented in Figure 3 is based on a systems model to both facilitate the study of transportation systems and complement an activities oriented system of learning.

The following are some general examples of activities that a transportation technology educator can use at the middle school level. The activities all fit into the systems model and are intended to provide the middle school transportation teacher with some established activities. Teachers can apply their current activities to the model and perhaps identify ways to improve them.

A. History Activities
   Research, design and build working models of early machines.
   Conduct an oral history of transportation changes locally.
B. Geography Related Activities
   Design travel plans or brainstorm efficient routes for travel.
   Design a world wide network to efficiently move goods and people.
C. Social Studies Related Activities
   Research costs of transportation as it effects products.
   Identify the caused by and effects of transportation on society.

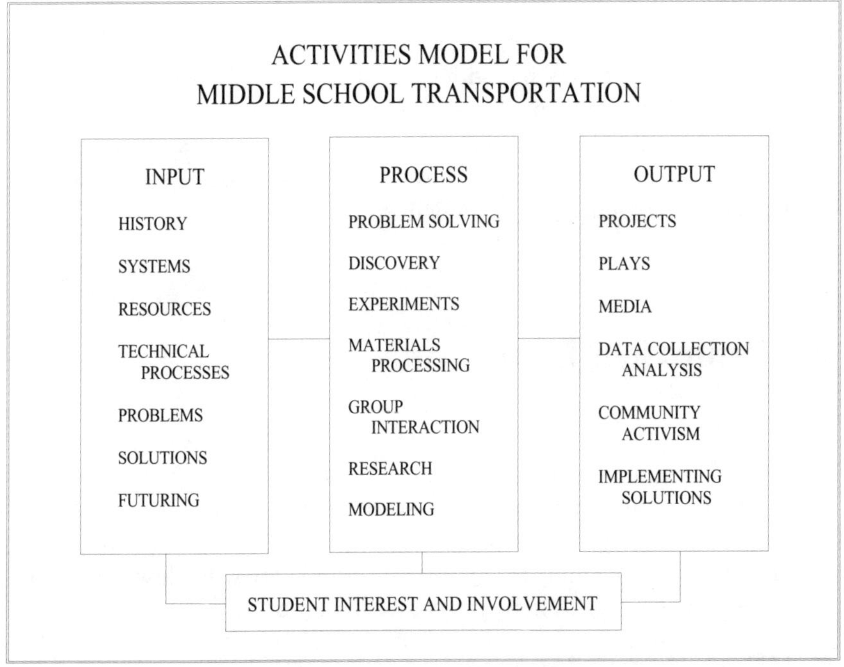

Figure 3

D. Science/Math Related Activities
   Build models and calculate mechanical advantage and efficiency.
   Conduct experiments on transportation and pollution.

E. Hands-on Project Activities
   Build radio controlled vehicles.
   Build vehicles to solve problems such as moving an object.

F. Computer Activities
   Design vehicles using Glide Path or Car Builder Software.
   Simulate flight using Flight Simulator or similar software.

Specific Examples of Middle School Activities

The following activities were developed by Tracey (1987) to provide the middle school technology education teacher with a working format to implement interdisciplinary study. The activities included in this chapter were chosen because they can be done free or with little cost. The few required materials can be readily found for purchase or recycled from other uses. An equipped laboratory is not necessary but with time, creativity and resources the activities can be made very elaborate. The specific focus of the activities are technology concepts that illustrate and use principles of mathematics and science. The activities can also be expanded to integrate language, social studies and other academic content by expanding them.

Air Pollution Detector

Purpose:

The transportation industry has created the ability to travel great distances as a result of the automobile and internal combustion engine. A by-product of this technology is pollution, which has caused government and industry to form regulations concerning this problem. This activity will allow the students to see the particles produced by the combustion process.

Sci/Tech Principles Involved:

Air Pollution, Incomplete Combustion, Particulate Matter

Fuels used by vehicles undergo a process of combustion. These fuels are usually fossil fuels which are carbon-based. Incomplete combustion of these carbons and hydrocarbons produce a variety of pollutants which take the form of gases and particulates. These pollutants may be dangerous to our environment producing serious health problems.

Equipment and Materials:

Two or three standard size glass or plastic microscope slides, flat stick or yardstick, vaseline (petroleum jelly), paper plate, jaw-type clip, nut and bolt, thumbtack and microscope.

Procedure:

A. Exhaust Indicator
   1. Tack a paper plate to the end of a yardstick or similar size flat stick.
   2. Smear the plate with vaseline.
   3. Holding the stick, move the plate near the exhaust pipe of a running car to collect particle matter.

4. Do this process for a new car and an old car without a catalytic converter.
5. Compare the particle matter for both.

B. Particle Collector
1. Bolt a jaw-type clip to a flat stick, such as a point stirrer about 12" long.
2. Smear a thin layer of vaseline over the top of the microscope slide and place it in the jaws of the clip.
3. Set the apparatus in a desired location, such as the production laboratory, making sure it will not be disturbed.
4. After several hours, a day, or a week examine the slide underneath a microscope. Keep sample slides in a plastic box for comparison.
5. Conduct this process in all of the technology laboratories in your school and compare results for each.

Results:

A. Exhaust Indicator

The particles produced by incomplete combustion take the form of gases and unburned carbons. These will appear on the paper plate sample in the form of soot. The older car without a catalytic converter will produce more soot than the newer car. This is an example of the automobile industry's effort to combat air pollution.

B. Particle Collector

The particles in the various technology education labs may take the form of saw dust, soot, plastic dust, and paper lint. These illustrate the need for proper ventilation of facilities to maintain a clean working environment.

Conclusion:

The air pollution problem is quite prevalent as a result of our technology. The results of these experiments indicate the various particle matter that is produced by incomplete combustion. The newer car produces less particle matter due to its emissions control and catalytic converter. When processing different materials such as wood, plastic, metal, and paper in the technology labs, particles are produced which contribute to air pollution. The students should be aware of the many environmental problems created by our technology and actively participate in observing and studying ways of correcting this problem.

Flight

Purpose:

Humans have always been amazed by flight. Our technology has enabled us to put people on the moon as well as travel at phenomenal speeds. This activity will allow students to experiment and observe the scientific principles involved in flight through design and construction of a wind tunnel and airfoil.

Scientific Principles Involved:

Aerodynamics, Streamlining, Friction. To understand flight, students need to learn some basic principles of aerodynamics. This should be done by studying the components of an airfoil. An airfoil can be divided into several parts: the leading edge, which separates the air; the trailing edge, which allows the air to rejoin; the chord, a straight line drawn from the lead edge to the trailing edge; the center line, dividing the airfoil into two equal parts; and the chamber, which is the convex curve of an airfoil rising from its chord.

Equipment and Materials:

Nine square one half gallon size milk cartons, a roll of masking tape, knife, an electric fan, a coat-hanger, 16 oz. soft drink bottle with cork, and various sizes of stiff paper.

Procedures:

A. Wind Tunnel
   1. Remove the tops and bottoms of the nine milk cartons and stack them on top of each other in rows of three to form a honeycomb.
   2. Bind the cartons together with tape and place them in front of the electric fan.
   3. When the fan is turned on, the tunnel is in operation and may be used for testing an airfoil.

B. Airfoil Construction & Design
   1. Take a piece of coat-hanger wire and bend it into an "L" shape.
   2. Place the short arm of the wire onto the cork of the bottle, which serves as a stand.
   3. Bend a piece of the paper into the shape of an "airfoil" or "wing" over the long arm of the wire.

4. Set the hanger and "wing" in front of the model wind tunnel, with the folded edge of the paper facing the air stream.
5. Turn on the fan.
6. As the blast of air blows against the paper airfoil, notice the position it takes.

Test:

A. Devise a number of other shapes and designs out of paper. Test each paper form by using the model wind tunnel. Which shape provides the best lift?
B. Have the students design cardboard models of airplanes. Use various aviation magazines and books in your school's library for research into various designs.

Results:

The airfoil is shaped in such a way that the pressure beneath it becomes greater than the pressure above, as the air stream flows past the upper and lower surfaces. The pressure beneath the airfoil creates lift, the force that sends the plane aloft and keeps it in the air. The wings of an airplane are shaped in this manner.

Conclusion:

The many designs of airfoils and airplanes created by technology education students will be affected differently as they begin testing with the wind tunnel. Some may flop and some may be very successful, the purpose however is that each student will design, construct, test and experiment with various scientific principles involved in flight.

Determining Horsepower

Purpose:

In technology education we use various types of equipment and machines to do work and produce products efficiently. In the areas of manufacturing, communication and transportation this principle is widely used. This activity will allow the student to understand the importance of work and the role it plays in producing goods and services efficiently for our society.

Sci/Tech Principles:

Energy, Force, Power and Horsepower. Energy is the ability to do work. Work can be defined as force exerted over a distance. This is simply moving something from one place to another a given distance at a given speed. Force is applied to perform work. The power produced by work is measured in horsepower. Horsepower is simply a unit of power, which is used to measure the rate at which work is performed.

Equipment and Materials:

Flight of stairs, students, a few hardbound books (example of load), tape measure, bathroom scale and stopwatch.

Procedures:

1. Measure the distance between the bottom of the stairs to the top of the stairs with the tape measure.
2. Have each student weigh themselves using scale.
3. Record each student's weight on a data sheet of paper.
4. One at a time have each student run up the stairs.
5. Time each student as they begin their run until they reach the top of the stairs with the stopwatch.
6. Record each student's time on a data sheet of paper.
7. Determine the amount of horsepower you produce.

Formula for horsepower:

$$\text{H.P.} = \frac{(\text{students weight}) \times (\text{stairway height})}{(\text{time required to run up}) \times (550)}$$

8. Now have the students run up the stairs a second time while carrying the stack of books (load).
9. The weight of the load should be added to the students weight on their data sheet.
10. Record the time it takes each students to run up the stairs with the load.
11. Determine the horsepower for the second run.
12. Compare the horsepower for run one and two.
13. What can be determined from the results?

Results:

The students who are carrying the stack of books use more horsepower to climb the stairs because of the load.

Conclusions:

The concept of work is involved in many applications to produce goods and services through specific technologies. These technologies produce units of power to do work at efficient levels.

Evaluation of Learning

Middle school philosophy limits competition and substitutes direct conferences and written evaluations for formal grading systems. Individualized instruction and evaluation recognizes the unique characteristics of each child and his or her own level of maturation and achievement. Comparisons with others as a means of evaluation should be discouraged. The goal of the middle school is to help students to feel capable, to want to learn, and know something about themselves and the areas of learning which they may find particularly rewarding. They should learn that more can be achieved through cooperation than through competition and that each person has unique characteristics which make him or her of special value. The organization and atmosphere created in middle schools should reflect these goals.

Teachers in middle schools are often dismayed by the unwillingness of many students to answer questions, volunteer to solve problems and stand out as an individual. Frequently, these attitudes can be traced back to earlier activities where children may have had discouraging experiences. When maturity occurs, the memory of earlier humiliations prevent children from risking similar occurrences even though they may now be ready to compete more effectively. This may also happen in an academic and social context.

One of the most difficult tasks in education to do well is the evaluation of students. Evaluation should be for the purpose of promoting further learning. It should be a positive supportive experience. Unfortunately, evaluation systems are often used for other ends, often involving fierce competition. Teachers sometime use grading systems to motivate, punish, or control. In this they frequently have parents as allies. It is assumed that students with poor grades will naturally work harder to achieve better grades. Good marks become the objective of learning. Technology education teachers in middle schools should use grades as a method providing additional student growth through learning.

Lab Facilities for Middle School Transportation

Although the topic of facilities will be covered in another section of this book it is worth mentioning a few considerations related to facilities for middle school transportation.

Bolyard and Komacek (1990) identified three options (including the unlikely totally new school) for changing existing facilities to teach transportation. The two remaining options were using a general industrial arts shop and in a worse case scenario a former power laboratory. Another option that may occur in middle schools is that technology education will have no dedicated laboratory or facility at all.

The middle school literature focuses on several physical areas of the school that will enable the technology teacher to implement a transportation program, unit or activities. All middle schools should contain computer laboratories, instructional material/ media centers, science laboratories and classrooms. The four major emphases of middle school technology education, correlated construction activities, awareness of technology, jointly planned and taught academic and technology courses, and tool use skills can all be taught by sharing these facilities.

Summary

The teaching of transportation technology holds great promise for middle school technology education. The major goals of the middle school focus on student's personal development, provide for the transitional nature of students, and include a wide variety of exploratory educational experiences. The middle school curriculum must be interdisciplinary with varied instructional methods including, problem solving groups, individualized projects, discovery learning and a range of media supported learning. Transportation technology education can provide all these opportunities for students and even more. Implementation of programs that teach the system of transportation will increase students awareness of technology, provide interrelated learning, and that teach basic skills and concepts create opportunities for students and their future.

REFERENCES

Asper, N.L. (1973). Technology through power and transportation. *Industrial arts and the challenge of an urban society*. Washington, D.C.: American Industrial Arts Association. pp. 296–297.

Bender, M. (1980). In H. Anderson & J. Bensen (Eds), *Technology and society: Interfaces with industrial arts*. Washington, D.C.: American Council on Industrial Arts Teacher Education. pp. 268–298.

Bloom, Benjamin S. (1976). *Human Characteristics and School Learning*. New York: Macmillan Publishing Co., Inc.

Bolyard, G. & Komacek, S. (1990) The learning environment for transportation education. In W. Tracey (Ed.) *Proceedings of technology education symposium XII*. New Britain: Central Connecticut State University.

Cuff, William A. (1967). Middle schools on the march. Bulletin of the National Association of Secondary School Principals. Volume 51, February, 1967, p. 83.

DeVore, P.W. (1970). Transportation technology: The identification of content and method. *Journal of Industrial Arts Education, 29*(6), pp. 18–22.

Eichhorn, Donald H. (1966). *The Middle School*. New York: The Center for Applied Research in Education.

Elkind, David. (1974). *Children and Adolescents*. 2nd ed. New York: Oxford University Press.

Fales, J.F. (1975). *Development and pilot test of a curriculum for transportation in Louisiana*. Unpublished doctoral dissertation, Texas A&M University.

Georgiady, Nicholas, P., Riegle, Jack, D., & Romano, Louis, G. (1973). What are the characteristics of the middle school, *The Middle School: Selected Readings on an Emerging School Program*. Chicago: Nelson-Hall Co.

Kleintjes, P.L. (1965). The transportation division. In W.E. Warner (Ed.), *A curriculum to reflect technology*. Columbus, Ohio: Epsilon Pi Tau.

International Technology Education Association (1985) *Technology education: a perspective on implementation*. Reston, VA: ITEA.

Moss, Theodore C. (1969). *Middle School*. Boston: Houghton Mifflin Company.

Rogers, Carl, R. (1969). *Freedom to Learn*. Columbus, Ohio: Charles E. Merrill Publishing Co.

Scott, Michael L. (1987). Serving mildly handicapped students in technology education. The Technology Teacher 45(3), pp. 5–9.

Tennessee Department of Education (1977). *Tennessee industrial arts curriculum model.* Smyrna: Educational Media Center.

Tracey, W.E. Jr. (1987). Science activities for technology education. Unpublished Paper. Norfolk, VA. International Technology Education Association International, Conference.

Virginia Department of Education. (1977). *Power and transportation technology.* Richmond: Industrial Arts Education Service.

CHAPTER 7

Transportation Technology Education in the High School

By Dr. Robert A. Daiber
(Technology Teacher & Chairperson at Triad High School, St. Jacob, Illinois)

Introduction

Teaching transportation technology in the high school provides opportunities for students to investigate, develop, and test transportation systems. A variety of instructional units can be included in transportation courses which pertain to the following: the history of transportation, important technical developments, the operation of vehicles, the shipment of goods and people, consumer information, and career awareness. Typically, class activities involve students encountering problem-solving or decision-making tasks regarding transportation systems. For example, students may be assigned to develop the most efficient route to move goods from one city to another. The transportation curriculum should be an equal part of the high school technology education program.

For some reason, the area of transportation is usually the most underdeveloped content area in a technology education program. McCrory (1980) indicated this curriculum deficiency may be due to the fact that transportation is not usually considered an industry and classroom teachers do not understand how to approach teaching it. In schools where teachers have been negligent or confused about developing transportation courses, auto mechanics and auto body classes may represent the transportation curriculum. Such classes misrepresent the transportation portion of a technology program. To provide direction for teachers interested in developing a transportation curriculum, the following sections of this chapter will explain what transportation technology is as a subject area, why it is important for high school students to study, and how it is taught.

Transportation Technology: A Program of Study

Transportation technology is an area of study which focuses on how people and products are moved within a society. The study of transportation technology involves students learning about the process by which transportation occurs. The *Jackson's Mill Industrial Arts Curriculum Theory* (1981) identified that the process of transportation included the stages of receiving, loading, transporting, unloading, and delivering. To graphically depict this process, a systems model is presented in Figure 1. The process of transportation occurs in four general environments (terrestrial, marine, atmosphere, and space). These four domains are areas of study used as content organizers for curriculum and instructional development.

A Rationale for Study

Transportation is a major technical adaptive system used by humans in society. The necessity to move people and goods is an age-old process which has become sophisticated in the high tech world we live today. The demand by society to be mobile is responsible for the sporadic growth of transportation systems this century. Transportation has personal, commercial, and governmental impacts on our world. Today, hundreds of people work in the field of transportation to build, operate, and service transportation systems. The lifestyle of the American society is dependent on modern and efficient means of transportation. For these reasons, curriculum developers of state technology education plans (Illinois, Indiana, Missouri, New York, West Virginia et al.)

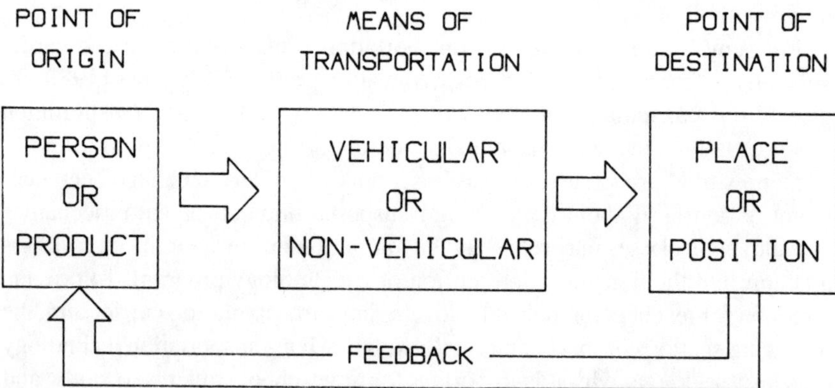

Figure 1: A transportation systems model for instructional development.

have included transportation technology as a subject area high school students should study as part of their technology education.

The transportation technology curriculum serves as an area of study where students can learn about the design and operation of transportation vehicles, the resources needed to operate transporting systems, the industrial implications, and the societal and environmental impacts. The goals of a transportation curriculum are to provide students with knowledge and information of this technological system. Studying transportation technology increases students' technological literacy dimension in that it broadens their vocabulary dimension and knowledge base.

To teach transportation technology to high school students effectively, the transportation curriculum should emphasize several objectives.

1. Students should learn about the many transportation systems in our world.
2. Students should become knowledgeable of the function of many different transportation vehicles.
3. Students should learn about the engineering and design of transportation systems.
4. Students should become competent in the use of general tool and material process tasks as related to transportation.
5. Students should receive instruction which relates math, science, and social studies content in transportation learning units.
6. Students should be introduced to the global business of transportation technology and the many related careers.
7. Students should become knowledgeable of the social, economical, environmental, and cultural implications transportation technology has on our world.
8. Students should investigate possible and probable future trends in transportation technology.

A Philosophical Statement

Technology educators (Savage, Sterry, et al., 1990) believe the study of transportation technology should be an integral part of all technology education programs because it is a part of the technological knowledge in our world. At the high school level, students should be presented with instructional content that will provide orientation units to all technological systems (grades 9–10), as well as, subject specific courses addressing transportation systems (grades 11–12). The nature of the transportation learning environment should be action oriented (learning by doing technology). Transportation class activities should involve problem-solving situations or opportunities for students to explore new technology. To implement a transportation curriculum, consideration must be given to an organized content structure.

A Content Structure for Transportation Technology

Developing a content structure for a transportation curriculum in a high school requires the teacher to establish a content outline and select appropriate instructional methods. Curriculum theorists (e.g. Gagne & Briggs, 1979; McNeil, 1985) agree that content is best presented to students simple to complex, familiar to unfamiliar, and concrete to abstract. This approach to establish a content outline presents teachers with a means to begin creating a scope and sequence for an operational curriculum.

Prior to the development of a curriculum, classroom teachers should review their state curriculum plans for transportation technology. The state plans often provide teachers with content outlines for courses that are recommended to be taught as part of their curriculum. If teachers find that their state does not have a curriculum guide, they may wish to review the national guides: *Jackson's Mill Industrial Arts Curriculum Theory, Industry & Technology Education—A Guide for Curriculum Designers, Implementers, and Teachers,* and *A Conceptual Framework for Technology Education.* By reviewing state and national curriculum guides, teachers can maintain continuity of their program scope and sequence with schools in their state and schools across the country.

Program Scope

The scope of the transportation program refers to the range or levels of learning units that will be provided by the curriculum. Transportation teachers may wish to begin developing curriculum by reviewing the suggested units provided by curriculum guides, or developing a list of key topics that would be practical for their transportation curriculum. In high school programs, the instruction will entail developing learning units for grades 9–12. These four grades may represent four levels of learning: awareness, realization, skill development, and investigation. The titles assigned to each level depicts the tasks outlined by a formal curriculum. The *Industry and Technology Education* curriculum guide suggests the scope of a technology program should:

> "... provide a smooth continuum which would allow a student to move from a beginning foundation phase, which includes basic concepts, knowledge, skills and attitudes necessary for continued learning. Then the student would move through a series of developmental experiences which serve as the transition from basic learning to the pursuit of specialized interests at the concentration or Level IV phase" (Sterry & Wright, 1984, p. 12).

Grade 9, the awareness level, needs to provide students with experiences in all areas of technology so they possess the ability to make connections between technological systems. For example, it is important that students understand the role transportation plays to manufacture large quantities of products for our society. Likewise, students need to realize that some new technology exists only because of the linkage between technological systems. The ability to launch and control the orbit of satellites in our atmosphere is responsible for the global communication which has made the world community much closer.

Grade 10, the realization level, should provide students with an understanding of the following transportation subsystems: terrestrial, marine, atmosphere, and space. Learning units in each of the subsystems may address historical developments, commonly used terminology, applications of the systems, societal and environmental impacts, and careers. The content taught in grades 9 and 10 should provide a basis for students to encounter more complex instructional units. Figure 2 provides a sample transportation course content outline.

Grade 11, the skill development level, should provide students with content that will develop their technical and social skills. At this level of instruction, students may receive instruction which pertains to the use of precision tools or test equipment. Likewise, students may receive instruction on the operation of specific vehicles or safety in traffic control systems. Other activities may involve developing social awareness programs regarding the disposal of used motor oil, tires, and batteries.

Grade 12, the investigation level, should provide students with detailed problem-solving exercises. A learning unit at this level might involve problem-solving a specific malfunction of control, guidance, or propulsion systems. In such an activity, students would need to understand the process of using service manuals, the proper tools for disassembling the system, the procedure for rebuilding the system, and the process for testing the system. Other learning units may involve more research and development to solve a proposed problem. Such an activity could request teams of students to design and develop vehicles that would run on a twelve volt DC motor and not exceed fifteen pounds in weight.

TRANSPORTATION TECHNOLOGY

I. INTRODUCTION TO TRANSPORTATION TECNOLOGY
   A. TRANSPORTATION AS A SYSTEM (IT IS RELATED TO COMMUNICATION, PRODUCTION, AND ENERGY UTILIZATION.)
   B. TRANSPORTATION AS RELATED TO WORLD CULTURE.
   C. TRANSPORTATION AFFECTING PEOPLES' LIVES IN THE U.S.
II. TRANSPORTATION TECHNOLOGY
   A. DEFINING TRANSPORTATION AS A SYSTEM.
   B. IDENTIFYING TYPES OF TRANSPORTATION.
   C. STUDYING THE PROCESS OF TRANSPORTATION.
   D. DEVELOPING A HISTORICAL TIME LINE OF TRANSPORTATION.
   E. LEARNING ABOUT THE TECHNICAL AND SOCIAL-CULTURAL AFFECTS OF TRANSPORTATION.
III. TRANSPORTATION SYSTEMS
   A. TERRESTRIAL SYSTEMS.
   B. AIR SYSTEMS.
   C. MARINE SYSTEMS.
   D. SPACE SYSTEMS.
IV. TRANSPORTATION AND THE FUTURE
   A. VEHICLE DESIGN.
   B. PERSONAL TRANSPORTING SYSTEMS.
   C. CARGO TRANSPORTING SYSTEMS.

Figure 2: A sample transportation course outline.

The learning units which are provided by the transportation curriculum should parallel the maturity of the student. A curriculum could be criticized for not providing difficult enough experiences for twelfth grade students; thus, the image of the technology program would be hurt. By providing learning units which are challenging and meaningful to the students' age group, teachers will hold the students' interest and more learning will take place. Figure 3 illustrates a scope of instructional units for a transportation curriculum.

Program Sequence

The decision regarding what content should be taught first in a technology education program involves sequencing the instructional units in a logical order. As discussed earlier in this section, technology content may best be taught simple to complex. With this in mind, course titles need to be derived which will represent the learning units taught at each level of instruction. Also, time frames will need to be established to determine the length of each course.

When developing a curriculum, numerous variables influence the framework of the curriculum. Such variables as the number of students enrolled in the program, number of faculty members available to teach, size of the facility, financial resources, and the philosophy of the school should be considered during curriculum development process. Various scenarios can be created of sequential programs for transportation technology. To provide direction for curriculum developers, the following curriculum models have been created.

Model 1—A Small-School Program. When only one instructor is available in the technology education program, a limited number of courses can be offered. This model represents an approach that may be used to establish a curriculum framework in such a situation. As illustrated in Figure 4, the sequence of classes includes Introduction to Technology, Transportation I, and Transportation II. The introductory course would provide instruction for all the technological systems. This course would involve four semesters of instruction in which each technological system would be taught for one semester. An overlap of instructional material from the awareness level, realization level, and skill development level would be included as instruction. The Transportation I course would focus on skill development tasks. This course would be offered

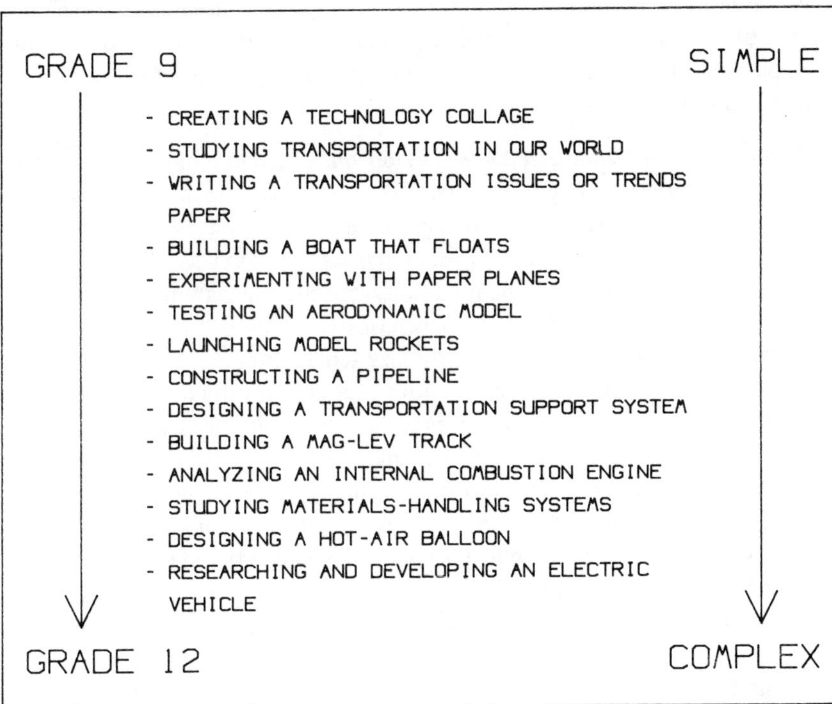

Figure 3: A scope of practical learning units for grades 9–12 that range from simple to complex.

COURSE TITLE	GRADE LEVEL	SEMESTERS ENROLLED
INTRODUCTION TO TECHNOLOGY	9-10	4
TRANSPORTATION I	11	2
TRANSPORTATION II	12	2

Figure 4: A small-school transportation model.

for one semester in which students would accomplish specific technical competencies to learn about the technology in transportation systems. Transportation II would involve twelfth grade students applying their skill development abilities to solve problems in transportation systems. This course may be developed around the concept of research and development in which students would be involved in designing and building transportation systems, or making innovations on existing transportation systems. Since this course would be part of the comprehensive school curriculum, it may include learning units (computer skills, writing assignments, etc.) which would reinforce students' general education.

Model 2—A Medium-Size School Program. In a medium-size school program, more courses can be offered because more than one instructor is available to teach classes. The medium-size school program may also have a larger and better equipped facility than a small-school program because of its financial resources. For example, the medium-size school program may have one area of its lab designed to teach transportation technology. Figure 5 illustrates the curriculum framework for a medium-size school program. Unlike the small-school program, the medium-size school curriculum offers the introductory technology course for two semesters rather than four. This allows another course, Transportation Systems, to be scheduled for tenth grade students. A course in transportation systems would instruct students about air, land, water, and space transporting systems. For example, students would learn how a railroad system operates. Commonly, this course would be offered for one semester so students could take another technology course such as production systems the second semester. At the eleventh grade, the course, Transportation Technology, is a skill development class. The general objective of this course is to teach students about the technology in transportation systems. This course is much more technical than the tenth grade course titled, Transportation Systems. The course outline for this class may include learning units regarding

COURSE TITLE	GRADE LEVEL	SEMESTERS ENROLLED
INTRODUCTION TO TECHNOLOGY	9	2
TRANSPORTATION SYSTEMS	10	1
TRANSPORTATION TECHNOLOGY	11	2
ADVANCED TRANSPORTATION TECHNOLOGY	12	2

Figure 5: A medium-size school transportation model.

aviation technology, automotive technology, diesel power systems, electric vehicles, solar-power systems, and space technology. Depending on the actual size of the school program, this year-long course could vary in complexity. The twelfth grade course, Advanced Transportation Technology, is a sequential class. The content of this course would involve students utilizing their skills to solve transportation problems, such as building an electric vehicle for entry in the Odyssey of the Minds competition.

Model 3—A Large-School Program. The large-school transportation curriculum offers more course options for students. Although the Introduction to Technology course and Transportation Systems course are much like the medium-size school program, the eleventh and twelfth grade courses may be quite different. Some large schools may develop articulation agreements with community college programs and offer courses in transportation-related subjects as part of their technology education curriculum. These "tech prep" programs offer one or two year courses in subjects such as auto mechanics, auto body, diesel mechanics, aviation mechanics, or heavy equipment maintenance. The large-school program may also offer sequential courses in transportation technology at the eleventh and twelfth grades. These courses would be for students who were not interested in continuing their education at a trade technical school, but are interested in pursuing a college degree in engineering, industrial technology, or business. Figure 6 illustrates the large-school program.

Instructional Methods

The strategies used to deliver content for transportation courses may vary according to the grade level and subject material. Schwaller and Kemp (1988)

COURSE TITLE	GRADE LEVEL	SEMESTERS ENROLLED
INTRODUCTION TO TECHNOLOGY	9	2
TRANSPORTATION SYSTEMS	10	1
TRANSPORTATION TECHNOLOGY I	11	2
TRANSPORTATION TECHNOLOGY II	12	2
OR		
TECH. PREP. PROGRAM (AVIATION. AUTOMOTIVE. DIESEL MECHANICS. HEAVY EQUIPMENT)	11-12	4

Figure 6: A large-school transportation model.

presented four delivery systems that practitioners may find useful to teach technology education. Their list included: a) formal presentations and demonstrations; b) group interaction; c) discovery, inquiry, and experimentation; and d) games and simulations. A teacher may select one or more delivery systems to accomplish an instructional unit. By reviewing these delivery systems, teachers may better understand how they may be applied to teach transportation technology.

Formal Presentations and Demonstrations. This instructional method is used extensively in classes where the teacher is providing new information to a class. Formal presentations may be used to begin a transportation lesson in which students are going to use a new piece of equipment. Following the explanation regarding how the device works, a demonstration is given which illustrates the device in action. The demonstration may be used to reinforce content provided earlier in the lesson. Formal presentations are also used to present factual information about data, resources, or historical events. This means of instruction may be most effective in introductory and skill development courses where students are learning concrete material.

Games and Simulations. Learning can take place in a relaxed atmosphere where students are having fun. Games and simulations are instructional methods that can stimulate student participation. In introductory courses to technology, games may be used as an action-learning strategy to help students remember terms, people, and events. Likewise, teachers may have students make simulations of actual transportation systems. Simulations can be done by building cardboard models, assembling paper cutouts, or using commercial kits such as Lego's. Modern software allows teachers to use computers for games and simulations. Computer programs like *Glidepath* and *Car Builder* are simulations that challenge students' cognitive abilities.

Group Interaction. An instructional method that attempts to get all students actively involved is group interaction. Whether the setting involves groups of two, four, eight, or larger, the interaction among the students encourages participation. Group interaction could be used in transportation classes at any level of the program. The teacher may find group interaction works well following formal presentations or demonstrations when students need to discuss ideas or issues relating to the lesson. Group interaction can also be used for group problem-solving activities. By allowing students to work in groups to solve problems, more ideas may be presented and more dialogue may take place to derive a solution to the problem.

Discovery, Inquiry, and Experimentation. These strategies provide a problem-solving atmosphere for transportation classes. Technical and social-cultural problems may be investigated by using these instructional methods. Discovery, inquiry, and experimentation provides students in advanced classes with challenging lab experiences, such as powering a vehicle with solar cells. These strategies actively involve students researching and testing ideas. The flexibility of this instructional method allows the teacher to use it for short- or long-term activities. These instructional techniques can be made adaptable for small or large labs.

The instructional methods teachers use should be compatible with their teaching style and the instructional unit. Teachers can enhance their transportation lessons by using supportive instructional technology and resources. VCR tapes, computer software programs, and learning modules can help teachers increase students' interests regarding learning units which otherwise would be abstract. For example, if a teacher was presenting a unit regarding the transportation systems used in industrial plants and presented the material entirely by formal presentations, the students may not fully comprehend the appearance of this plant. However, if the teacher provided a formal presentation on the topic, showed a VCR addressing industrial transportation systems, and involved students in building models of transportation systems for an industry; students may have a much better understanding of industrial transportation because they were involved in the lesson.

Transportation Technology and the School Curriculum

The transportation curriculum should add a new dimension to the school curriculum and reinforce the content taught in related school subjects. The integration of technology education courses with academic subjects is a growing trend in secondary schools. Maley (1986) developed illustrations regarding the integration of various technologies with math, science, and social studies as examples for classroom teachers. Transportation courses offer an interdisciplinary appeal to numerous areas of the curriculum such as science, math, business, consumer education, geography, and other subjects which may relate to the movement of people or goods. While transportation is easily integrated with other subject areas, it also has its own unique content dimension which is outlined by the technical and social/cultural content it provides for students' technology education.

High school teachers who are involved in curriculum development activities need to understand that the courses they presently teach can be transformed into a technology program in which part of the curriculum is transportation. The teachers also need to know how to integrate this content with the total school curriculum. The following sections address these areas of concern.

Teachers Developing Transportation Curricula

How do teachers develop new curricula? If a state curriculum guide is available, it is generally the first resource reviewed by teachers as the formal curriculum to develop. However, teachers sometimes have ideas and concerns of their own which may influence them to modify the curriculum to meet their local school districts' needs. The compromised curriculum is commonly referred to as an operational curriculum because it is what works in the classroom.

The following program model is an example of an operational curriculum that could be used to teach transportation technology in a high school. This particular example illustrates how teachers could use a mid-size curriculum model as cited earlier in this chapter and include other content which pertains to energy and power systems. In this particular example, the school may have had a quality power mechanics or automotive program. Some of the information taught in such courses can be made applicable in a transportation curriculum. This school may not have been able to offer an individualized course in energy technology so it also included energy content in the transportation sequence. To explain the structure and content of this transportation curriculum the following example is inclusive of a sequence of classes, course descriptions, and content outlines for each course.

This transportation curriculum includes a sequence of four courses: Introduction to Transportation, Energy and Power Systems, Transportation Systems, and Advanced Transportation Technology. The classes are offered for grades 9–12 as follows:

Introduction to Transportation	9th grade	1/2 semester
Energy/Power/Transportation	10th grade	1 semester
Transportation Technology	11th grade	1 semester
Advanced Transportation Technology	12th grade	2 semesters

Introduction to Transportation. This course should provide students with general information regarding the history, growth, and future development of transportation. Students should participate in a variety of laboratory and classroom activities to learn about the ways products and people are moved in our world. Learning units in this course should emphasize expanding students' vocabulary and introducing them to hands-on /minds-on activities. The instructional content of this course should also attempt to show the relationship between transportation, production, communication, and energy systems.

The following is a sample topical outline regarding the content this course might address:

I. Introduction to Transportation Technology
   A. Defining transportation as a technological study
   B. Explaining the process by which people and products are transported
   C. Identifying vehicles used in today's world
II. The History of Transportation
   A. Developing a time line of significant technical developments
   B. Identifying social impacts which resulted from transportation developments
   C. Researching possible future trends in the field of transportation
III. The Transportation Systems in Our World
   A. Air transportation
   B. Land transportation
   C. Water transportation
   D. Space transportation
IV. Transportation Modes to Distribute People and Goods
   A. Air travel
   B. Railways
   C. Barges, ships, and ferries
   D. Highways and subways

E. Pipelines
F. Material handling devices
V. The Relationship of Transportation and Other Technologies
A. Communication needed for transportation systems
B. Transportation needed for production systems
C. Energy used to power transportation systems
VI. Issues and Trends in Transportation
A. Social impacts of transportation on lifestyles
B. Environmental impacts of transportation
C. Federal transportation regulations
D. New transportation trends for the 21st century
VIII. Transportation Careers

Transportation Systems. The transportation systems course should provide students with information regarding the technology used in land, air, water, and space transportation. Students should learn about important events which lead to specific technical developments. The course would also provide information regarding safety, regulatory measures, and laws that govern transportation systems. Some specific technical content would be included in each instructional unit to explain the general engineering principals behind the propulsion, guidance, and support systems of vehicles. At the completion of this course, students should be knowledgeable of the operation of the major transportation systems in our world. Likewise, they should be aware of the role each plays in moving people and products to a desired destination.

The following is a sample topical outline of the content this course might address:

I. Transportation Systems in Our World
A. Personal transportation systems
B. Commercial transportation systems
C. Governmental transportation systems
D. Recreational transportation systems
II. Land Transportation Systems
A. Early land transportation (sleds, carts, wagons, and coaches)
B. Rail systems (trains, trolley cars, subways, and transit systems)
C. Highway systems (automobiles, buses, and trucks)
D. Cycles and all-terrain systems (bicycles, motorcycles, mopeds, and three-wheelers)
III. Water Transportation Systems
A. Early water transportation (canoes, rafts, sailboats, clipper ships, and vessels)

  B. Inland transportation (barges, tugboats, towboats, riverboats, and fishing boats)
  C. Ocean vessels (oceanliners, merchant ships, tanker vessels, and submarines)
  D. Hydrofoil craft

IV. Air Transportation Systems
  A. Early transportation (biplanes, dirigibles, and prop planes)
  B. Commercial airliners (light aircraft, jet aircraft, and rotary-wing aircraft)
  C. Military aircraft transportation (cargo planes, fighter planes, and helicopters)

V. Space Transportation
  A. Early unmanned-spacecraft
  B. Manned-spacecraft
  C. The skylab projects
  D. The space shuttle series

VI. The Social-Cultural Impacts of Transportation Systems
  A. Changes in lifestyles
  B. Changes in values, beliefs, and attitudes
  C. Governmental transportation controls
  D. Transportation and its impact on new careers

VII. Future Transportation Systems
  A. Personal rapid transit
  B. Electric automobiles
  C. Space planes
  D. Hovercrafts
  E. Jetpacks

Energy, Power, and Transportation Technology. This course would provide students with a working knowledge of the relationship between energy, power, and transportation technology. In this course students are involved in working with mechanical, electrical, fluid, and computerized systems. Students are also involved in learning about the use of gasoline-, diesel-, nuclear-, and solar-powered vehicles. Throughout the course, students would be involved in labs which address how these systems work.

The following topical outline illustrates the content which could be taught in this course:

I. Energy and Power Needed for Transportation
  A. Engines used in transportation vehicles
  B. Motors used in transportation systems
  C. Fuels for powering transportation systems

D. Safety in energy, power, and transportation

II. Energy Resources
   A. Renewable resources
   B. Nonrenewable resources
   C. Inexhaustible resources

III. Energy Conversion and Measurement
   A. Scientific laws and principles
   B. Mechanical energy and power
   C. Electrical energy and power
   D. Fluid energy and power
   E. Nuclear energy and power

IV. Power Systems
   A. External combustion engines
   B. Internal combustion engines
   C. Solar power
   D. Wind power

V. Transportation Vehicular Operations
   A. Propulsion systems
   B. Control systems
   C. Guidance systems
   D. Suspension systems
   E. Vehicular support structures

VI. Automation in Energy, Power, and Transportation
   A. Applications of synchronized systems
   B. Applications of microprocessors
   C. Applications of fluid actuators
   D. Applications of sensors and controllers

VII. Components in an Automated Transportation System
   A. Programmable controllers
   B. Conveyors
   C. Elevators
   D. Trams
   E. Augers
   F. Machines
   G. Robots

VIII. New Developments in Energy, Power, and Transportation
   A. Digital instrumentation
   B. Ceramic-based engines
   C. Computerized-guidance systems
   D. Synthetic lubricants
   E. Recycled products

Advanced Transportation Technology. An advanced course in transportation technology should be based on research and development. Students would be involved in problem-solving activities which pertain to technologies associated with automotive, aviation, mass transit, waterway travel; as well as, material handling systems such as robots, conveyors, elevators, augers, and pipelines. The skills students would learn in this course would help them to analyze problems and apply their knowledge to formulate solutions and solve the problems. This advanced technology course could be a technical preparation class for students planning to pursue a community college program or enter a four-year university program in industrial technology.

The following is a sample topical outline which describes the content that could be included in this course:

I. An Overview of the Development of Transportation Technology
   A. Foundational technical developments in transportation
   B. Changes in transportation technology
   C. Transportation careers of yesterday, today, and tomorrow
II. Innovations in Commercial Transportation Systems
   A. Receiving and loading facilities (terminals, stations, docks, and freight yards)
   B. Holding and storing facilities (warehouses, lockers, stockyards, and bins)
   C. Moving facilities (cranes, forklifts, dollies, carts, trucks, trains, ships, and planes)
   D. Delivery (couriers, shippers, truckers, and express services)
III. Transportation Safety
   A. Federal regulations and policies
   B. Maintenance and service regulations
   C. Safety precautions for motorists, cyclists, and commuters
IV. Maintenance and Service Procedures for Transportation
   A. Automotive technology
   B. Aviation technology
   C. Marine vehicle technology
   D. Material handling technology
V. Transportation Research and Development
   A. Innovation in automotive technology
   B. Innovations in aeronautics
   C. Innovations in marine technology
   D. Designing alterative transporting systems
VI. Designing and Building Alternative Transportation Systems
   A. Electric vehicles

B. Solar- and wind-powered vehicles
C. Light rail networks
D. Lighter than airship (LTA)

VII. Issue and Trends in Transportation
A. Aerodynamic bodystyling
B. Fuel-efficient vehicles
C. Trailers on flat cars (TOFC)
D. The space program
E. Commercial air travel and financial bankruptcy

VIII. New Frontiers in Transportation Technology

Teachers Integrating Transportation Content

By integrating transportation content with other subject areas, the school curriculum is more "socially relevant and personally meaningful" (McNeil, 1985, p. 161). Transportation is a very diverse subject area that can be interrelated with science, math, history, geography, general business, consumers education, and most other areas of the secondary school curriculum. How the integration is done and what content is integrated are two decisions teachers must make to relate transportation with the school curriculum.

The integration of transportation and academic subjects can be accomplished through articulated and cooperative efforts. In ideal settings where a technology teacher and an academic teacher work equally, the academic teacher provides students with lessons on theory and the technology teacher has students put the theory into practice. If articulation can not be established between academic and technology teachers, some level of cooperation is needed to correlate the academic and transportation subject matter. McNeil (1985) stated there are five typical arrangements for facilitating integration: a) concentration, b) correlation, c) integration of a tool subject, d) field study, and e) comprehensive problem solving. Each of these techniques can be examined as a means to integrate transportation and academic subjects.

1. Concentration is a method of integration which is student centered. Students are not overburdened with extensive course loads so they can see the integration of subject areas. In a present-day high school, students may be enrolled in four to five courses and have one hour of time to be involved in activities to integrate their studies. In today's schools, special programs for talented and gifted students provide time for integrated activities.

2. Correlation is an integration technique in which teachers from different courses (transportation, science, and social studies) teach similar concepts at the same time. For example, the transportation teacher may provide an instructional unit regarding the historical development of vehicles, while the social studies teacher lectures how the train, steamboat, and automobile changed the world socially, economically, and politically. At this same time, the science teacher may teach about the theory of the internal and external combustion engines. The relationship between the content taught by one teacher reinforces the content taught by the other teacher.

3. Integration of subjects involves one subject area including content from another subject area. For example, math or science concepts can be taught in a transportation course. This is the most typical form of integration that has been presented to technology teachers. The September 1984 issue of *The Technology Teacher* provided a math-science-technology interface lesson in which students were assigned to calculate the mass, momentum, acceleration, average force, and impluse of a high impact technology vehicle (see Figure 7).

4. Content can also be integrated by drawing on information from another field of study. Transportation technology content might be included in a chemistry course to explain the emission of gases from an automobile's catalytic converter.

5. Comprehensive problem solving is an integrated approach which requires students to use knowledge from various subject areas to derive a solution for the problem. For example, suppose students were confronted with the problem to redesign a sail for a boat. Students would need to use historical, scientific, and mathematical information to solve this problem.

The content which is to be integrated by subject areas should be meaningful to the instructional unit. As mentioned earlier in this section, integrating content should add more relevance and meaning to the learning unit. When teachers consider the integraton of transportation technology with other subjects they may wish to begin with those subjects that offer practical integration. Such subjects as science, math, geography, general business, and consumer education can be integrated with transportation courses to create meaningful learning units. The following are examples of practical integrated learning activities. The explanations of each should provide insights for teachers to develop other integrated units.

Science offers many avenues for integration with technology subjects because much technology content is applied science. In most every science-based course (general science, biology, chemistry, and physics), content could be integrated with transportation courses. For example, the study of general science

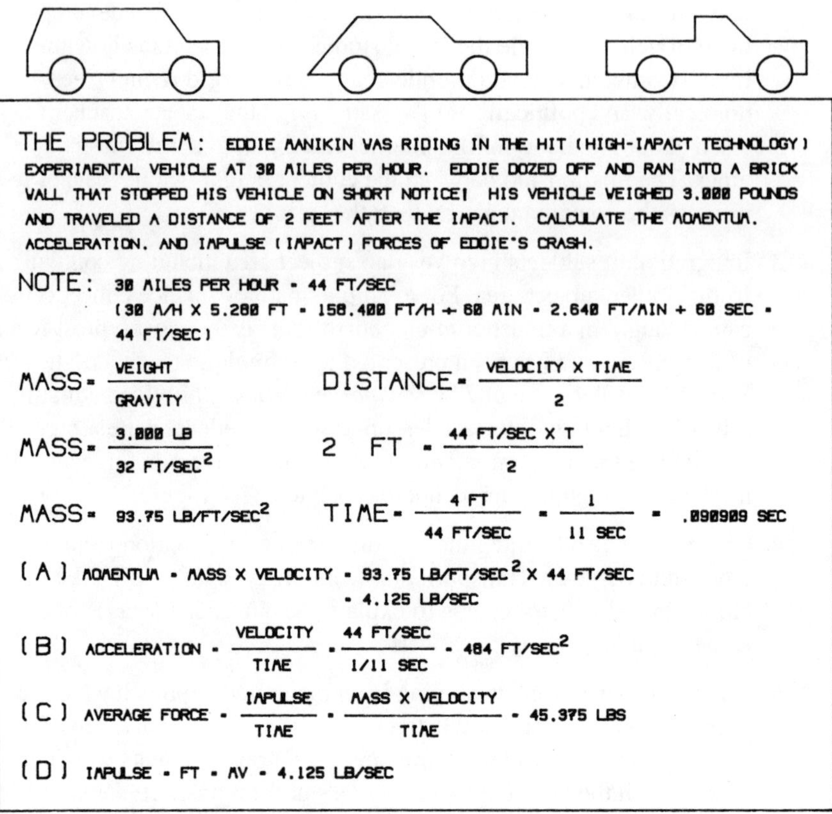

*Figure 7: An example problem for integrated learning units (*The Technology Teacher, *1984, p. 21).*

may relate to an introductory of transportation course in that both courses could address the effect of transportation on the earth's atmosphere. A relationship of biology to a course of transportation systems may integrate by examining features of the human anatomy that allows people to operate vehicles safely. A chemistry course could be integrated with a Transportation I course by students participating in labs which examine chemical reactions such as that between lead and sulfuric acid in an automobile battery. Another science-technology link can be made between an advanced transportation technology course and physics. Studying about the propulsion of vehicles offers many meaningful learning units to discuss physical concepts such as energy, work, force, drag, and thrust.

Math also offers many opportunities for integration with transportation subjects. In all basic calculations used to solve problems, some form of general math is used. Likewise, basic algebra is often applied to solve for an unknown variable such as in distance, rate, and time problems (distance = rate × time). Other math courses such as geometry and trigonometry may be used to calculate the size or design the shape of components for transporting systems. A simple example could be calculating the size of a cylinder for an engine.

Subjects such as geography also provide opportunities for integrating content with transportation courses. A geography and transportation teacher may develop a unit concerning the transportation routes in a given region. Geography and transportation could also be integrated with a U.S. History course in a unit which identified the great American trails and the means of transportation used by settlers. This unit might include information regarding how vehicles were built to travel across the rough terrain.

Transportation can be integrated with general business courses through lessons on operating transportation businesses. The general business teacher could assign students to determine the cost of operating a trucking firm, delivery service, bus company, or an airport. In this activity the students would use their business management skills and knowledge of transportation systems.

Since everyone in our society uses some form of personal or commercial transportation, consumer education can be integrated with transportation courses. Learning units which address purchasing a vehicle, buying insurance, making air line reservations, or renting a moving van are all possible topics to develop integrated activities.

Many benefits can result from integrating content from two or more courses. The teachers who are involved in integrating subjects may observe:

1) students better understand the relationship between school subjects;
2) students see course content more relevant to their personal lives; and
3) students who tend to be unmotivated in academic classes become active learners.

The means by which schools integrate subject areas must be designed around their constraints of course schedules, faculty interests, and the instructional leadership provided by the principal. If good communication is not present among faculty members, integration would be very difficult to coordinate. Most student learning in transportation courses would take place by individual or group learning activities. The following section presents several learning activities that could be used to teach transportation technology.

Student Learning Activities in Transportation Technology

The instructional design for transportation activities involves hands-on activities to reinforce concepts which are delivered through formal presentations, demonstrations, or reading assignments. Transportation activities may focus on technical, engineering, math, or science concepts. In some instances, an activity may dwell on one concept such as designing an airport. In other activities, a multiple number of concepts may be included such as designing, building, and testing a vehicle. The types of activities that can be created for teaching transportation vary on a large continuum. Posthuma (1989), a classroom teacher, developed 101 transportation activities that are practical for high school students. Among his list of activities was the following: construct a model space shuttle, build a monorail system, service a bicycle, and plot a ship's course. When creating transportation activities, it is important to consider the various instructional technology options available.

Hands-On Learning Activities

Transportation technology is like other technology education courses in that the classroom setting is action oriented. The hands-on learning activities help to develop a technical knowledge base for students by providing them with specific transportation information and psychomotor skills. Teachers should not limit their activity designs to building objects from raw materials. Numerous activities can be developed from commercial kits ready to be assembled. Popular items which are advertised in vendor's catalogs (Pitsco, IASCO, & Paxton/Patterson, 1990) include power planes, mouse trap cars, and model rockets. In addition to kits, building sets such as Legos provide endless activities which are limited only by the teachers' and students' imaginations. Also, an assortment of software exists on the market which challenges the students' problem-solving and decision-making skills through simulation programs (e.g. *Car Builder* and *Glidepath*).

Other hands-on activities such as building paper models can be very simple but very effective. The level of technical competency should not be under estimated because soft activities involving paper, scissors, and tape are used in advanced classes to build models. Students can learn a great deal about design and quality appearance through building models. In advanced transportation courses, it is important that students are involved with full-size transportation vehicles for real-to-life problem-solving experiences. Servicing vehicles such as bicycles, motorcycles, and automobiles can attract students' personal interests in transportation classes.

Reinforcing Concepts

Transportation activities are a means to reinforce basic concepts students should learn in technology education and the academic curriculum. General tasks which involve measuring, separating, forming, fastening, and finishing processes are transferable to accomplish other hands-on tasks. Student activities may involve such tasks in an activity like building a CO_2 race car, or involve only one specific task such as measuring the speed of the CO_2 race car. In both instances concepts are being reinforced through the activities.

Students can also gain an understanding of designing, developing, modeling, testing, and evaluating through transportation activities. These concepts are essential to understand the engineering involved in any transportation system. The concepts provide a conceptual framework by which teachers can deliver instruction to enhance students thinking skills.

Other transportation concepts which are math and science based can be reinforced by activities which will help students understand the principles being taught. Each transportation system (land, air, water, and space) is designed with the basic principles in mind. For example, aerodynamics, propulsion, and control are three concepts considered when designing all modern-day land vehicles. Likewise, the concepts of lift, drag, thrust, and gravity are essential in building an airplane that will fly. Furthermore, without understanding the concept of buoyancy, ships and barges could not transport large volumes of cargo. Today's space age only exists because aeronautical engineers understand the gravitational pull in our universe and the force it takes to launch a vehicle into orbit. These concepts which have just been mentioned are essential to include in transportation activities. Figure 8 illustrates a graphic depiction of these concepts to help students better understand them. The following sample activities are examples of learning units which may be used for teaching land, air, water, and space transportation.

Sample Activity 1

Activity Title: Transporting Goods Transcontinental

Activity Objectives:

1. To teach students in introductory courses about the various modes of transportation that are used to move freight across a continent.
2. To involve students with decision-making tasks to select routes and modes of transportation.
3. To integrate mathematical calculations with transportation by having students add up the cost of transporting freight.

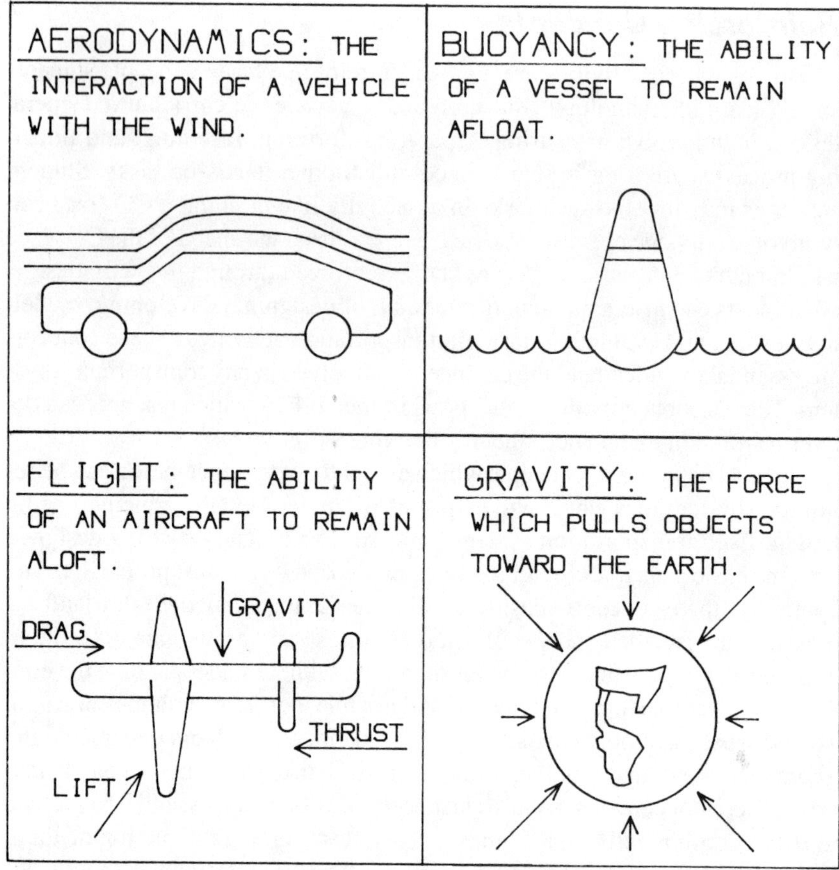

Figure 8: Key concepts in transportation systems.

Activity Description:

In this activity, students will develop a map to move freight transcontinental. To begin the activity, the class should be divided into small groups. Each group will need to select a form of freight to transport, indicate the point of origin, determine the destination point, identify the modes of transportation to move the freight, select the routes of travel, and estimate the cost of transportation. As a final result of this activity, students should have developed graphic examples of the routes of travel used to move their freight from the point of origin to the destination point. Each time a different mode of transportation is used, a graphical example of the vehicle should appear on the map. The teacher will need to obtain highway, railway, waterway, and airport maps for students to use. This activity can best be completed on poster board or large sheets of paper.

Sample Activity 2

Activity Title: Designing an Aerodynamic Automobile

Activity Objective:

1. To involve tenth or eleventh grade students in designing an aerodynamic model.
2. To develop students' ability to use computer-design programs.
3. To enhance students' technical skills through building models.

Activity Description:

This activity will involve students using a computer-design program to create a graphical design of an aerodynamic automobile. Any user-friendly CAD program or design software is acceptable for this activity. Students will use their designs to build an aerodynamic model. Each student will build a model and test it for aerodynamics in a wind tunnel. The models can be framed from craft sticks and then covered with paper mache to enhance the body styling. Model wheels should be attached to the chassis to complete the vehicle's appearance.

Sample Activity 3

Activity Title: Installing an Electronic Ignition System

Activity Objectives:

1. To teach eleventh or twelfth grade students about the importance of electronic technology in transportation.
2. To provide students with hands-on experience to install electronic ignition components.
3. To advance students' technical knowledge of ignition systems.

Activity Description:

Students can learn about the function of electronic ignition systems by installing an ignition module in a two-cycle small engine. By using available small engines with traditional breaker points, the teacher should have students in groups of two remove the flywheel and install the ignition module as indicated by the directions provided with it. Next, the students should assemble the engine and attempt to start it to see if their installation was successful.

Sample Activity 4

Activity Title: Building a Boat that Floats

Activity Objectives:

1. To provide ninth or tenth grade students with the opportunity to experiment with buoyant materials.

2. To provide students with hands on problem-solving tasks.

3. To encourage students' creativity in designing a marine transportation vehicle.

Activity Description:

In this activity, students are challenged to design a boat that will float and propel itself a given distance. Students should be encouraged to use any type of material that is at their disposal. This activity involves students combining technologies to build a functionable boat. The propulsion system could be a propellor or paddle wheel driven by a small nine volt dc motor or a mechanical source such as the tension of a rubber band. This activity should be completed individually by students. The teacher may wish to restrict the size of the boats to accommodate the marine testing environment available in the lab. This activity should provide students with numerous problem-solving tasks.

Sample Activity 5

Activity Title: Boat Hull Testing

Activity Objectives:

1. To teach ninth or tenth grade students about different shapes of boat hulls.

2. To involve students in designing a hull, testing the hull, and calculating the payload-to-hull ratio.

3. To familiarize students with common marine transportation terminology.

Activity Description:

The teacher will provide each student with a 2 x 4 blank approximately 8 inches long. Each student will be required to select one of the six basic hull shapes (flat bottom, vee bottom, round bottom, cathedral, gull-wing, or multiple hulls) for designing a boat. Next, each student will shape the blank according to the hull design. In addition to shaping the outside of the boat, students will need to hollow out the inside of the boat. This may be done by routering or chiseling the wood. An area inside the boat should be created to carry a heavy payload since the goal of the activity is to see which hull shape is the most efficient. Next, each student should weigh the boat hull to measure the mass of the vessel itself (gross tonnage—GT). Then the boat should be loaded to capacity with weight (metal flat washers are recommended). When the boat is about to sink or capsize, stop adding weight. Next, each student should weigh the cargo to determine the dead weight tonnage

(DWT). The ratio of gross tonnage—GT / dead weight tonnage—DWT will provide a payload-to-hull weight ratio. The data obtained is a percentage which may be used to compare the different hull shapes. This activity can be concluded by students plotting their ratios on a chart and discussing their results.

Sample Activity 6

Activity Title: Designing a Free-Throw Plane

Activity Objectives:

1. To teach twelfth-grade students about the principles of aeronautics.
2. To engage students in creating a geometrically-designed aircraft.
3. To observe the performance of aircraft in flight.

Activity Description:

In this activity, students will use white bonded paper (8 1/2 x 11) to design a paper airplane. On the sheet of paper students should layout the fold lines which will be used to fold their planes. It is important that the design is completed accurately and the angle of each fold is recorded. After the planes are designed, they should be folded and tested. If a wind tunnel is available, students should place their planes in the tunnel to visually observe the lift and drag of their plane designs. Next, students should measure the length of the wing span and the fuselage. After the dimensions are recorded, each student should fly their plane and record the length of the flight. As part of a class discussion, students should display their planes and report their results. The class may analyze if there is a relationship between the geometrical design and the flight distance.

Sample Activity 7

Activity Title: The Rocket Launch

Activity Objectives:

1. To teach eleventh or twelfth grade students about space technology.
2. To integrate transportation with other subjects such as mathematics, physics, astronomy, and psychology.
3. To involve students in a problem-solving exercise that requires design and construction of a model rocket.

Activity Description:

This activity will require students to design and build a model rocket. Teachers may find it beneficial to allow students to work in groups of two or three because of the amount of time it will take to complete this project. The body of the rocket may be made from balsa wood, plastic, or paper-based material. Metal materials of any nature are discouraged for safety reasons. It may be beneficial to provide students with design examples prior to beginning this activity. The sample designs will give the students ideas to begin creating their rockets. During the actual construction of the rocket, the teacher should integrate math and physics concepts. For example, it would be meaningful for the students to calculate the total power of their rocket engine which is expressed in terms of impulse (I). This can be calculated by using the average thrust (f) and multiplying it by the time of the thrust duration (t). The formula $I = f \times t$ will help students realize how math and physics relate to space vehicles. The final phase of this activity is launching the rockets and gathering data. A recording should be made of the flight time for each rocket. The conclusion of this activity should be made with a class discussion about the success of the rocket designs. Related discussions which may be part of this activity might pertain to the psychological training astronauts receive which prepares them to deal with isolation, fear, and space distortion.

Sample Activity 8

Activity Title: Space Shuttle Experiments

Activity Objectives:

1. To teach ninth and tenth grade students about the function and use of space shuttles and space stations.
2. To provide students with a unit in creative thinking.
3. To involve students in a group problem-solving experiment.

Activity Description:

The teacher will need to provide students with a review of general information regarding the space shuttle missions. A video tape or slide series regarding space shuttles could be used to provide students with visual illustrations and information about the appearance and operation of modern spacecraft. Next, the teacher should divide the class into groups of four and assign each group to design an experiment that could be conducted in space. The teacher may wish to cite examples of previous experiments such as the tomato seed experiment which involved transporting tomato seeds into space and then issuing them to schools to plant. Each group of students should prepare an explanation of their experiment. As part of the activity, the teacher may assign the students to develop a poster that illustrates the phases in which their experiment could be conducted. This activity should be concluded by having each group present their experiment to the class.

The sample activities which have been presented can be used as learning units in a high school transportation program. In order for such activities to be conducted in a lab setting, some modifications to an existing school shop facility are necessary. The following section explains how instructional facilities can be adapted to teach transportation technology.

Instructional Facilities to Teach Transportation Technology

Transportation courses are commonly taught in one of two facilities. In a small-school program, all technology subject areas share a general laboratory facility. In larger schools, the power mechanics or auto mechanics facility may be used to teach transportation technology. If some laboratory revisions are not made in both of these settings, the facilities will be inadequate to teach transportation. Bolyard and Komacek (1990) stated that reorganizing an existing facility is important, but radical changes are needed to influence the attitudes and expectations of students, administrators, and teachers. If traditional equipment remains: "students see the old facility and expect the old curriculum" (p. 5).

Developing a Transportation Facility

A transportation facility will require more diversity than a traditional school shop. Most school shops were designed to be material and process areas. To begin renovation of a traditional facility, the teacher may want to consider the following:

1. Sell or discard equipment and supplies which are outdated, take up space, and have little value to the instructional program.
2. Seek advice from educational consultants for facility plans or visit programs which have renovated their facilities.
3. Reorganize the remaining equipment in the facility so there is room for an instructional/design area, production area, testing area, and storage area.
4. Repaint the facility to provide a contemporary appearance. A new learning environment can be enhanced by wall murals, posters, and displays.
5. Purchase needed equipment and supplies to teach transportation.

The task of renovating a facility is not simple or inexpensive. It is very important that teachers develop a design of the facility they want to create. Teachers may find it beneficial to create a facility plan that outlines the changes and establishes a work schedule to accomplish the facility renovation. In most instances, a complete facility renovation is a multiple-year project. Teachers may wish to inquire about program development funds from state, regional, or local funding agencies.

Since the tranportation labs developed in the 1990's will be exemplary in nature, all facility developers should feel free to be innovative in their approach. To provide teachers with some guidance to revise facilities, the following information is offered regarding facility organization and equipment.

Technology educators (Boulard & Komacek, 1990; Siciliano & Wright, 1990, et al.) who have developed models for the teaching and learning environment of technology education have agreed in their facility recommendations that an instructional/design area, production area, testing area, and storage area are needed. These four areas provide a great deal of continuity for learning units which may be taught in other technology education classes. Figure 9 illustrates a design model for a transportation lab.

The instructional/design area provides the setting where the teacher can deliver formal presentations and interact with students regarding assignments. This area also offers a place for design work to be done by students. In remod-

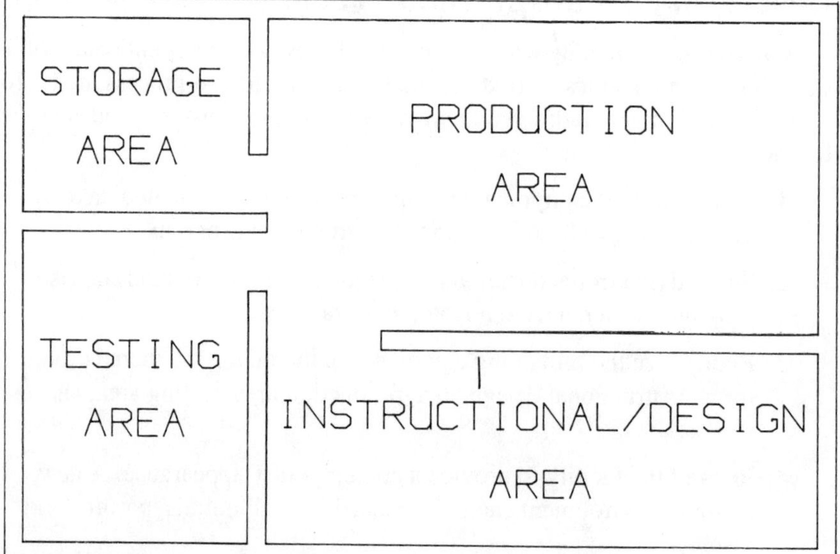

Figure 9: A model transportation facility.

TESTING AREA	PRODUCTION AREA	INSTRUCTIONAL/ DESIGN AREA
AIR-FILM TABLE	BAND SAW	COMPUTER-AIDED DESIGN SYSTEM
BALANCE SCALE	C-CLAMPS	COMPASS
CO2 CAR LAUNCHER AND TRACK	COMBINATION BELT/DISC SANDER	DRAWING BOARD
COMPUTERS	COMBINATION SQUARE	MODEL CAR
CONVEYOR SYSTEM	DRILL BITS	MODEL ENGINE
DYNAMOMETER	DRILL PRESS	MODEL PLANE
ENGINE ANALYZER	GLUE GUNS	MODEL ROCKET
HYDROTEST TANK	GRINDER	MODEL TRAIN
MAG-LEV TRACK	HAND SANDERS	MODEL VESSEL
MOTOR SPEED CONTROL	HAND SAWS	MODULAR FURNITURE
ROBOTIC SYSTEM	HAND SEAMERS	OVERHEAD PROJECTOR
WIND TUNNEL	POP RIVET GUN	PROTRACTORS
WIND SPEED INDICATOR	RULES	TRIANGLES
	SCRATCH AWLS	
	SOLDERING IRON	
	STRIP HEATER	
	TIN SNIPS	
	TRY SQUARES	
	VACUUM FORMER	
	WORK TABLES	

Figure 10: Practical equipment for a transportation facility.

eling the facility, it is recommended that tables (rectangular or oval) are installed rather than individual seats. These tables can be used by students as a meeting area to discuss class assignments. This area also serves as a clean environment where written materials, calculations, or printouts may be reviewed.

A production area is needed to make models, perform service tasks, or conduct other lab activities which may involve building, assembling, or finishing procedures. In the production area, a general assortment of material and processing equipment is needed. Versatile equipment such as a band saw, drill press, grinder, and belt-disc sander should be included. Highly specialized equipment such as a wood shaper is not needed and should be removed to make room for more applicable equipment.

In the testing area, most new types of equipment will be located. A wind tunnel, hydrotank, conveyor, robot, measuring scale, torque convert, speedometer, and diagnostic engine analyzer are examples of equipment that might be included in this lab area. It is important to note that this equipment is of a different nature than material and processing equipment. This equipment requires an environment that is clean and is designed for testing purposes. Figure 10 provides a listing of possible equipment to include in a transportation laboratory.

The fourth main part of the transportation technology facility is the storage area. This dimension of the lab houses supplies for the activities, as well as, stores projects students are designing and building. Storage areas are essential to manage a technology education facility. Well-designed storage areas can enhance the appearance of a lab area. In facilities where supplies and projects are not properly stored, they become disorganized, damaged, and present a poor lab appearance. Teachers can construct large storage areas by framing the area with 2 x 4 lumber and covering it with 1/2 inch particle board or plywood. By painting the storage areas and applying transportation designs to the door fronts, the storage areas can be an attractive asset in the facility. Figure 11 illustrates a design for a practical storage area.

Changing the Instructional Facility Environment

Once the transportation facility has been established a new environmental stigma is present. The instructional area no longer presents the atmosphere of a shop setting, rather a designing, building, and testing laboratory. As depicted by the activities which take place in daily classes, the transportation lab is an action-oriented facility. Students who participate in transportation courses should establish a new perception and attitude about this learning area. The image this area of study portrays should attract the attention of students and teachers who were not previously interested in school shop activities. The goal of all technology teachers should be to integrate technology studies with other subjects in the school curriculum.

Summary

Transportation technology can be a dynamic part of a high school technology education program. In order for curriculum development to occur in transportation technology, teachers need to direct more of their thinking in this area of study. The technology areas of communication and production are further developed than transportation because of the similarities in these areas to previous industrial arts courses (drafting, electronics, wood, and metal). As teachers become more involved in teaching transportation, changes in labs will become more evident. Transportation is an essential part of our high tech culture and has a valuable place in the technology education curriculum.

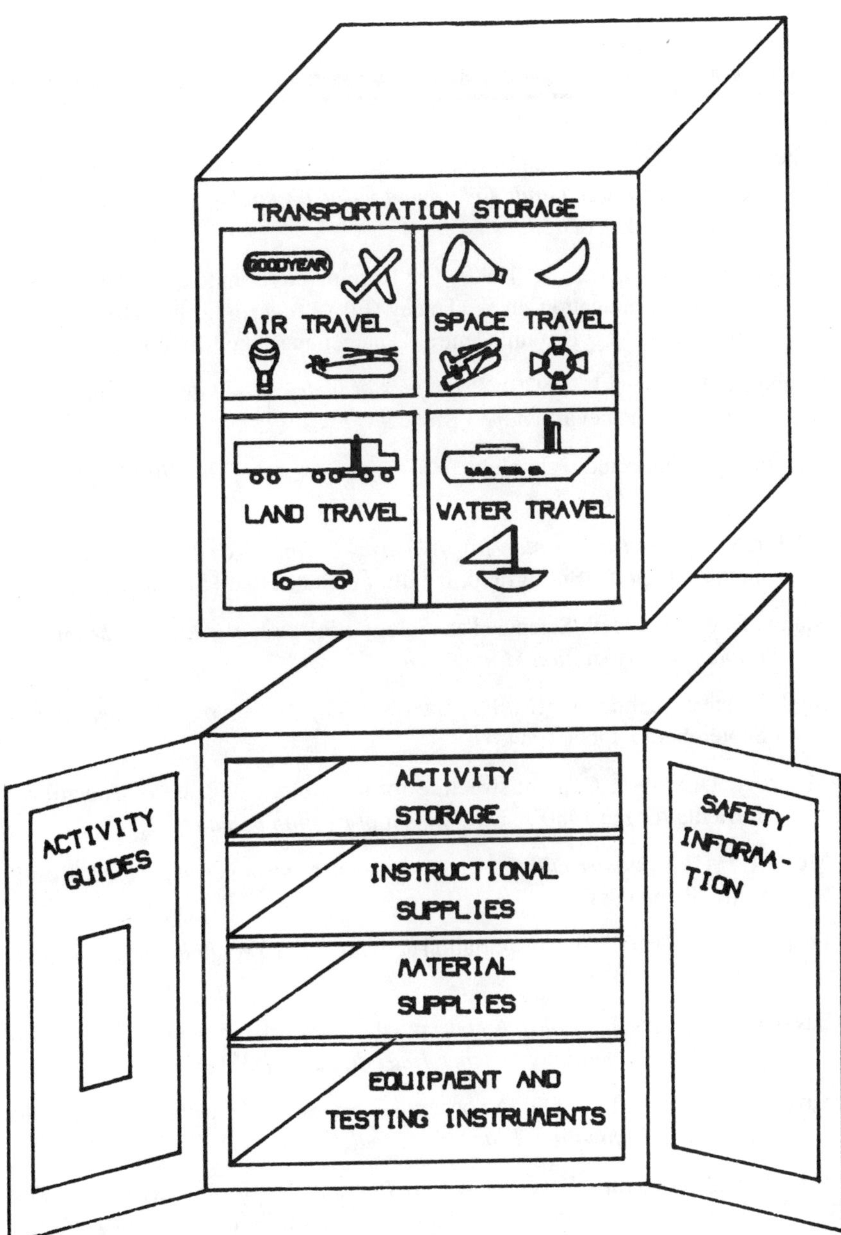

Figure 11: A well-designed storage unit can enhance instruction and lab appearance.

REFERENCES

Bolyard, G. & Komacek, S. (1987). Boat hull design & testing. *Teaching Activities and Resource Guide for Educators of Technology*, West Virginia Department of Education.

Bolyard, G. & Komacek, S. (1990). The learning environment for transportation technology education. In W. Tracey (Ed.) *Proceedings of technology symposium XII*. New Britain: Central Connecticut State University.

Gagne, R. & Briggs, L. (1979). *Principles of instructional design*, 2nd ed. New York: Holt, Rinehart and Winston.

Integrating science and technology. *Progress: Journal of the Illinois Vocational Association*, *2* (3), 7.

ISBE (1987). *The Illinois plan for industrial technology education: An implementation guide*. Springfield, IL: Illinois State Board of Education.

Maley, D. (1986). Math/Science/Technology Projects. *International Technology Education Association Monograph*.

Math-Science-Technology (M/S/T) Interface. *The Technology Teacher Journal*, September/October 1984.

McCrory, D. (1990). Content structure for technology education: Toward new curricula for the 1980's. *The Journal of Epsilon Pi Tau*, *6*(2), 27–34.

McNeil, J. (1985). *Curriculum: A comprehensive introduction*, 3rd ed. Boston: Little, Brown & Co.

Posthuma, F. (1989). 101 transportation activities. *The Technology Teacher Journal*, February 1989, 34.

Savage, E. & Sterry, L. (1990). A conceptual framework for technology education Part 1. *The Technology Teacher Journal*, *50*(1), 6–11.

Savage, E. & Sterry, L. (1990). A conceptual framework for technology education Part 2. *The Technology Teacher Journal*, *50*(2), 7–11.

Schwaller, A. & Kemp, W. (Eds.). (1988). *Instructional strategies for technology education* (Council on Technology Education, 37th Yearbook). Mission Hills, CA: Glencoe Publishing Co.

Siciliano, P. & Wright, P. (1990). Teaching construction systems: Responses to the "facilities" question. In W. Tracey (Ed.) *Proceedings of technology symposium XII*. New Britain: Central Connecticut State University.

Snyder, J. & Hales, J. (Eds.). (1981). *Jackson's mill industrial arts curriculum theory*. Charleston: West Virginia Department of Education.

Wright, T. & Sterry, L. (Eds.). (1984). *Industry & technology education—A guide for curriculum designers, implementors, and teachers*. Langsing, IL: The Technical Foundation of America.

CHAPTER 8

Transportation Technology Teacher Education

By Dr. David L. Rouch
(Assistant Professor at Ohio Northern University)

Introduction

Transportation curricula is increasingly receiving attention in the technology education curriculum. However, transportation continues to be the least developed and implemented of the content organizers of communication, construction, manufacturing, and transportation. One deterrent to the implementation of transportation curricula is that very few of the technology teacher education institutions have provided good models of transportation curricula for its pre-service teachers. When one considers the commonly held belief that teachers tend to teach the way they were taught and what they were taught, it should be of no surprise that the limited implementation of transportation exists as it does. It is essential that pre-service teachers have the opportunity to learn about, experience, and practice the concepts of transportation technology if they are ever expected to teach such curricula as future teachers.

This chapter will be broken down into three major sections. The first section will look at the philosophical basis for transportation curricula by providing a look at the history, characteristics, rationale, and distinctions between energy, power mechanics, and transportation. The second section will take a brief look at the status of current transportation technology teacher education. Finally, the last section will propose a suggested model for transportation technology teacher education programs.

Philosophical Basis for Transportation Curricula

A Historical Perspective of Transportation Curricula

To clearly understand the content, nature, and significance of transportation curriculum in technology education, it is imperative that curriculum developers understand what has taken place in the years preceding contemporary technology curricula. According to Schubert (1985) "To be ahistorical, devoid of perspective of one's past, is indefensible. If people have thought and worked in one's area of concern, one must take responsibility to learn about what has gone on before" (p. 9).

The roots of contemporary transportation curricula can be traced back through the history common to the industrial arts/technology education profession. An early antecedent to transportation curricula came at the Paris higher technical school of *Ecole des Ponts et Chaussees* in 1747 where the aim was to train engineers for both bridge and road building (Bennett, 1926, p. 345). Later on at the *Ecole Centrale des Arts et Manufactures* (started in 1829) special courses were offered in the study of steam engines and railroads (Bennett, 1926, p. 346).

The Moscow Imperial Technical School, which was initially patterned after the *Ecole Centrale des Arts et Manufactures*, later developed its innovative class instruction system for teaching the mechanic arts. The Moscow Imperial Technical School is credited with the first pedagogical class of instruction where railway engineers were taught the workings and manufacture of steam engines (Bennett, 1937, p. 15). This model of class instruction made famous at the 1876 centennial exposition greatly influenced the early development of industrial arts. The main contribution of these regarding transportation curricula, however is that there was increasing support for education aimed at developing the knowledge of the transportation technology that was so drastically shaping their lives.

In the last half of the 19th century the manual training movement lead by Calvin Woodward was the first major effort toward placing relevant, practical experiences into the public high school curriculum in the United States. Woodward often criticized school curricula that utilized the traditional Latin Grammar School content and method for educating its youth. He suggested "put the whole boy in school" and give him some practical experiences that will benefit him in many ways, rather than a schooling which is abstract and has little direct application to life. Woodward proposed a curriculum that included drafting, woodworking, metalworking, and foundry along with the traditional subjects of science, language, and mathematics. Woodward (1896) felt this was an important mix for all boys to develop all the faculties of their mind.

Woodward's manual training school had no organized instruction concerning the operation of mechanical things; however, students who went through such schooling were capable of many skills for which they were not directly instructed as was evidenced by manual training graduates who were able to make mechanical repairs through casual analysis (Woodward, 1905). The only exposure that manual training students had in power or transportation was in terms of learning how the machines they were using worked and possibly in the final project they made for graduation from the manual training school (e.g. some students made working steam engines as their final project) (Woodward, 1896).

The lack of emphasis by Woodward on a transportation content is most likely due to the fact that transportation was powered mostly by horses, mules, donkeys, oxen, people, etc. with the exception of steam engine powered locomotives and ships. Consequently, learning about steam engines was of a trade specific knowledge not needed by the general public. Therefore, the main contribution of Woodward was that general technical training was seen to be important for all students and not just tradesmen.

With the development of the gasoline engine and the growth of the automobile industry in the early 1900's, it became increasingly important for the general public to know how this "horseless carriage" mechanical contraption worked so they could efficiently use and maintain it for their transportation needs. A review of articles in the industrial arts education journals of the time by DeVore, Maughan, and Griscom (1979) reveals that in the decade 1910–1920, articles about gasoline engines, automotives, electricity, and automotive repair subject matter were quite common.

Even though in practice, content relative to transportation was finding its way into the industrial arts curriculum, many were opposed to such a practice. In the classic definition of industrial arts by Bonser and Mossman (1923), such content was purposefully delimited from such study. The classic definition of industrial arts by Bonser and Mossman reads as follows:

> The industrial arts are those occupations by which changes are made in the forms of materials to increase their values for human usage. As a subject for educative purposes, industrial arts is a study of the changes made by men in the forms of materials to increase their values and of the problems of life related to these changes (1923, p. 5).

The key delimiter in this definition is "changes made in the forms of materials." Transportation provides place utility not form utility and so therefore is eliminated from such a study of industrial arts.

Although philosophically industrial arts did not include a study of transportation, auto mechanics-type courses were offered out of public demand to learn about the automobile. Henry Ford's mass production of the automobile made it possible for the commoner to afford the "Tin Lizzie" automobile. With such wide-spread use, it was intriguing for students and their parents to learn about the mechanical wonders of the family automobile.

The 1926 curriculum of Janesville, Wisconsin Junior/Senior high school contained a shop mechanics class and four auto mechanics classes. At the Senior high school level the aims of the auto mechanics classes were to "(a) give a thorough understanding of the operation of an automobile engine, (b) care and repair of the engine and car, (c) correct use of tools and an appreciation of accuracy in workmanship, (d) honesty of workmanship or doing well and thoroughly the job in the places where they can not be seen, and (e) training the pupil for auto mechanics as a vocation" (Lamoreaux, 1926, p. 43).

From these aims, it can be seen as explicitly stated that such a curriculum which included auto-mechanic types of courses were oriented more toward the vocational viewpoint and not considered necessary for all students. This is a typical view of auto mechanics courses even today as many consider auto mechanic-type courses as a component of vocational education. This is quite possibly why Bonser was so strongly against including transportation subject matter in the industrial arts curriculum.

The Prospectus for Industrial Arts in Ohio (Warner, 1934) suggested a "Laboratory of Industries" (general shop) to teach the industrial arts. The major contributor to the prospectus, William E. Warner, saw industrial arts "defined as but one of the practical arts where studies about agriculture, commerce, and the home are included as well" (p. 19). With this perspective of industrial arts, Warner saw subject content to involve: "the individual pupil and his needs, the current social-economic forces which affect the status of our current civilization and should affect education, the material or enduring cultures of all time which are represented by the substance contributions of all people" (p. 19). This meant that the service utilities of communication and transportation were important social-economic forces which needed attention in the public schools of Ohio. The prospectus dealt with the vocation issue of auto mechanics in industrial arts by suggesting a broad perspective of auto mechanics by building it into a study of transportation. Some of the purposes pointed out with this broader viewpoint are as follows:

1. Automobiles should be considered in a perspective of transportation.
2. All vehicles should be studied for their influence on various civilizations which included their use.
3. The relative values of different types of transportation may be judged in terms of what is best, fastest, most economical, safest, whether it be a: horse and buggy, train, automobile, bus, ship, airplane, or dirigible.

4. Learn something about the raw materials used in various types of transportation and of their origins (pp. 88, 89).

According to Towers, Lux, and Ray (1966) "The laboratories of industries was to provide an understanding of the characteristics of industry of the time. Exactly what these characteristics were and just how they might be incorporated into a program of study never became clear" (p. 107). Therefore, it was now philosophically acceptable in some circles to use the transportation organizer for content in the study of industrial arts but the exact working out of such curriculum had not been translated into practice. This resulted in a continuation of auto mechanics programs in many of the public secondary schools.

By the time World War II was over, it became increasingly evident that industry had undergone extensive changes. The 1947 presentation by Warner and several graduate students at the American Industrial Arts Association convention was an effort to reflect these changes and was called A Curriculum to Reflect Technology. This proposal utilized a socio-economic approach to determine subject matter divisions. This was done by regularly examining census and other economic data to discover large divisions of subject matter which included: Power, Transportation, Manufacture, Construction, Communication, and Management. In this case, transportation and power were seen as separate entities. Transportation was seen to embrace "The study of the various carriers: automobile, locomotive, ship and plane, . . ." and ". . . the intimate connection between automobile and highway, ship and port, airplane and navigation" (Kleintjes, 1965, p. 25). On the other hand, power was supported as a study in that "it is basic to all mechanization and technical development" (Lisack, 1965, p. 21). The major divisions in the study of power consisted of (a) sources, (b) generation, (c) transmission, and (d) utilization.

Kleintjes (1947) was successful in implementing the transportation curriculum at Oswego, New York. This is the first known instance where the transportation organizer was used at the teacher education level for organizing content. However, the use of the transportation organizer did not come into wide-spread use. In reality the Oswego program was way ahead of its time and was an exception rather than the model for future transportation programs.

However, Fales and Kuetemeyer (1982) criticized the transportation curriculum developed by Kleintjes to be "heavily oriented to vehicles and to the mechanics of the vehicles." This was most likely due to the abundance of activities readily available with the automobile. This also was a strong force in the prevailing name given to such curriculum—power and transportation (Asper, 1973, p. 297).

In 1948, the Florida State Department of Education Guide to Teaching Industrial Arts accepted the power and the transportation divisions of the

Curriculum to Reflect Technology. A study of transportation was seen important in that "Recorded history testifies to the importance of man's mastery of transportation; his ability to move by more than manpower his person and his goods from place to place" (Florida State Department, 1948, p. 28).

Throughout the 1950's the transportation curriculum organizer continued to receive philosophical support. The extensive changes in the transportation sectors of society provided impetus for several other masters theses after Kleintjes. These provided further conceptualization of transportation curricula at various levels of the public school industrial arts curriculum. However, except for Kleintjes, none were concerned with the preparation of teachers.

Tierney's (1949) masters thesis focused on identifying land transportation activities and the implication of such activities on the teaching of transportation in industrial arts secondary school programs. He found there was an abundance of possibilities for teaching transportation content. Tierney's suggestions for activities were for the construction of various land transportation devices such as carts, wagons, scooters, toy trucks, etc.

Belton (1949) investigated the contributions of transportation in the society of the time by reviewing the transportation literature of the time. His conclusion was that such content is appropriate and important for a comprehensive study of industrial arts.

Another masters thesis (Aman, 1951) pointed out that the units of instruction for a transportation program should be based on the processes and procedures of transportation rather than on project construction. The activities of Aman's line of thought were based on the service and repair of various transportation devices along with model design and the operation of transportation vehicles.

Each of these masters theses were completed at The Ohio State University under the inspiration of William E. Warner. Therefore, it can be seen that starting with the Ohio Prospectus in 1934, Warner carried great influence on encouraging the use of the transportation organizer for industrial arts content. Such influence carried on through to Delmar Olson's dissertation which was also developed during the tenure of Warner.

Delmar Olson's book entitled *Industrial Arts and Technology* (1963) which was an adapted version of his Doctoral Dissertation at The Ohio State University called for a study of transportation along with seven other major categories for industrial arts content. Olson wrote "Transportation development in the United States is an integral part of all industrial development. It has become as essential in the American way of living as has Communications" (p. 137). The influence of the earlier works in transportation curriculum development at Ohio State by Tierney (1949) and Aman (1951) can be clearly seen as Olson saw the study of transportation to "include both the manufacture of the equipment and the operation of the transportation systems" (p. 137).

In the 1960's and 1970's the transportation organizer began to show up in the scheme of other curriculum developers. The American Industry project (Face and Flug, 1965) gave support for using the transportation organizer for industrial arts curricula. Transportation was one of the 13 major concepts of American Industry which were deemed necessary for students to experience to enable them to understand industry. More support came from DeVore (1970) who wrote an article in the Journal of Industrial Arts Education in support of using the transportation organizer and suggested using a taxonomy for organizing such content for transportation. The taxonomy suggested by DeVore was primarily focused on the hardware of transportation systems, i.e. the propulsion, guidance, control, structure, suspension, and support systems of transportation devices. In the same issue as DeVore's article was an article by Alexander (1970) which described two different methods for developing the transportation curriculum. In one of the methods he suggested using the common core of transportation knowledge taught in other fields of endeavor such as civil engineering, business and logistics, and social studies. The other method he suggested and supported was based upon the process method which was based on DeVore's taxonomy and the systems inherent in the taxonomy.

One major ideological setback occurred to the transportation organizer when the Industrial Arts Curriculum Project (IACP) chose to use the organizers of construction and manufacturing for curriculum development (Towers, Lux, and Ray, 1966). The rationale for these two organizers was that everything in the man-made world is either manufactured or constructed. The study of transportation was not left out of the IACP curriculum, it in fact received more attention in its broad concept than transportation was receiving in most industrial arts programs of the day. In IACP, transportation was dealt with in how materials were transported to the place of production, either on-site (construction) or in-plant (manufacturing). Transportation however, was seen as just a support to industry and not significant to the point of including it as a major area of study.

Bender, (1973) working as an advisee of DeVore, developed taxonometric structures for alternative energy propulsion devices which could be used as a basis for transportation curricula. The findings were helpful in that it brought to the attention of transportation curriculum developers that focusing only on the reciprocating internal combustion engine when other alternatives are likely to take the place of the inefficient engine in the future is a narrow and limiting concept of transportation curricula.

Fales (1975) developed an activity centered conceptual course based upon the management and production of transportation creating time and/or place utility in the movement of cargo or passengers for his dissertation. Fales' work was an innovative shift from transportation curricula which was focused on the automobile and the other hardware of transportation systems. This signaled that there was a feeling of dissatisfaction with what had previously been developed, and that the broad knowledge of transportation was being seen as an increasingly significant part of the industrial, technological society.

Even with the developing trend toward transportation classified curricula, there was empirical evidence that it was not being offered extensively in industrial arts secondary school programs. A study by Schmitt & Pelley (1966) revealed there were only 152 industrial arts classes entitled transportation out of the 18,882 schools surveyed with industrial arts programs. Other evidence that the transportation organizer was not being used in public school programs was found from a more recent status study of industrial arts course offerings in the Standards for Industrial Arts Programs Project (Dugger, 1980). This study indicated that of the three sample groups comprising a total of 5,259 industrial arts classes, only eight classes were reported as "transportation" and an additional 46 were reported as "power/transportation". Clearly, these statistics give evidence that transportation subject matter continued to be untapped in its general sense.

It is therefore seen that in the 1960's and 1970's that even though the transportation organizer was being philosophically accepted by more and more people, in practice, transportation curriculum was not being widely disseminated and implemented. The continued acceptance of the transportation organizer was due likely to the idea that many saw how transportation had transformed their very lives.

In brief summary, it can be seen that up to the late 1980's the trend toward the transportation organizer for technology education subject matter content has been evolving through the years beginning with technical, engineering type schools where infrastructures were designed and steam engines and other propulsion devices were studied and manufactured. Transportation curricula began to show up in the local public school curriculum in response to the advent of more sophisticated transportation devices made available to the public. Depending on the particular school, the focus of the curriculum in most public schools has been toward the study of power mechanics, automotive service and repair, energy/power utilization, construction of transportation devices, alternative energy conversion systems, or the study of transportation systems. Only recently has there been a shift in the focus of the transportation organizer toward the study of the productive processes of transportation systems which produce time and/or place utility.

Rationale for Transportation Curriculum

Although transportation has been identified as one of the major content areas by two major curriculum consensus building efforts (Hales & Snyder,

1981; and Savage & Sterry, 1990) of the technology education profession in the last ten years, transportation's place in the technology education curriculum is not accepted by all. This should not be the case. When one considers the economic, social/cultural, and environmental impacts and importance of transportation to today's society, transportation as a viable content is easily defended.

The economic influence of transportation alone provides a strong rationale for transportation content. Nearly 20% of the gross national product (Smith, 1985) and 30% to 75% of the cost of a manufactured product may be attributed to transportation (Sule, 1988). These revealing numbers are supported by other ideas that indicate the importance of transportation to today's society.

All the materials and objects seen in one's home or place of work have been transported to its present location. This includes all the materials used in the construction of one's dwelling as well as the materials used to manufacture the vehicle that transported the materials to one's dwelling. The all-encompassing nature of transportation in society is further explained by Coyle, Bardi, and Cavinato (1986) in the following statement:

> Transportation is one of the tools required by civilized man to bring order out of chaos. It reaches into every phase and facet of our existence. Viewed in historical, economic, environmental, social, and political terms, it is unquestionably the most important industry in the world. Without transportation, you cannot operate a grocery store or win a war. The more complex life becomes, the more indispensable are the elements of transportation systems (p. 4).

Talley (1983) further provides insight into the importance of transportation by stating that "life in a modern city would be impossible without adequate transportation to bring to it the goods needed for its existence as well as to provide for the movement of goods and individuals within its boundaries" (p. 2). The development of the suburbs and the changes that go with them is a direct response to the freeway system that makes them possible. Transportation in our time has caused changes in the way we live, the people we know, the location of our cities and their shape, the environment, the economic system, and in the political system (Talley, 1983, p. 3). Yu (1982) also points out the pervasive influence of transportation on all fabrics of society with the following statements:

> Transportation is a principal component of the economic, social, cultural, and political structures of our society and thus a vital factor in a civilization. The economic development of any geographic area, whether it is a nation, region, state, or city, will find transportation a very important

> influence. . . . Parts of the world that have developed economically the earliest and fastest are those where there had been developed adequate transportation (pp .1, 2).

The growth of air travel and transport itself is a clear example of how transportation has heavily influenced the structures of our society. For example, it is possible for a midwesterner to take a three-day weekend vacation to ski in the mountains of Colorado or relax in the sun of the beaches of the Bahamas. Also, it is possible to take a vacation to distant countries and be exposed to and influenced by different cultures. The expectations and ability to have overnight delivery service from coast to coast has only served to make one even less patient and place more demanding expectations on such services. A few examples of the impact of air travel and transport are: the jobs created, the cultural exchange, the relocation of homes to make room for airports, the constant sound of aircraft in the sky no matter how remote the location, the loss of lives due to transportation related accidents, and the opportunity to have fresh exotic fruits and vegetables from distant parts of the world.

We live in a society where transportation is so much a part of our lives that we have taken it for granted. "Picture life without transportation; consider how people's lives would change if their environments extended no farther than as far as they could walk" (Stephenson, 1987, p. 12).

These realizations about transportation are only the "tip of the iceberg" of what must be understood by today's youth. This idea is brought out emphatically by the former secretary of the U.S. Department of Transportation, John Volpe (1970) with the following remarks: "It is essential that young people confidently understand the transportation systems that are so large a part of their daily lives. This is especially true if we are to make those systems responsive to public needs and human objectives" (p. 5).

All individuals are involved in the decision making process for transportation that effects the fabric of our transportation systems. They are classified by Stephenson (1987) as "carriers, users, the government, and other interested parties such as taxpayers and non-users affected by environmental or other transportation-caused problems" (p. 6). Stephenson points out that so many groups with so many conflicting expectations results in confusion and "decisions, strategies, and trade-offs will be made; the challenge is to make the best ones" (p. 7).

Unless all people from every walk of life are informed about the role of transportation in their lives, wrong decisions will be made. There will continue to be inefficient use of our natural resources, increased time expenditure for our transportation needs, and higher costs for transporting cargo and people to the desired destination.

Characteristics of Contemporary Curricula

The 1980's has been a period for change in the technology education profession. The national professional organization, the American Industrial Arts Association (AIAA) officially changed its name to the International Technology Education Association (ITEA) at the 1985 House of Delegates meeting. Although the name change may have been a little bit premature, since many programs have changed in name only, there has been an abundance of curriculum development and revision activity in an effort to reflect the technology of contemporary society. Such activities as computer aided drafting design (CADD), computer aided manufacturing (CAM), and robotics/automation have found their way into the curriculum.

Of primary concern when developing new curricula is the need to decide what logically should be selected as the content for such curricula. Bensen (1988) points out four methods used for structuring technology education curriculum. These include the conceptual, behavior analysis, problem-solving, and systems approach. The conceptual approach uses taxonomies to structure content into conceptual categories, and hierarchies. The taxonomy is used to show where a particular concept fits into the discipline. An advantage of the conceptual approach is that it "promotes inclusiveness and ensures a holistic study of technology. The goals of the program, rather than the concepts themselves, dictate the nature of the study" (Bensen, 1988, p. 173).

The behavior analysis method is an approach that selects content based upon what an individual needs to survive in the technological world. These life tasks are those skills it takes to be a home owner, citizen, decision maker, and consumer. The content would be taught in this method by giving the student learning and doing experiences in these life tasks (Bensen, 1988).

The problem solving method is a content selection method that bases the curriculum on the theory of "process as content." In this method it is acknowledged that it is impossible to teach students everything about technology, especially in contemporary society where the gaining of new knowledge is growing exponentially. If the student can understand the process of problem solving, they will be able to solve most technological problems no matter what the specific technological content is. Waetjen (1989) points out that problem solving is a teaching technique as well as a method for selecting curriculum.

The other method for selecting content is the systems method. In this method, content selection is based upon the systems model where the parts of technological systems are studied as part of a system. A system is seen as more than the sum of its parts because it is an "interacting whole" where if one component of the system is changed, it will have repercussions for the rest of the system.

These methods of curriculum content selection are indicative of the changing focus of industrial arts to technology education. How have these changes affected the transportation organizer? The next section will discuss how traditional power mechanics compare to contemporary transportation curricula.

Distinctions Between I.A. Power Technology and Transportation Technology Education

Power, power mechanics, energy/power, energy and transportation, and power transportation are the most common traditional descriptors of curriculum that has lead up to the transportation content organizer. In the years since the development of the Jackson's Mill Curriculum Theory (Hales & Snyder, 1981) it has become fashionable for programs to change the name of courses and programs to make it appear as though their programs are up-to-date and in line with contemporary curriculum development in the field. However, many times the changes occur in name only, while the content and learning activities of the curriculum continues to be the same as before.

In the mid 1970's the transportation organizer in curricula was side-tracked by the global energy crisis that was taking place at the time. As the result of energy shortages, a new focus on energy use and conservation efforts emerged. The literature was full of many articles dealing with building solar energy devices and other practical energy conservation suggestions for the home. Alternative energy enthusiasts grew quickly in number being mainly concerned with utilizing and developing renewable and inexhaustible energy sources. This worldwide concern for energy had a major effect on industrial arts, social studies, and science education. Suddenly there were no illusions regarding the fact that our fossil fuel based energy supply was limited and that people needed to be educated about efficient energy usage, transmission, conversion, and alternative energies. Many industrial arts teachers started to implement solar energy and other alternative energy units into their courses. These units had much success because they were new, exciting, and practical in the midst of the energy crisis. Soon many textbooks were written and projects and activities were developed for use in energy classes. Most of these courses have been included under headings such as power, energy, or alternative energy.

This matter has had great influence in the industrial arts profession as efforts have been made in the early 1980's to develop a consensus for industrial arts curriculum. The Jackson's Mill Industrial Arts Curriculum Theory (Hales and Snyder, 1981) has suggested the use of transportation along with communication, construction, and manufacturing as the major organizers for subject matter. These organizers were selected in that they are the major human adaptive systems of endeavor in industry and technology. Although the Jackson's Mill Curriculum Theory was supposedly a national consensus building effort, most states have adapted the theory to meet their particular philosophy. For instance, states such as Minnesota and Illinois have broken out the two areas of energy/power and transportation into two separate organizers for their industrial technology state curriculum plan. Other states such as Indiana and Utah combine energy/power and transportation into one organizer for curricula. Therefore, it can be seen that there are many differing opinions regarding where the transportation organizer should fit into the technology education curriculum and whether it should be combined as a subset of energy and power mechanics or if it should be a single, distinct organizing category.

Power mechanics, energy, etc. (energy/power) have significantly different approaches to transportation in content selection and basic strategies. As shown in Figure 1, the organizer for transportation curricula is human adaptive systems. This content organizing scheme was identified by Jackson's Mill (Hales & Snyder, 1981) as the basis for industry and technology education content. The focus of transportation content is to design and develop the most efficient system for transporting goods or people from one place to another. On the other hand, energy/power is not a system but is literally defined as the ability to do work (energy) and the rate of doing work (power). Energy is an input into transportation systems to enable the movement of people and/or cargo. Likewise, power technology is used and can be measured as the people and/or cargo are moved.

Energy/power curricula have a focus on service, repair, and control of mechanical, electrical, and fluid power transmission devices. Sources of energy,

	Transportation	Energy/Power
Organizer	Human adaptive system	Efficient ways of doing work or ability to do work
Purpose	Efficient movement of goods and/or people	Service, repair, and control
Content	• Designing/developing transportation systems/vehicles. • Learn about modes of transportation • Investigate impacts of transport • Scheduling routes • Rate making/transporting costs • Preparing for move, moving, and completing the move. • Management of transportation	• Learn how mechanical, electrical, and fluid power transmission devices work • Research sources of energy • Experiment with various types of energy converters to learn how they operate
Strategies	• Understanding systems; inputs, processes, outputs, and feedbacks • Application of problem solving	• Understanding devices • Experimentation • Apply scientific principles

Figure 1: Comparison of transportation and power mechanics.

and energy converters, and learning the application of scientific principles are also major components of energy/power. Some programs use the automobile and/or small gasoline engine as the emphasis for teaching such curricula. Conversely, transportation is much broader in content. The emphasis is on the design and development of efficient transportation devices and developing an understanding of the different modes of transportation. Scheduling, rate making, on-board vehicular systems and the study of the impacts of transportation are the focus. Problem solving should be an emphasis of transportation curricula while developing an understanding of energy/power devices is the emphasis for energy/power curricula.

Status of Current Transportation Technology Teacher Education

As was alluded to earlier in the chapter, there exist very few programs that are preparing pre-service teachers to teach transportation technology. A cursory review of the *Industrial Teacher Education Directory* (Dennis, 1990–91) reveals what teacher education programs are identifying their program offerings as. Of the 242 institutions listed in the yearbook, only 22 had faculty listed who taught transportation, power transportation, energy/transportation, or energy/power/transportation. On the other hand, 68 institutions had faculty listed who had taught power mechanics, power, energy, or energy/power. It should be pointed out that there are several other institutions that reported automotive mechanics as a course taught by their faculty.

Rouch (1989) reported that in personal communication with several teacher education institutions, unsolicited responses to correspondence included statements such as "our transportation course exists in name only and is really only a power mechanics course." Therefore, the number of institutions reporting transportation as a subject taught in their programs does not necessarily reflect the number of programs who are actually teaching transportation content.

The few teacher training institutions that do have transportation in their curricula may be classified into two types of programs. One program type has transportation coursework that is designed for teacher education students only. These programs have a sufficient number of students in their teacher education program to offer transportation courses that deal not only with the development of technological skills in transportation but the unique things a pre-service teacher needs to be involved with and know regarding teaching transportation technology. The other type of programs are those who have a mix of students in a core of introductory technical courses. Some of the students are pre-service teachers and others are preparing for work in industrial management-type positions. The focus is on the development of technological skills in transportation with little or no consideration for the context that these skills will be applied.

Of the two types of programs described above, one where courses can be designed for a well defined audience is the most desirable. However, because of uncontrollable factors, it is often necessary to operate programs context free. The next section of this chapter will look at what an ideal transportation technology teacher preparation program should look like.

A Model for Transportation Technology Teacher Education

Much of the curriculum development that has taken place in the content organizing area of transportation has been based upon past professional experience, and knowledge which is limited to the backgrounds of those who are designing such programs. The goal of this section is to propose a model for transportation technology teacher education programs that is grounded in the developing knowledge bases for teacher preparation institutions.

The curriculum content for teacher preparation may be broken down into three major components: General Education, Content Specialty Studies, and Professional Pedagogy Studies. According to the new NCATE Standards (1987) these three components must have strong ties to the "World of Practice." Figure 2 illustrates how the three major components of the teacher preparation curriculum is related to the world of practice. This is of critical importance to the education of teachers as it is important that pre-service teachers are able to relate abstract classroom knowledge to realistic clinical and field-based situations of a variety they are being prepared to teach in.

General Education

According to the NCATE Standards (1987) "Education students should have a solid grounding in general education that will allow for concentration on professional and specialty studies." It is the intent of NCATE that teachers be recognized and respected as learned and well-educated individuals by professional men and women. Years ago, teachers were the only individuals of the community that had received any formal education past the grade school level. However, this is no longer the case as a higher and higher percentage of people in the community have had some formal education including and past

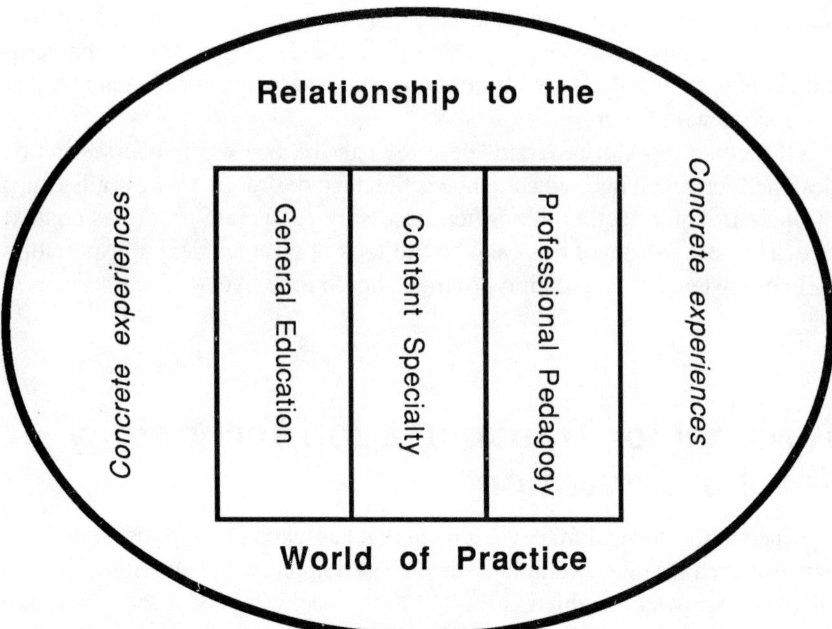

Figure 2: Relationship of teacher education curriculum to the world of practice.

the secondary school level. Conant (1963) provides an additional rationale for inclusion of general education in the teacher education curriculum. "There is moreover, an important practical reason for certain studies: almost any teacher inevitably faces the necessity of dealing with subjects outside his area of specialization, not only in his classroom but also in conversation with students. If he is largely ignorant or uninformed, he can do much harm" (p. 93). Teachers are to serve as good models of well-educated persons for their students. Also, if teachers have a solid general education, it can serve to strengthen, enrich and undergird their own teaching specialty areas, freeing them to think critically and apply specialty knowledge to related areas of study.

The content of the general education component is much debated among scholars and therefore the attempt to solve that argument will not be made here. However, it should be pointed out that many schools have general stipulations for meeting basic education requirements that includes a potpourri of courses from the humanities, social sciences and natural sciences. Regardless of what one's view is regarding the content of general education, such an arrangement for general studies is unlikely to deliver well rounded and broadly educated individuals.

According to NCATE Standards (1987) "The general education component is a well-planned sequence of courses and experiences that includes theoretical and practical knowledge gained from studies in communications, mathematics, science, history, philosophy, literature and the arts" (p.38). It is clear that programs who wish to be in compliance with NCATE standards for accreditation, have some pretty clear guidelines as to what subjects should be chosen for general education. However, the precise number and levels of courses should be based upon the content specialty. This will provide the opportunity for pre-service students to gain complementary knowledge to their teaching specialty to increase the possibility of continued intellectual growth (Smith, 1980). General education courses such as economics, physics, technology and society, and introductory management are courses that should be required of pre-service transportation teachers.

Professional Studies

This component of the teacher education curriculum should include the development of generic knowledge and skills in pedagogy. According to NCATE Standards (1987),

> the professional studies component(s) for the preparation of teachers provides knowledge about and appropriate skills in learning theory, educational goals and objectives, cultural influences on learning, curriculum planning and design, instructional techniques, planning and management of instruction, design and use of evaluation and measurement methods, classroom and behavior management, instructional strategies for exceptionalities, classrooms and schools as social systems, school law, instructional technology, and collaborative and consultative skills (p. 40).

Common professional course offerings include: educational psychology, educational foundations, curriculum, special methods, teaching and learning theory, and introduction to teaching. These courses are generally offered by a general educational department (with the exception of teaching specialty methods). One problem that has existed over the years with this component is that students have difficulty applying the abstract knowledge gained in these courses to practical situations. This can be explained by the fact that pre-service teachers have not had the concrete experiences that make it possible for them to make sense of what they are learning.

The development of field experiences along-side such courses is a great help in rectifying this situation. However, it is important that these field experiences are purposeful and closely monitored so that pre-service students are not simply sitting for hours in classrooms bored stiff at what they are observing and maybe not even knowing what they are to be observing.

The student teaching or internship experience is a very critical component to the preparation of technology teachers. McCrory (1986) points out the need to place student teachers in places where they can implement recently learned skills and ideas of technology education. If the students do not have the opportunity to explore innovative ideas and make some mistakes in their student teaching experience, it is doubtful that they will be innovative as teachers on their own. One problem associated with this is that there are very few opportunities for student teaching placement in the area of transportation. It is important that exemplary programs in transportation and the other content organizing areas be developed near teacher training institutions so that student teachers have some idea what facilities and curriculum should look like for teaching technology. The Holmes Group Proposal (1986) strongly supports the upgrowth of professional development schools that is analogous to teaching hospitals in the medical profession. This will provide an environment where research, experimentation, and practice of university faculty, practicing teachers, and administrators can develop exemplary learning institutions.

Course offerings

The specialty methods courses taught and supervised by the major department should give pre-service teachers the chance to investigate, experience, implement and execute skills, ideas, and processes relative to a teaching career in technology. The Undergraduate Studies committee of CTTE has prepared a monograph (Henak, 1989) that has provided a structure for a model undergraduate technology teacher education program. The following courses are proposed by Henak:

Course Title: Teaching Technology

Course Description:

Students work individually and in collaborative groups to investigate a career in teaching Technology, begin developing a philosophy of teaching relevant to technology, and gain an understanding of the historic development, terminology, and curriculum development processes in Technology.

Intended Learning Outcomes:

1. Describing a career in teaching Technology.
2. History of Technology.
3. Differentiating terminology in the field of Technology.
4. Developing a Philosophy of Teaching.
5. Describing curriculum development processes used in Technology.

Course Title: Methods for Teaching Technology

Course Description:

Problems of developing and implementing instructional strategies, preparing evaluation instruments, managing the physical environment, and maintaining a cooperative classroom environment. Topics developed in the context of field experiences whenever possible. (Note: this course should be taught in the major department with the credit hours used to satisfy the professional requirements.)

Intended Learning Outcomes:

1. Describing the characteristics of a group of learners.
2. Communicating the rationale, objectives, structure, and intended outcomes of a Technology course.
3. Developing an instructional strategy for teaching problem solving through a problem solving approach in which technical content and activities are emphasized.
4. Designing an evaluation system for a Technology course.
5. Designing and managing the physical environment for a Technology course.
6. Managing classroom behavior.
7. Producing instructional media.
8. Teaching value/moral issues within a Technology context.
9. Teaching futuristics in the Technology classroom.
10. Teaching students with special needs.
11. Developing and implementing a safety program in Technology laboratories.

Course Title: Curriculum Development in Technology

Course Description:

Emphasizes contemporary approaches to Technology, curriculum development, and the preparation and use of instructional media. Students plan and execute a teaching unit in a public school setting.

Intended Learning Outcomes:

1. Developing criteria for evaluating Technology curriculum materials.
2. Evaluating and selecting instructional units in Technology.
3. Developing and implementing instructional units in Technology.
4. Preparing and using instructional media (pp. 38–39).

Specialty Studies

The specialty studies component of the curriculum must provide for the attainment of a "high level of academic competence and understanding" (p. 39) in the areas in which pre-service students plan to work or teach (NCATE, 1987). Of primary concern is that a well formulated plan is developed to deliver curriculum that will meet the standards of professional learned societies. The NCATE approved ITEA/CTTE guidelines (*Basic Program in Technology Education*, 1988) for technology teacher education programs define and establish transportation content as follows: "Efficiently using resources to obtain time and to attain and maintain direct physical contact and exchange among individuals and societal units through the movement of material/goods and people" (section 3.2.4). In short, Transportation is an economic productive activity which has as its goal to provide time or place utility of materials, products, or people. Therefore, as a content area of study for Technology Education, the focus must be on studying the most efficient technical means by which this is accomplished. Many teachers who claim to teach transportation are only teaching a small segment of the efficient technical means of producing time or place utility. Additionally, the observed tendency in such courses and supportive curricular materials is to pick "hands-on" activities from a grab-bag that are "neat things to do" but often times do not go very far in teaching the broad concepts that are unique to transportation technology and are essential for future teachers to understand.

According to the Jackson's Mill curriculum theory (Hales & Snyder, 1980), within the process portion of the universal systems model are found the concepts, principles, generalizations, and unifying themes of technology. A knowledge of such provides one with a knowledge of the efficient technical means utilized in transportation. The knowledge of these appropriate technical means or processes is called "technology." One part of the process portion that is often neglected is management. The knowledge of effective and efficient management in transportation is critical to developing appropriate technical means. Clearly, both the Jackson's Mill curriculum theory and the Industry and Technology (Wright & Sterry, 1983) curriculum guide point out that the experiences in transportation should be included from both the productive and management activities of the system. For this reason, management concepts relative to transportation should be introduced into the content of each course.

Courses

The CTTE monograph: *Elements and Structure for a Model Undergraduate Technology Teacher Education Program* (Henak, 1989) suggests offering three transportation courses. One of the courses is an introductory course, another is a systems management type course and the other one is research and

Transportation Teacher Education		
Introduction to Transportation Technology	Transporting Systems	Transportation Research and Development

Figure 3: Technological courses for transportation teacher education.

development oriented. The most recent research of Transportation Technology Teacher Education (Rouch, 1989) has been implemented into course titles, descriptions, and intended learning outcomes. The intended learning outcomes have been adapted from a list of outcomes empirically validated by a select group of experts in transportation (Rouch, 1989). Figure 3 shows the breakdown of courses in the transportation sequence. Those planning to teach transportation should take all three courses. All technology teacher education students should be required to take at least the first two levels of courses.

Course Title: Introduction to Transportation Technology

Course Description:

An introductory survey course of the basic concepts, history, modes and methods, efficient utilization, and the transportation technology vehicular subsystems of guidance, control, structure, suspension, propulsion, and support. Also emphasized in this course is the application of the universal systems model to transportation and how transportation has impacted our lives socially, culturally, environmentally, and economically.

Intended Learning Outcomes:

1. Recognizes various modes of transportation and their characteristics.
2. Understands the significance of transportation in the historical development of society.
3. Comprehends the relationship of transportation to communication, construction, and manufacturing.
4. Analyzes the negative and positive impacts of transportation on the environment.
5. Comprehends the technical means by which humans accomplish the movement of materials, goods, and people.
6. Demonstrates safety consciousness in regards to transportation devices.
7. Knows the receiving, holding/storing, loading, moving, unloading, and delivering techniques utilized in transportation for different modes.
8. Performs as a wise consumer in regards to transportation activities.
9. Knows the various types of energy sources, storage devices, and power transmission systems used in vehicles.
10. Understands the guidance, monitoring, control, propulsion, structural, and suspension systems used with transportation devices.
11. Evaluates the guidance, monitoring, control, propulsion, structural, and suspension systems used with transportation devices.

Course Title: Transporting Systems

Course Description:

The primary emphasis of this course will be in the planning, organizing, directing, and controlling management functions as related to transportation systems. Logistics, scheduling, rate making, plant/facility location, routing, packaging, JIT, and legislation.

Intended Learning Outcomes:

1. Appreciates the vast network required to support transportation systems.
2. Understands the application of computer technology to transportation system design, control, monitoring, and evaluation.

3. Understands the transportation processes of receiving, holding/storing, loading, moving, unloading, and delivering.
4. Knows the recent operational, technological, and managerial developments utilized in transportation technology.
5. Comprehends transportation economics and the cost of moving goods, people and materials.
6. Understands the impact of transportation on facility location.
7. Evaluates the efficiency of intermodal transportation systems.
8. Understands how societal values and economics affect one's choice of particular transportation modes.
9. Demonstrates management skills needed for planning, organizing, and controlling transportation processes.
10. Evaluates the routing of transportation traffic lines.
11. Knows the function of various transportation agencies and regulatory organizations.
12. Understands transportation documentation procedures.

Course Title: Transportation Research and Development

Course Description:

This is an advanced level course that emphasizes the analysis, design, and development of transportation devices and/or systems. The problem solving system model will be used as the technological inquiry method for analyzing and developing an efficient transportation system.

Intended Learning Outcomes:

1. Identifies issues and problems related to transportation.
2. Utilizes problem solving skills for transportation related problems.
3. Evaluates transportation systems for their energy utilization efficiency.
4. Demonstrates logical decision making skills regarding transportation issues.
5. Knows the variables to be considered in designing an efficient transportation system.
6. Knows the methodology to evaluate future transportation innovations and developments.
7. Uses transportation technical literature.
8. Analyzes the methods utilized in transporting materials, goods, and people.

Activity Selection

As was stated earlier, transportation is the least developed area of the technology education curriculum. One of the unique features of technology education is that it is a "practice oriented" or "action based" program. Therefore, one of the problems that has been evident with transportation curriculum has been the inability to develop activities that are unique to transportation. The tendency has been to repackage traditional automotive mechanics activities and change the name of courses to transportation. The writer does not deny the importance of the automobile and its possible merit as a study of technology, math, and science concepts but it clearly does not constitute the study of the productive processes of transportation.

Another tendency has been to focus activities on the research and development aspects of various types of transportation vehicles. Such a strategy is no different from the research and development that goes into other manufactured or constructed products. Consequently, it is important that the purpose of an activity is to apply an understanding of the research and development process to transportation and the unique problems and components of design that are peculiar to transportation. DeVore (1970) has developed a conceptual taxonomy of the technical systems of transportation devices. This taxonomy provides the transportation researcher the major elements for analyzing and developing transportation systems. However, when developing activities, it must be kept in mind that the purpose of a transportation system is to produce place utility of people and/or goods and materials in a timely and efficient manner through the productive processes of receiving, loading, moving, unloading, delivering (Hales & Snyder, 1981). One of the critical aspects often not dealt with in transportation activities is the application of the management techniques of planning, organizing, directing, and controlling. Transportation activities should give students the chance to learn about and apply management techniques, technical systems, and how they apply to the various modes of transportation. Also, the students should research and study the impacts of transportation on the technological, sociological and biological environments. Figure 4 shows a model that represents the breadth of content for transportation technology teacher education. Activities should be chosen that will enable students to understand transportation technology as a whole, not just some small, isolated part of transportation. Following is a list of ideas for activities (Rouch,1990) that have been collected from various sources.

Some Possible Transportation Related Activities:

1. Test the flight stability of model aircraft.
2. Determine the actual cost of moving a person or product from one

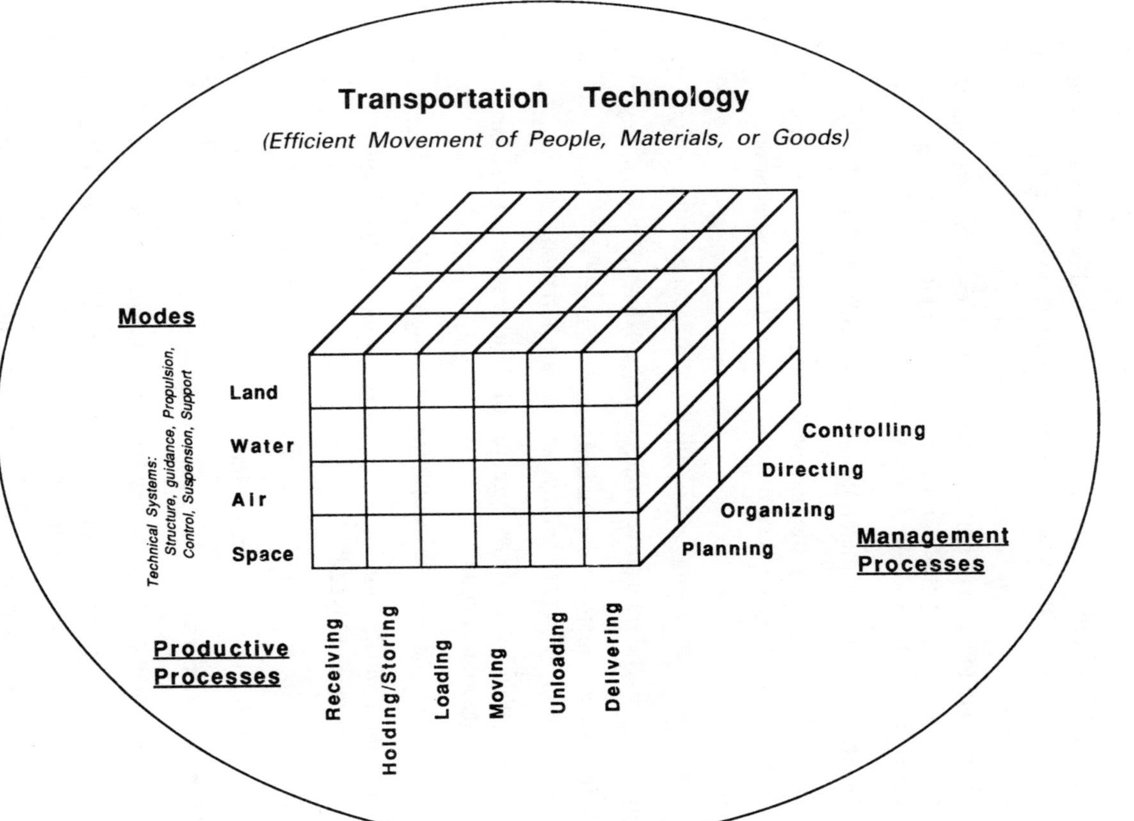

Figure 4: A model for transportation technology.

point to another point by figuring the cost of gasoline for the distance traveled, the wages to be paid to the driver, the cost of maintenance and wear and tear on the vehicle, and the insurance and tax expenses for operating the vehicle.

3. Calculate the energy utilization rate for carrying people using several modes.
4. Critically analyze the transportation system used in a manufacturing plant for moving materials, and parts from one point to the next point.
5. Investigate location of cities, churches, factories, and/or schools. Research why some particular industry is located in their city, or why their city was built where it is.
6. Determine where the materials came from to build their laboratory.
7. Determine if their city should develop a mass transit system or suggest changes that should be made in an existing transportation system.
8. Trace the modes used to get gasoline to the local gasoline station.
9. Identify several transportation agencies and determine what they do.
10. Find out how many of the student's parents would be without a job if there ceased to be petroleum powered transportation.
11. Disassemble, measure, analyze, rebuild, and reassemble the parts of a small gasoline engine.
12. Plan the airline flight schedules for incoming and outgoing flights.
13. Have individuals apply for a transportation job and interview prospective employees.
14. Build an electric motor.
15. Investigate the purpose of the interstate commerce commission.
16. Develop a record sheet to be used for delivery documentation.
17. Trouble-shoot problems on the family automobile or lab engine.
18. Develop a suspension system for a vehicle that will produce the smoothest ride on a bumpy surface.
19. List some transportational professional organizations and find out who composes the membership.

20. Find out possible transporting services available to the disabled, elderly, and poor in your area.
21. Study Europe's train system and investigate reasons why Europe's system has continued to flourish and the United States system has almost become an extinct species.
22. Plot a ship's course by looking at possible routes.
23. Construct a model river barge and calculate its draft.
24. Identify, design, and evaluate on-site material handling equipment.
25. Operate a model pipeline complete with pumping stations.
26. Given a product to be moved to a particular location, pick the proper mode for shipping the product.
27. Design and build a mouse-trap spring powered vehicle.
28. Reconstruct the scene of a traffic accident to determine factors that caused the accident.
29. Design, analyze, build, and fly a paper airplane.
30. Plan a trip to anywhere in the world. Determine what to pack, what vaccinations are required, what modes of transportation will be required, how much the trip will cost, how long you will be gone, and what places you will see.
31. Design a barge hull.
32. Overhaul a bicycle.
33. Obtain E.P.A. data on air quality as influenced by transportation devices.
34. Evaluate automobile usage by average number of passengers per car.
35. Build a steam engine.
36. Design a packaging system for a particular product by considering the weight, protection requirements, shipping and handling methods, temperature requirements.
37. Design a wind-powered vehicle.
38. Given a map of a particular city determine the best route from point A to point B.
39. Given a particular package size and weight, determine what method of shipment is the most economical, UPS, U.S. Postal service, or express mail.

40. Develop a time-line of historical developments in transportation.

41. Investigate the spin-offs from the NASA space program.

42. Program a robot to move parts from one location to another location.

43. Do a Delphi study on the use of the electrical vehicle in the future.

44. Design a scale model of a mass transit system for your particular city.

45. How to buy a car, including negotiating, consulting consumer reports, financing, etc.

46. Construct a Maglev Train.

47. Write a scenario on future transportation.

48. Design and build a propeller driven car.

49. Schedule the delivery of construction materials to a site.

50. Build and fly a hot air balloon.

51. Build and launch a model rocket.

52. Use a wind tunnel to test the efficiency of various shapes of vehicles.

53. Build a car that is powered by a brick that swings down and hits the car. The car is to carry an egg the farthest distance. The car that carries the egg the farthest distance without breaking it is the best design.

54. Design and build a monorail system.

55. Design and build a CO_2 cartridge powered car.

56. Go to the library and find out what transportation related periodicals are available.

57. List different types of fuels used in automobiles and determine how octane number rating influences efficiency and determine the relative efficiency of alternative fuels for automobiles.

58. Investigate displacement and buoyancy of a clay ball that is reformed into a boat shape.

59. Complete dynamometer, horsepower, and torque measurements of various types of engines.

60. Assess the bus routes on your campus and make a report of recommendations for changes or reassignment of buses.

61. Design and build a barge that will carry 5 lbs. of sand in a waterway 10" deep.
62. Given several possible locations for a manufacturing facility and the number of and distance of deliveries to be made to and from the facility, determine the best location for the facility.
63. Analyze the traffic flow on a highway that requires a new bridge.
64. Visit a transportation engineer's office to see how the traffic is controlled and monitored.

Nature of Laboratory and Other Facilities

As can be readily seen from the discussion that has taken place thus far in this chapter, there are far reaching consequences for the transportation laboratory. This should be seen as an opportunity, not a liability. Students may participate in developing any laboratory apparatus that may be required for activities. This will give the pre-service teacher some valuable experience revising the set up for a lab, something every technology teacher needs to be able to do. Also, another way of viewing this is that instruction should not be limited to a clinical or on-campus laboratory. Some activities are more appropriate and should take place in a real world setting as is suggested by NCATE. Activities such as traffic flow analysis, scheduling, and rate making should take place in real world situations. Other possibilities are that a field based component can be a required part of teacher preparation courses by having pre-service students design and develop transportation learning activities that can be taken out to schools of the local community.

Conclusions

Transportation is clearly a very important part of the technology education curriculum. Each teacher education institution needs to take on a leadership role in providing pre-service experiences in transportation to their students. This will enable their graduates to implement transportation activities into their future teaching situations. Also, teacher education institutions need to be active in the schools of their general community, offering assistance in setting up exemplary transportation technology programs, and providing inservice training workshops. Once exemplary programs have been established, the development of other programs will follow as pre-service students can be placed for field experiences and student teaching to observe and be involved with the nature of transportation subject matter. Presently, few have such an opportunity and thus, little change has taken place nationally in the development and implementation of transportation curriculum. Now is the time for change to an exciting, activity based, comprehensive transportation technology program.

REFERENCES

Alexander, W. F. (1970). A concept of transportation for industrial arts. *Journal of Industrial Arts Education. 29*, 6, 12–17.

Aman, C. H. (1951). An industrial arts transportation program for secondary schools. An unpublished masters thesis, The Ohio State University, Columbus, Ohio.

Asper, N. L. (1973). Technology through power and transportation. In *Industrial arts and the challenge of an urban society* pp. 296–301. Washington D.C.: American Industrial Arts Association.

Babbie, E. R. (1973). *Survey research methods*. Belmont, California: Wadsworth Publishing Company Inc.

Basic Program in Technology Education. (1988). NCATE approved curriculum guidelines. Reston, Virginia: International Technology Education Association.

Belton, W. L. (1949). Transportation: A content study for industrial arts. An unpublished masters thesis, The Ohio State University, Columbus, Ohio.

Bender, M. (1973). Alternative energy systems for the automobile: implications for content derivation for teaching transportation technology, (Doctoral dissertation, West Virginia University, 1973). *Dissertation Abstracts International, 34*, 3940A.

Bennett, C. A. (1926). *History of manual and industrial education: up to 1870.* Peoria: Bennett.

Bennett, C. A. (1937). *History of manual and industrial education: 1870 to 1917.* Peoria: Bennett.

Bensen, M. J. (1988). The transition from industrial arts to technology education. In R. F. Brandt (Editor), *The content of the curriculum* (pp. 167–180). Washington D. C.: Association for Supervision and Curriculum.

Bonser, F. G., & Mossman, L. C. (1923). *Industrial arts for elementary schools.* New York: The Macmillan Company.

Conant, J. (1963). *The Education of American Teachers*. New York: McGraw-Hill.

Coyle, J. J., Bardi, E. J., & Cavinato, J. L. (1986). *Transportation* (2nd Ed.) St. Paul, Minnesota: West Publishing Company.

Dennis, E. (1990–91). *Industrial Teacher Education Directory*, CTTE and NAITTE. Department of Industrial Technology, University of Northern Iowa, Cedar Falls, Iowa.

DeVore, P. W. (1970). Transportation technology: the identification of content and method. *Journal of Industrial Arts Education. 29*, 6, 18–22.

DeVore, P. W., Maughan, G. R., & Griscom, W. E. (1979). Influence of technology on industrial arts subject matter. In G. E. Martin's (Ed.) *Industrial arts education: retrospect, prospect.* Bloomington: McKnight.

Dugger, W. (1980). *Standards for industrial arts education programs project.* (DHEW-funded project). Virginia Polytechnic Institute and State University.

Face, W., & Flugg, E. R. (1966). The American Industry Project. Menomonie, Wisconsin, Stout State University.

Fales, J. F. (1975). Development and pilot test of a curriculum for transportation in Louisiana, (Doctoral dissertation, Texas A&M University, 1975). *Dissertation Abstracts International 36*, 2686A.

Fales, J. F., & Kuetemeyer, V. F. (1982). Transportation: toward a balanced curriculum. *Man/Society/Technology* March, pp. 2–4.

Florida State Dept. of Education. (1948). A brief guide to teaching industrial arts in the secondary schools.

Hales, J. A., & Snyder, J. F. (Eds.) (1981). *Jackson's Mill industrial arts curriculum theory.* AIAA.

Henak, R. (Chairperson). (1989). *Elements and Structure for a Model Undergraduate Technology Teacher Education Program.* A monograph of the Council on Technology Teacher Education.

Illinois State Board of Education. (1984). *Transportation technology curriculum guide.* Springfield, Illinois: Department of Adult, Vocational and Technical Education, Research and Development Section.

Industry and technology education. (1983). A guide for curriculum designers, implementors, and teachers. Technical Foundation of America, Illinois.

Kleintjes, P. L. (1947). A transportation program in industrial arts. An unpublished master's thesis at The Ohio State University.

Lamoreaux, E. S. (1926). Industrial arts curriculum for Janesville junior and senior high schools. Wisconsin.

Lisack, J. P. (1965). Power division. In W. E. Warner *A curriculum to reflect technology.* Columbus, Ohio: Epsilon Pi Tau.

McCrory, D. (1986). Is student teaching the weak link in technology teacher education? *Journal of Industrial Teacher Education, 23*, 4, 56–57.

NCATE Standards, Procedures, and Policies for the Accreditation of Professional Education Units (1987). Washington, D. C.: National Council for Accreditation of Teacher Education.

Olson, D. (1963). *Industrial arts and technology*. New Jersey: Prentice-Hall.

Rouch, D. (1989). The rating of curricular learning outcomes by a select group of transportation professionals for transportation technology teacher education. An unpublished doctoral dissertation at The Ohio State University, Columbus, Ohio.

Rouch, D. (1990). Racing into the Future with a Comprehensive Knowledge of Transportation Technology. Presentation at 1990 ITEA conference, Indianapolis.

Savage, E. & Sterry, L. (1990). A conceptual framework for technology education. *The Technology Teacher. 50* 1, 6–11.

Schmitt, M. & Pelley, A. (1966). *Report on nature of programs, teachers, and students in industrial arts*. (DHEW-funded project). Washington: Department of Education.

Schubert, W. H. (1985). *Curriculum: perspective, paradigm, and possibility*. New York: Macmillan.

Smith, B. O. (1983). Curriculum content. In R. S. Brandt (Ed.) *Fundamental curriculum decisions*. Association of Supervision and Curriculum Development Yearbook.

Smith, F. (1985). *Transportation in America* (3rd Edition). Washington D.C. Transportation Policy Associates, July, p.2.

Stephenson, F. J. (1987). *Transportation USA*. Reading, Massachusetts: Addison-Wesley Publishing Company.

Sule, D. R. (1988). *Manufacturing facilities, location, planning, and design*. New York: McGraw-Hill Book Company.

Talley, W. K. (1983). *Introduction to transportation*, Cincinnati: South-Western.

Tierney, W. P. (1949). Land transportation: A study of pupil activities and teaching implications for industrial arts programs in secondary schools. An unpublished masters thesis, The Ohio State University.

Tomorrow's teachers: a report of the holmes group. (1986). East Lansing, Michigan: The Holmes Group Inc.

Towers, E. R., Lux, D. G., & Ray, W. E. (1966). *A rationale and structure for industrial arts subject matter*. U. S. Office of Education.

Volpe, J. A. (1970). Transportation technology: a new dimension. *Journal of Industrial Arts Education, 29*, 6 p. 5.

Waetjen, W. B. (1989). *Technological problem solving*. Reston, Virginia: International Technology Education Association.

Warner, W. E. (1934). *A prospectus for industrial arts in Ohio*. State Department of Education and Ohio Education Association.

Woodward, C. M. (1896). *Manual training in education*. London: Walter Scott.

Woodward, C. M. (1905). Manual training: Theory and method. *The Outlook. 81*, 927–932.

Yu, J. C. (1982). *Transportation Engineering, Introduction to Planning, Design, and Operations*. New York: Elsevier.

CHAPTER 9

The Learning Environment for Transportation Technology Education

By Dr. Stanley A. Komacek
(Associate Professor at California University of Pennsylvania)

and

Mr. Gary Bolyard
(Assistant Professor at Fairmont State College, Fairmont, West Virginia)

This chapter focuses on environmental planning considerations for the design of learning environments for transportation technology education. It is not a plan or blueprint for a laboratory facility, but a discussion of curricular and instructional factors affecting the design of the learning environment.

Environmental planning is a prerequisite to laboratory facility planning. Brown (1990) established the difference between facility planning and environmental planning. He described facility planning as the "determination of equipment and furniture, lighting and color specifications, chalkboard and bulletin board peripherals, and a variety of other aspects that are architecturally specific" (p. 143). Environmental planning, on the other hand, "establishes the philosophical guidelines for facility planning by studying carefully the implications of such things as size, lighting, and furniture" (p. 143).

Brown also made a very important point that deserves repeating; "environmental planning for communication technology courses is still new and exploratory" (1990, p. 143). While Brown's focus was communication technology, it should be evident to anyone involved in designing learning environments for technology education that his statement applies to the other technology education system areas as well; especially transportation. Most technology educators would agree that the transportation area is lagging behind the other systems areas in terms of curriculum development and implementation. Rouch documented the evolution and significance of transportation curricula in 1989. DeVore provided a taxonomy of transportation for the identification of content and method in technology education in 1970. The *Jackson's Mill Industrial Arts Curriculum Theory* document (Snyder & Hales) identified transportation as a major curriculum organizer for technology education in 1981. Despite these facts, "transportation is probably the least understood and least accepted by teachers in terms of developing and implementing curriculum in their classroom" (Helsel & Jones, 1986, p. 193). This lack of understanding and acceptance may have lead to the popular "slash" courses (i.e., energy/power/transportation) in technology education that often combine transportation with energy and the more traditional power technology curricula. The lag in curriculum development and lack of understanding has also hampered the design and establishment of learning environments for transportation technology education. This chapter will attempt to provide several ideas that may be used by teachers who are considering the development of a learning environment for transportation technology education. The chapter focuses on a learning environment used exclusively for transportation technology education at the high school or teacher education levels; not general technology laboratories typical of middle/junior high school programs or combination energy/power/transportation laboratories commonly found at various grade levels.

A Curriculum Structure for Transportation

The design of the learning environment should be based upon an accepted curriculum design. A transportation curriculum structure, including a taxonomy of transportation and a list of characteristics of technology education, helps identify the basic concepts and content covered in a transportation course. Also, the taxonomy and characteristics will serve as the basis for the development of a definition of transportation technology education. The definition also contributes to the curriculum design.

Taxonomy of Transportation

The taxonomy in Figure 1 can be used to identify the basic curriculum structure for a general transportation systems or introduction to transportation course. Briefly, the course content would address the basic concepts presented on the taxonomy. In this chapter, the taxonomy is limited to its basic elements.

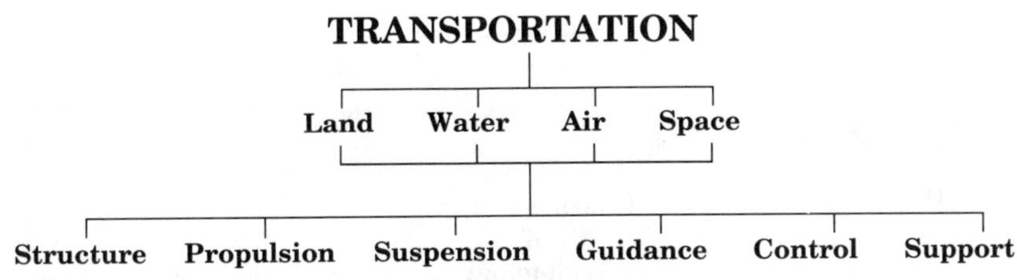

Figure 1: Taxonomy of transportation technology.

Chapters 1 and 2 provide more detailed descriptions of the taxonomy. The taxonomy organizes transportation by four environmental mediums (land, water, air, and space) and six constant technical transportation subsystems (structure, propulsion, suspension, guidance, control, and support). The rationale for the focus on environments and technical subsystems is well documented (Bender, 1983; Colelli, 1989; DeVore, 1970; Komacek, 1988; Snyder & Hales, 1981). This structure is accepted by most curriculum developers as evidenced by the dedicated transportation courses designed with the environmental mediums as the main units of instruction and the technical subsystems studied in each unit (Illinois State Board of Education, 1984; Texas Education Agency, 1983; West Virginia Department of Education, 1988).

A well balanced transportation course would draw content from all the topics identified on the taxonomy giving each fair and appropriate, if not equal, treatment and coverage. Such a balance eliminates the justification of traditional power technology courses and the popular combination or slash courses mentioned earlier, which focus too heavily on one limited aspect of the taxonomy, namely propulsion.

Characteristics of Technology Education

In addition to the taxonomy, several characteristics of technology education contribute to how transportation can best be taught (see Figure 2). The characteristics are recurring themes appearing repeatedly throughout most technology courses, including transportation.

Most of the characteristics are basic to technology education. However, one misunderstood characteristic is modeling. Scale working models (model rocket or Metric 500 car) and profile models (paper airplane or balsa glider) are often used in transportation. Other types of modeling include mathematic models (miles per hour or miles per gallon formulas), graphic models (schematics, diagrams, charts), and computer models (computer simulation software). Operating with full-scale, fully functional prototypes is often not practical when economic and time factors are considered. Engineers employ various types of models in their design and research and development work to save time and

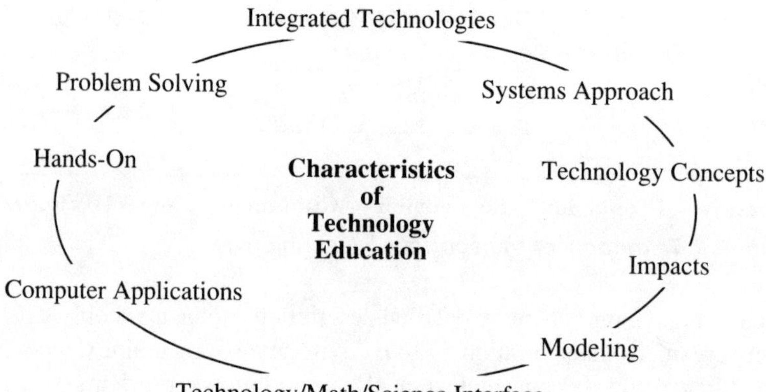

Figure 2: The characteristics of technology education are reoccurring themes in all technology courses.

money. Students in technology education courses, particularly transportation, often emulate this practice without realizing the connection with the real world.

Definition of Transportation Technology Education

The definition of any subject area can be used as a guide in the development of curriculum materials, learning activities, and thus, the learning environment. The definition of transportation technology education below ties together the content and organization of the taxonomy, the dynamics of the systems approach, and several characteristics of technology education. Transportation technology education is defined as:

> The study of how people use the elements of technology (resources) to design and produce technical systems for the purposes of moving freight and passengers, safely and efficiently, in land, water, air, and space environments, and the impacts these systems have on technological, societal, and biological systems (Bolyard & Komacek, 1990, p. 4).

This definition, which differs slightly from accepted international definitions of transportation technology education, has been used effectively as a guide in curriculum development by several transportation technology teachers.

How to Change Facilities

Many ideas for changing industrial arts facilities to teach technology are in the technology education literature (Bender, 1978; Brown, 1990; Daiber &

Gerstenecker, 1981; Daiber & LaClair, 1986; DeVore & Lauda, 1976; Durkin, 1986; Gemmill, 1989; Jones, 1985; Listar & Schiffman, 1986; McCrory, 1985; Polette, 1991; Reynolds, Schwermin, & O'Hare, 1982–83). Most of the ideas are typical of the "reorganization" approach suggested by Jones:

> We do not need to re-equip our facilities to implement technology education. On the contrary, we need to reorganize existing facilities, get rid of the useless equipment, [and] make the remaining equipment adaptable to future class needs (1985, p. 20).

A smaller group of writers has expressed a more radical approach to facility change, as suggested by Durkin and McCrory. Durkin said "[technology education] demands a rethinking of the very essence of what constitutes an instructional facility" (1986, p. B-21). McCrory was more direct when he said ". . . most of our old industrial arts lab equipment is worn beyond repair, so lets scrap it and start over" (1985, p. 29).

Many teachers implement technology education by reorganizing facilities and phasing-in new curriculum over time, but making radical changes has certain merits. There are numerous examples of teachers trying to implement transportation technology education in a power technology laboratory. Often, they make moderate advances in the early part of the change, only to be hampered by the old familiar equipment of power technology. Keeping old equipment while changing the curriculum can lead to a dependence on the old equipment. When students see the old facility they expect the old curriculum. This results in the traditional equipment dictating the curriculum and hampering curriculum change. Making radical changes in the learning environment can assist the teacher in making curriculum modifications by influencing the attitudes and expectations of students, administrators, and teachers.

Changing attitudes and expectations are an important part of the change to technology education. In many instances the industrial arts "shop" image may be retarding efforts to update the curriculum. Changing the facility is one important step in changing attitudes and expectations.

Options for Changing to Transportation

There are three options for changing from industrial arts facility to a laboratory for transportation technology education. The first option, and ideal situation, would be to have a completely new transportation facility built as part of a renovation or new building program. Very few new comprehensive transportation technology laboratories are under construction today. Therefore, at this time, it is difficult to identify all the specific elements that would go into a new transportation facility. However, the following descriptions should provide some guidance and insight for teachers fortunate enough to be involved in renovation or new building projects.

The second option is to reorganize an existing industrial arts facility. Most good transportation programs are "in-transition" and faced with reorganizing or converting an old industrial arts shop, usually a power technology laboratory, into a transportation laboratory. Given these reorganization and in-transition conditions, an industrial arts general shop may be preferable to the power technology laboratory for the conversion. The general shop, with tools and machines that can be used for a variety of materials and processes, can be very useful for transportation technology, and other systems. Polette (1991) described the value of modifying an existing general shop:

> Since the structure of general technology relies . . . on learning about . . . systems theory and critical thinking processes used to analyze the nature of a system, a general technology laboratory organization somewhat reminiscent of the industrial arts general shop (but substantially modernized and updated) has been considered. The advantage of this general facility is that the diversity of machines, tools, and materials permits a multitude of different activities to be conducted simultaneously (p. 26).

There are several examples of technology teachers who have successfully implemented transportation technology in reorganized industrial arts general shops (Bolyard & Komacek, 1990; Bolyard, 1991; Culver, D., Moats, T., Zirkle, S., & Kessler, R., 1990; Komacek, 1987; Mickitsch, 1991; Spencer & Straub, 1991). Starting with a learning environment not readily identifiable with power technology is one example of making radical facility changes.

A final choice for conversion to a transportation laboratory would be a power technology laboratory. The conversion from power technology to transportation may seem like the most logical process, but may be the least desirable of the three options described here. Some teachers feel there are too many "white elephants" in power technology facilities, such as hydraulic floor car hoists, automotive engine analyzers, and fluid power benches. These white elephants can impede the change process and perpetuate the traditional expectations and images. Car hoists, engine analyzers, and power benches are valuable and important equipment, for vocational programs. For the in-transition transportation technology teacher, they may hinder the change process. Making radical changes in the learning environment can have a dramatic impact on the expectations of students, administrators, and even the teacher in the changed facility.

Of the three options just described, the preferred option, and most radical, is building a new, state-of-the-art transportation facility. Given the realities of reorganization and conversion, prospective transportation teachers might consider the positive aspects of converting a general shop. Whatever option chosen, or provided, teachers who must convert an old industrial arts facility into a new technology education facility should consider the comments of Todd (1987):

> our old facilities are becoming less and less supportive to change and improvement. I have seen a lot of teachers who are implementing very inventive technology activities for their students but often being hamstrung by facilities that obstruct or limit such inventiveness. The experience of this growing group of innovators foretells the demise of the standard facilities that we have known for 50 years or more (p. 8).

Learning Environment Instructional Areas for Transportation

A comprehensive transportation learning environment would encompass five instructional areas:

1. Group Meeting/Design Area
2. Research Center
3. Prototyping Lab
4. Dynamic Testing Area
5. Storage

This chapter does not provide a list of tools, machines, equipment, and furniture, a suggested floor plan, or specifications for minimum square footages. Educators interested in such listings, plans, and specifications should review the many state laboratory facility planning or curriculum guides for technology education that contain such information (Dyrenfurth, 1987; Indiana Industrial Technology Curriculum Committee, 1989; Technology Education Association of Pennsylvania, 1988; West Virginia Department of Education, 1988). In this chapter, the five areas listed above will be described with examples of the types of student activities conducted and representative equipment and furniture found in each area.

Group Meeting/Design Area

The Group Meeting/Design Area would be used for large and small group meetings and design activities, such as drawing, sketching, and modeling.

Many traditional industrial arts facilities have stand alone classrooms with individual student tablet-arm chairs (chair and desk combinations). Removing the tablet-arm and replacing them with work center classroom furniture (reconfigurable rectangular or round tables and chairs) would provide optimum usage of this type of space. The furniture in the room could be arranged for large group meetings, (similar to traditional lecture sessions) and rearranged for small group brainstorming sessions where solutions to design problems would be discussed.

Also, large table surfaces, rather than small tablet-arm chairs, make this area useful for design and modeling activities such as drawing/sketching plans for a vehicle, or assembling a small model robot or vehicle from prefabricated parts.

To stimulate student interest, imagination, and expectations, color posters and photographs, scale models, and examples of previous student work could be displayed on the walls or suspended from the ceiling.

Around the perimeter of this area would be computers on reconfigurable (possibly rollable) tables or built-in counters rather than individual learning carrels. Tables would provide adequate space next to the computers where robotic or conveyor systems could be placed for interfacing activities. Also, open tabletops permit several students to gather around to view computer-controlled transportation processes or for small group activities. Individual learner carrels, with their built-in sides and back, are too limiting in this respect.

Since this is the design area, the priority for computer usage would be computer-aided drawing and design activities. A CAD or CADD package similar to the one used in the communication laboratory could be available. Also, word processing and computer graphics software could be available for writing research papers, letters for technical information, and/or drawing quick design sketches. Computer modeling software; such as Car Builder(c), Design Your Own Train(c), Glide Path(c), Flight Simulator(c), or other transportation simulation-type software would be available in this area. Finally, a spreadsheet and/or database program would be handy for compiling, sorting, and graphing performance data for student vehicle projects.

When discussing computers, the question of which type to purchase surfaces. A basic guideline is to purchase software with the desired features first, then get the required computer. Probably, most laboratories should have a variety of computers. One author of this chapter has a mix of IBM-compatibles (used primarily for interfacing activities and database management), Apple IIe's (used primarily for word processing, simulations, and tutorials), and Macintoshes (used primarily for simulations, graphics, and instructional materials development) in his transportation teacher education lab.

All the activities conducted in the Group Meeting/Design Area are relatively clean in nature, which supports the "clean room" suggested by Polette (1991). However, a supply of brown craft paper or cardboard should be available to protect tabletops from glues, adhesives, and utility knives. Carpeted or tiled floors would be nice in this area and adequate lighting should be provided for the design and smaller modeling activities. Additional pieces of equipment found in this room might include a visual media projection screen, a VCR and monitor (on a rollable cart), and other media equipment (slide projector, film strip projector, etc.) needed for large group meetings. Average sized point-of-use storage space will be needed in this area for the media equipment. Smaller storage space will be needed for software, videos, slides, and traditional drawing tools (T- square, triangles, scales, etc.). Overhead wall cabinets above the computer area work nicely for storage.

Research Center

The Research Center should provide students with access to technical information related to transportation. Quite often, this type of area is identified and described in the technology education literature. Technology is information-based and students of technology need access to information. Educational studies suggest that when student research is required, the research materials should be provided in the classroom (Englehardt, 1988). Simply telling the students that a library may be found down the hall does not work.

In appearance, the Research Center would be a clean area similar to the Group Meeting/Design Area. To prevent interference from adjoining areas, the center should be a separate room, if possible, or have acoustical wall partitions to absorb noise. Having a separate room would provide the added security needed in this area to prevent unauthorized removal of materials.

Book shelves would be needed to hold technical books, textbooks, activity-type books and activity manuals from textbooks. Catalogs could be available from vendors of transportation-related components and supplies.

Vertical files could be used to house information on activity ideas from the Center for Implementing Technology Education and other sources, technical brochures (new car brochures, technical specifications on engines, etc.), and background information from magazine articles. A magazine rack should be provided to hold *Popular Science, Popular Mechanics, Air & Space, TIES, Discovery, R/C Modeler,* and other transportation- and technology-related magazines.

Also, the Research Center should contain an audiovisual carrel for individual use of videos, slides, or film strips. Headphones could be provided to limit noise. A computer with a database of the materials in vertical files and/or book and magazine racks would aid researchers. Tutorial software on transportation-related topics could be available. The ultimate, a CD-ROM system, would be nice, but very few disks are available at this time on technology education topics.

Prototyping Lab

The Prototyping Lab is where students turn their design ideas and research findings into reality. In an ideal situation, the Prototyping Lab would have two distinct areas; a Production Area (for preparing prototype and model parts and components) and an Assembly Area (for assembly of the models).

Production Area. The Production Area of the Prototyping Lab would be a dirt- and noise-producing area containing several pieces of traditional general shop-type tools, machines and equipment; such as saws, lathes, drill press, welding equipment, finishing booth, etc. Although this is traditional equipment, in most cases only one or two pieces of each type are needed, depending upon the student activities. For example, the CO_2 car (Metric 500 racer) is a proven transportation activity that requires some band saw time for each student. Even with this activity though, two band saws should be sufficient. For a dedicated transportation lab where scale modeling activities are the focus, down-sized precision production equipment, similar to the Dremel(c) and Hegner(c) lines, may be more appropriate than the larger traditional woodworking machines.

Another consideration may be the inclusion of a CAM system to produce airfoil sections, boat hull ribs, or concept car profiles from designs created on the CAD system in the Group Meeting/Design Area. Using such a system would reinforce the concept of integrated technologies.

Since this is a dirt producing area, dust collection and ventilation systems should be provided.

Assembly Area. The Assembly Area is slightly cleaner than the Production Area. Here, students would take the components and parts made in the production area and assemble a prototype or model. This area would have benches with vises in large open spaces. Instead of the traditional square woodworking benches, smaller reconfigurable benches might be preferred. The square benches can be cut in half to produce two smaller rectangular benches. They will still provide storage cabinets underneath and can be moved together if needed for working on larger prototypes. Electricity and compressed air could be provided with overhead supply lines.

Both the Assembly Area and Production Area would have a concrete floor. Probably, the Production Area should have a noise absorbing design as well. A large tool cabinet located within proximity of the Production and Assembly

Areas would facilitate student access to tools from either area. A wide selection of power and hand tools, including the latest in portable cordless tools and pneumatic tools, could be provided.

Dynamic Testing

This area would be used for testing vehicles and other transportation systems made by students. This may be the most important part of the lab in terms of teaching technology. Here, students get the opportunity to see if their ideas work. A variety of specialized testing equipment (see Figure 3) would be provided in this area. Several pieces of equipment on this list must be teacher- or student-produced, since vendors do not currently supply them. The wind tunnel, a relatively new piece of technology education equipment available from several vendors, is a vital piece of equipment for transportation studies. A

- **Articulated cut-away model engines**
- **Bicycle test stand**
- **C02 Car race track**
- **Computer-controlled materials handlers**
- **Conveyor systems**
- **Glider launcher**
- **Go-kart (educational)**
- **Hydrotest tank**
- **Mag-Lev train track**
- **Monorail test track**
- **R/C Car demonstration board**
- **R/C Vehicle testing area**
- **Robotic system**
- **Rocket engine test stand**
- **Slot car-type race track**
- **Small engine dynamometer**
- **Small engine analysis station**
- **Wind tunnel**

Figure 3: Specialized equipment for the dynamic testing area.

good wind tunnel could have a multitude of uses, including testing vehicles for coefficient of drag, analyzing laminar flow with smoke visualization techniques, investigating lift capacities on airfoil sections, checking the stability of model rockets, and studying performance characteristics on parachutes; to name a few. This handy tool can even be used by the construction teacher to study the effects of wind on building designs.

The specialized pieces of equipment in the Dynamic Testing Area would only be used a few days or weeks in each course. They should be flexible enough to be moved and stored when not in use. As an example, the hydrotest tank may be used only three to four days in a semester-long course. There are several ways to store equipment that is not used often. They can be placed around the perimeter of the room, wheels can be fastened to cabinet bases for rolling into a storage area, or the equipment can be suspended from the ceiling. One innovative approach is to use wall storage. Large adjustable shelving brackets could be installed on one wall in the lab. Tanks, tunnels, stands, etc. can be mounted on shelving and simply hung on the wall when not in use. This idea has the advantage of the public relations work the equipment can do while it is hanging on the wall. If equipment is stored away, only the teacher and students will see it when in use. However, when out in full view of any visitors, the equipment may prompt questions and statements that could lead to more understanding. Simply having equipment out and visible changes the appearance of the lab and thus the expectations of visitors.

Any specialized tools needed when working on dynamic testing equipment could be put in kits. Also, moveable panels allow for easy inventory, storage, and student use.

Storage

Throughout the descriptions above, specialized storage was mentioned for each area. However, a central storage facility may be needed for the following:

1. large storage shelves for student work-in-progress, such as go-karts, human-powered vehicles, and hovercrafts,
2. large storage shelves or cabinets for go-kart kit components, bicycle parts, small gasoline engines, electric motors, etc.,
3. small storage (plastic storage bins on shelves or in cabinets) for wire, small electric motors, batteries, model rocket parts, solar cells, switches, etc.,
4. large shelves to store materials such as lumber, plywood, tubing, pipe, etc., and

5. storage cabinets with shelves for supplies, such as welding rod, adhesives, finishes, fasteners, etc.

The supplies storage should serve as a warehouse of parts and components for a wide range of student research and development projects.

Storage is critical to the efficient operation of any technology course. However, to keep the size of a dedicated storage area to a minimum, every available space throughout the laboratory should be utilized. Having storage at the point-of-use, as mentioned in the descriptions of each area, is one way to obtain maximum space utilization. Overhead mezzanine storage in the central storage area is another good idea.

Selecting and Evaluating Equipment

As mentioned earlier, curriculum design should guide the design of the learning environment. Curriculum design also guides the selection and evaluation of equipment. Tools and machines should be purchased to match the planned student learning experiences. Referring back to the taxonomy of transportation and the characteristics of technology education will provide additional guidance in this process. In addition, the equipment program should be flexible enough to adapt as new tools and machines for technology education are developed and brought to the market.

Relationships Between Instructional Areas

As mentioned earlier, comprehensive tool lists and minimum square footage requirements are not provided in this chapter. However, the bubble diagram below shows some general size and location relationships among the five instructional areas. As shown in the diagram, the Group Meeting/Design Area could be located close to the Research Center, the Prototyping Lab would be located close to the Dynamic Testing area, and Storage would be centrally located. The rationale for these relationships is based on the movement of students between the areas. The following table lists those movements and what students might be saying as they move between areas.

One additional consideration is for a door (a garage door or large double door) that opens to the outside from the Prototyping Lab and/or the Dynamic

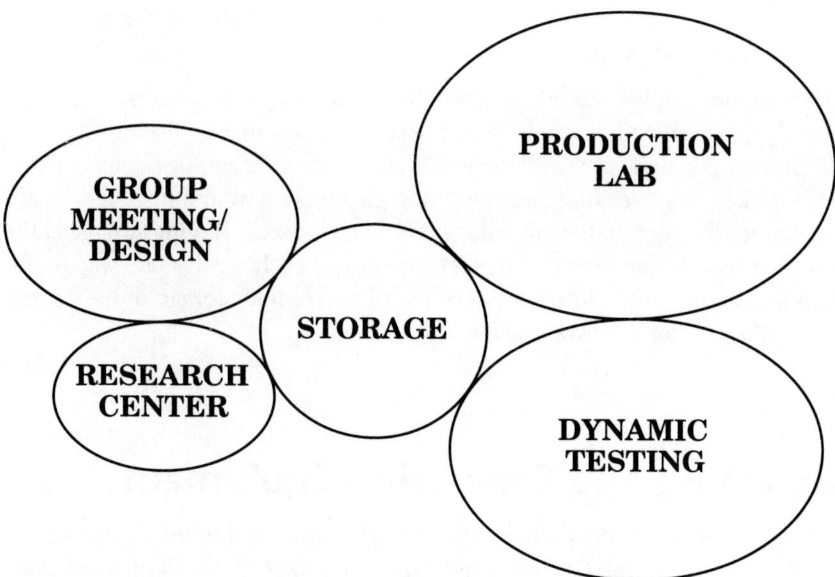

Figure 4: Bubble diagram of the five instructional areas.

Testing Area. This door would facilitate the movement of vehicles (i.e. human-powered vehicles, hovercrafts, go-karts, model rockets, profile model cars and planes, RC vehicles, etc.) and students to outdoor areas for additional performance testing.

Funding

Many authors have written about the costs of implementing technology education. Several have stated that technology education is no more expensive than industrial arts (Dugger, Pinder, & Bame, 1985; Jones, 1984; Wright &

Moving from...	Student says:
...Design to Research	"I need information."
...Design to Storage	"Do we have the size component I need?"
...Prototyping to Storage	"I need another one of these parts."
...Prototyping to Dynamic Testing	"I've built it, let's test it!"
...Dynamic Testing to Storage	"I broke this part in testing, I need another one."

Figure 5: Rationale for the relationship among the five instructional areas.

Sterry, 1984; Dulaney, 1981; Listar & Schiffman, 1986). Jones summarized this point of view; "In public school programs where Technology Education has been implemented, it has been determined that the new program can function with the existing budget allocated for the old program" (1984, p. 20).

In order for a program to continue with funding similar to its existing budget, old pieces of equipment will need to be replaced with new pieces gradually over time. This may seem counterproductive when the advantages of radical change are considered, but the reality of school budgets suggests such a transition.

Summary

The curriculum structure for transportation technology education should guide the design of the learning environment. A taxonomy of transportation and the characteristics of technology education should be considered.

Dramatic changes in the learning environment could result in new and different attitudes and expectations on the part of students, administrators, and teachers and thus facilitate curriculum changes.

A comprehensive learning environment for transportation technology education would include five instructional areas; (1) Group Meeting/Design Area, (2) Research Center, (3) Prototyping Lab, (4) Dynamic Testing Area, and (5) Storage. The design of each area and the equipment available should be determined based upon an analysis of curriculum structure and the appropriate student learning activities for transportation technology education.

REFERENCES

Bender, M. (1978). Planning a physical learning environment for the future. *Journal of Epsilon Pi Tau. 4*(2), 5.

Bender, M. (1983). Transportation systems: Environmental and technical. In DeVore, P. W. (Ed.). *Introduction to transportation.* Worcester, MA: Davis Publications.

Bolyard, G., & Komacek, S. A. (1990). The learning environment for transportation technology education. In Tracey, W. E., Jr. (Ed.). *Technology education symposium XII.* Worcester, MA: Davis Publications and New Britain, CT: Central Connecticut State University.

Bolyard, G. (1991, April). *Teaching transportation: Content and activities.* Unpublished paper presented at the Spring Conference of the Department of Industry and Technology of California University of Pennsylvania, California, PA.

Brown, R. (1990). Establishing the communication teaching and learning environment. In Liedtke, J. A. (Ed.). *Communication in technology education: 39th yearbook of the Council on Technology Teacher Education.* (pp. 139–164). Mission Hills, CA: Glencoe/McGraw-Hill Publishing Co.

Colelli, L. A. (1989). *Technology education: A primer.* Reston, VA: International Technology Education Association.

Culver, D., Moats, T., Zirkle, S., & Kessler, R. (1990, March). *Renovation of a technology education facility.* Unpublished paper presented at the Fairmont State College Technology Education Facility Design Seminar, Fairmont, WV.

Cummings, P. L., Jensen, M., & Todd, R. (1987). Facilities for technology education. *The Technology Teacher. 46*(7), 7–10.

Daiber, R. A., & Gerstenceker, D. (1981). Technology education at Triad. *School Shop. 40*(8), 41–46.

Daiber, R. A., & LaClair, T. D. (1986). High school technology education. In Jones, R. E., & Wright, J. R. (Eds.). *Implementing technology education: 35th yearbook of the American Council on Industrial Arts Teacher Education.* (pp. 95–137). Encino, CA: Glencoe Publishing Co.

DeVore, P. W. (1970). Transportation technology: The identification of content and method. *The Journal of Industrial Arts Education. 29*(6) May–June, 18–22.

DeVore, P. W., & Lauda, D. P. (1976). Implications for industrial arts. In Smalley, L. H. (Ed.). *Future alternatives for industrial arts; 25th yearbook of the American Council on Industrial Arts Teacher Education.* (pp. 1237–162). Bloomington, IL: McKnight Publishing Co.

Dugger, W. E., Pinder, C. A., & Bame, E. A. (1985). Technology education standards: Prospect/retrospect. In Andre, N., & Lucy, J. (Eds.). *Proceedings of Technology Education Symposium VII: Technology education; Issues and trends.* (pp. 49–53). California, PA: California University of Pennsylvania.

Dulaney, J. C. (1981). The superintendent's role as advocate of curriculum change. *School Shop. 40*(8), 45–46.

Durkin, J. (1985). The new facility: Rethinking the essence. *Technology: An implementation resource catalog from TransTech Systems.* San Diego, CA: Creative Learning Systems.

Dyrenfurth, M. J. (1987). *Missouri industrial technology education guide.* Columbia, MO: University of Missouri-Columbia.

Englehardt, D. F. (1988). Can space motivate [or demotivate] science teachers? *Council on Educational Facilities Planning Journal.* July/August.

Gemmill, P. R. (1989). From unit shop to laboratory of technologies. *The Technology Teacher.* 1–10.

Helsel, L. D., & Jones, R. E. (1986). Undergraduate technology education: The technical sequence. In Jones, R. E., & Wright, J. R., (Eds.). *Implementing technology education: 35th Yearbook of the American Council on Industrial Arts Teacher Education.* (pp 171–200). Encino, CA: Glencoe Publishing Co.

Illinois State Board of Education (1984). *Transportation technology curriculum guide.* Springfield, IL: Illinois State Board of Education; Bureau of Adult, Vocational, and Technical Education.

Indiana Industrial Technology Curriculum Committee. (1989). *Indiana industrial technology education curriculum: Tool and equipment guide.* Indianapolis, IN: Indiana Department of Education.

Jones, R. E. (1985). *A primer on technology education.* Unpublished paper presented at the meeting of the International Technology Education Association, San Diego, CA.

Komacek, S. A. (1987). Consider transportation technology. *TEAP Journal. 35*(4), 5–9.

Komacek, S. A. (1988). Transportation technology education: What should be taught? *TEAP Journal. 36*(1), 19–22.

Listar, G., & Schiffman, P. (1986). Technology programs: Greece, New York. *The Technology Teacher. 46*(1), 15–18.

Mickitsch, J. (1991, April). *Transportation technology: High school level.* Unpublished paper presented at the Spring Conference of the Department of Industry and Technology of California University of Pennsylvania, California, PA.

McCrory, D. L. (1985). What is the nature of technology education? In Andre, N., & Lucy, J. (Eds.). *Proceedings of Technology Education Symposium VII: Technology education; Issues and trends.* (pp. 27–32). California, PA: California University of Pennsylvania.

Polette, E. (Ed.) (1991). *Planning technology teacher education learning environments.* Reston, VA: Council on Technology Teacher Education of the International Technology Education Association.

Reynolds, D., Schwermin, R., & O'Hare, J. (1982–83, Winter). We're starting to implement the Illinois plan for industrial education. *Illinois Industrial Educator. 2*(4), pp. 6–8.

Rouch, D. L. (1989). The rating of curricular learning outcomes by a select group of transportation professionals for transportation technology. Unpublished dissertation, The Ohio State University, Columbus, OH.

Snyder, J. F., & Hales, J. A. (Eds.) (1981). *Jackson's Mill industrial arts curriculum theory.* Charleston, WV: West Virginia Department of Education.

Spencer, R., & Straub, J. (1991, April). *Transportation technology: High school level.* Unpublished paper presented at the Spring Conference of the Department of Industry and Technology of California University of Pennsylvania, California, PA.

Technology Education Association of Pennsylvania. (1988). *Pennsylvania industrial arts/technology education facility planning guide.* Harrisburg, PA: Pennsylvania Department of Education.

Texas Education Agency. (1983). *Transportation systems.* Austin, TX: Texas Education Agency, Occupational Education and Technology.

West Virginia Department of Education. (1988). *West Virginia technology education curriculum: Transportation.* Charleston, WV: WV Department of Education, Bureau of Vocational, Technical, and Adult Education.

Wright, T., & Sterry, L. (1984). *Industry and technology education: A guide for curriculum designers, implementors, and teachers.* Lansing, IL: The Technical Foundation of America.

CHAPTER 10

Providing Assessment for Transportation Technology Curricula

By Dr. Anthony F. Gilberti
(Assistant Professor at St. Cloud State University)

What is Assessment?

During the past ten years, there has been an increasing amount of emphasis placed on the topic of assessment. Despite this emphasis, there appears to be no consensus on exactly what topics and processes assessment comprises. Should assessment be concerned with the performance of individual students or groups of students, the quality of instructional practices, or the performance of departments or the institution itself?

Assessment Defined

Dictionary definitions contain similarities that to assess is to place a value on something. This is usually in financial terms. Such definitions are not centered on educational assessment. Although the outcomes of educational assessment (e.g., a student's degree class) may influence the salary received (Rowntree, 1987).

Assessment in education may be thought of as a means by which an individual(s) provide information about students' change and development, accountability of educators and instructional practices and the cost-effectiveness and goals of departments or institutions. The field of evaluation perhaps offers a more meaningful and conceptually clearer means to think about assessment. In this field, a distinction is made between formative and summative evaluation. Formative evaluation is used for the purposes of improving and/or developing an activity, program, person or product. Summative evaluation is used to determine accountability or resource allocation for programs, certification, and the selection and placement of students. Summative evaluation may further be used to make decisions about merit raises and promotions for faculty. In a similar fashion, institutions may perform assessments to improve what they are doing (formative) or make decisions concerning resources, institutions, programs, faculty or students (summative). It is the position taken here that assessment may be defined as the systematic process of data collection and analysis for the purpose of making an informed decision. Davis (1989) illustrated the differences between formative and summative assessment in Table 1.

FORMATIVE VERSUS SUMMATIVE ASSESSMENT		
Feature	***Formative Assessment***	***Summative Assessment***
Purpose	Improvement or development of activities, programs, products, people	Accountability, resource allocation; selection, placement, certification; pay and promotion decisions
Audience	Internal decision maker: program or department administrators; individual faculty	External decision maker: central administrators; government officials; accrediting bodies; public
Scope	Diagnostic, detailed, specific assessments	Global assessments
Timing	Ongoing or during a program or sequence of study	Before and after or simply at the completion of a program or sequence of study
Sources of Information	One or more	Multiple and diverse
Emphasis	Suggestions for improvement	Overall judgments

Table 1 *(Davis, 1989, p.9)*

Assumptions of Assessment

Despite one of the commonly held beliefs in the literature of assessment, tests and examinations are not the only means of evaluation. One could imagine a variety of assessment situations ranging from the informal, casual, to the highly structured and even ritualistic. An example of this informal assessment may be the evaluation process that takes place between individuals in everyday conversation. In such an event, each person is assessing and responding to the emerging understanding and attitudes that are presented.

In a classroom situation, however, the participants may be more directed to specific tasks and goals. As assessment becomes the purpose of the event taking place, the formality becomes even greater. Perhaps the highest degree of formality is reached when a person is required to perform in a testing situation—a quiz, interview, practical or written exam (Rowntree, 1987).

Assessment can be obtained without measurement that implies absolute standards. It may be appropriate for a given situation to simply observe whether an activity, program, person or product exhibits a discernible trait than what had previously been noted. This would require no form of competitive findings from one person to another. Nor would it require a hierarchical ranking of the comparisons made. Tough (1986) distinguishes between testing and appraisal:

> How does the child walk and run? What is the quality of his movement? What kind of control does the child have of fine and intricate manipulation and of movement that needs concentration of strength and effort: What is the child's general coordination of movements like? Is he awkward and ungainly or does he move easily and smoothly without apparent effort? Many of these qualities would defy measurement, and many would defy comparison with other children. But all could be appraised, i.e. described in terms which build up a picture of what the child is like (p. 32).

Assessment is not the same as grading. With grading, a letter or number is used to symbolize the quality of the work, and it is used as a comparison with the work of other students. This type of grading cannot take place without prior assessment. The nature and quality of the aspect under study must be determined before it is labelled as a suitable symbol.

Just as examinations are a means of assessment, grades represent possible outcomes. Yet, grades are not the only possible outcomes. Assessment is a precondition for diagnostic appraisal. With diagnostic appraisal, one can ascertain the strengths or weaknesses and identify emerging needs or future direction. Diagnostic appraisal enables educators to validate the teaching/learning process.

Models of Assessment

Two models of evaluation which could be used as assessment tools in the transportation technology curriculum area are CIPP and DEM. CIPP is the acronym for Context, Input, Process and Product (Stufflebeam, et al. 1971). Context evaluation involves the processes in selecting objectives. Input evaluation is concerned with the evaluation of, and selection from, a number of alternative strategies for achieving specific objectives. Process evaluation is used to evaluate the implementation of the strategies selected, and Product evaluation is used to determine the degree the objectives have been achieved. DEM is the acronym for Discrepancy Evaluation Model (Provus, 1971). Assessment with this model involves making decisions based on a determination of the differences or discrepancies which exist between the established standards and actual performance. Using either of these forms of evaluation will provide a comparison of the way things are with how they could be. While these are only two models of evaluation, there are numerous others available. The point is that valid models for evaluation and assessment involve the same essential components. These components are: a specification of goals and objectives; a method for the attainment of the goals and objectives, a development or selection of measurement tools, an analysis and interpretation of results and a means to redesign and implement changes. Lorber and Pierce (1983) illustrated these components as the Logical Instructional Model. Figure 1 graphically depicts this model.

Setting Goals and Objectives

When setting goals and objectives, the planning of an instructional procedure should begin with the instructional results. With this as a starting point, the transportation technology educator should ask: What should students be able to do after instruction? This is perhaps the most difficult aspect in the planning for instruction.

In every society there are specific cultural, student and subject-matter considerations that must be taken into account when curricula is designed and goals and objectives are decided upon. Technology educators, therefore, must consider these specific needs in relation to their community. Having done so, the educator must then organize these needs according to their importance, and use them in the selection and writing of instructional goals and objectives to satisfy these needs.

Having developed the overall goals, technology educators must further justify the inclusion of each objective so that it specifies the instructional intent. Each objective should specify exactly what a student will be expected to do or perform as a result of the instruction/learning received. Usually stated in terms

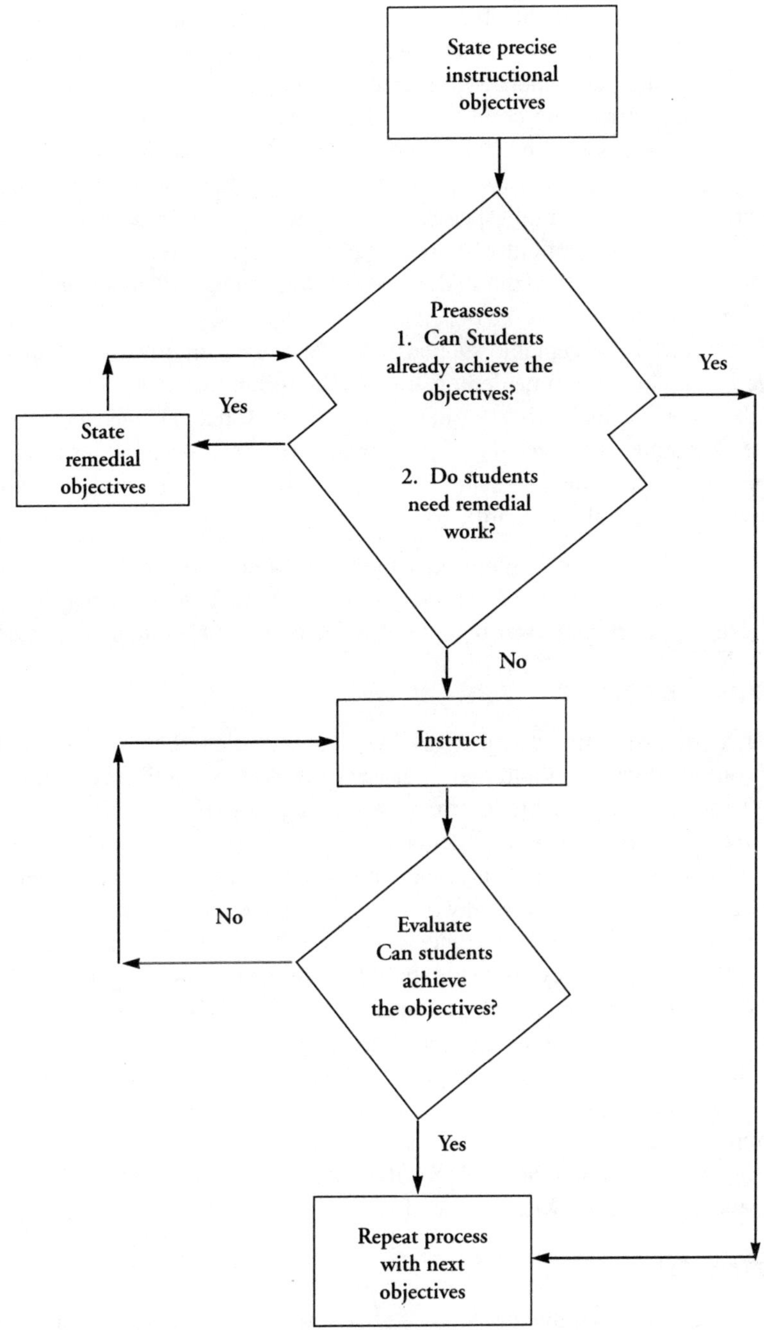

Figure 1: The Logical Instructional Model (Lorber and Pierce, 1983, p. 4).

of observable behavior, the objectives further provide both the student and the educator with the means by which the behavior is to be demonstrated (the conditions) and the performance level that is to be obtained (the minimum acceptable standard). The conditions refer to the setting, use of equipment, laboratory devices or time limits under which the observable behavior will occur (Lorber and Pierce, 1983). The technology educator in the transportation area for example, might specify using a dynamometer in an objective concerning the measurement of force or power. Again, the function of the conditions are to clarify to the student the constraints that will affect the demonstration of the behavior to be observed.

The minimum acceptable standard is concerned with how "well" the observed behaviors are to be demonstrated. The minimum acceptable standard may be stated in qualitative or quantitative terms. It may also use both qualitative or quantitative elements. The following is an example of an instructional objective that contains the elements of observable behavior, conditions and a minimum acceptable standard:

> The 12th grade technology education student in a laboratory situation will set-up and use the dynamometer in a safe manner to measure to a 70% accuracy level the power output of a selected internal combustion engine.

Preassessment

Once the instructional objectives have been developed, the transportation technology educator should then preassess the students' abilities. Preassessments can provide valuable information with regard to two specific questions. The first concerns whether students already possess the specific competencies. If it is found that students already possess the skills necessary to demonstrate the stated competencies, it would be pointless to proceed with the planned instruction. Should the determination be made that students can perform as required, the technology educator should move them to new objectives.

The second area where preassessments are useful is in providing information with regard to student need for remedial work. If it is noted that students lack the basic skills needed to begin working for the achievement of the stated objectives, the technology educator will have to design remedial objectives and learning situations that would provide students with the necessary background to progress (Lorber and Pierce, 1983; Rowntree, 1987). Again, this process can be viewed graphically with the use of the Logical Instruction Model, Figure 1.

Instruction

There are innumerable procedures for improving instruction. Some procedures deal with specific instructional activities and the methods of making them interesting and effective. Other procedures deal with the principles of learning. Bigge and Hunt (1968) have illustrated several basic principles that psychologists and educators generally accept when initiating the learning sequence. Bigge and Hunt wrote:

> Improving the efficiency of learning means establishing situations in which maximum change of insight or behavior may occur in a given time. In the learning process, active participation of learners is highly advantageous over passive reception. Effective, active participation is promoted through observance of some rather specific principles (p. 456).

These principles include: Student readiness, presenting meaningful material, motivation for learning and the role of practice in retention.

Student Readiness

An individual is ready to learn something when they have acquired sufficient physiological and psychological maturation that not only can they learn, but they also want to learn. As Bigge and Hunt (1968) noted, until a person is matured physically, it is difficult to determine what extent the incomplete development is hampering intellectual learning skills. While specific readiness figures are given for a student to perform a physical or intellectual task, these can be misleading. Some students may be ready to read at age three while others may not exhibit this readiness until eight years of age. Similar problems can occur at all age levels or at specific developmental tasks. Bigge and Hunt illustrated this point:

> Studies indicate that there is nothing to be gained by starting youngsters on a particular learning task earlier than readiness normally permits. Regardless of whether readiness for a particular task hinges primarily on genetically controlled maturation or primarily on experience and desire, most children, if started at a task much earlier than it is normally learned in our culture, do not learn it well, if at all. They tend to flounder, making gains which are offset by retrogressions. The one who is started on the same task at the optimum time may learn so much more rapidly that he quickly catches up with the child started earlier. This apparent fact should not be taken as a denial of the point made earlier; a number of subjects now normally reserved to high school or college could be taught effectively in elementary school if there were good social reasons for doing so (pp. 457–458).

Presenting Meaningful Material

Concepts and learning material which is meaningful to students in transportation technology education will be remembered better than material which is not. Meaningfulness consists of the relationships between facts, generalizations, rules, and concepts which students view as important and useful in a contemporary society. Making learning meaningful is a matter of selecting the appropriate content and helping students to see its applicability in the situations for which they are concerned. Since American culture has been characterized as technological, the function of our educational system (and particularly technology education) should provide citizens (students) with the insight and understanding to solve the problems resulting from the social, technical and environmental interface.

Citizens in a democracy should be able to understand the relationship of their local community to their state, nation and world community. Since technology education deals with the use of theoretical knowledge, and technology is in part a social process, citizens need to examine the many facets of responsible decision making to the problems encountered in a democracy. These problems might include population growth, toxic waste, greenhouse gases, timber reduction, land degradation, the use of natural and human resources and moving beyond the throwaway society. This examination requires a broad understanding from numerous curricula areas and disciplines. A study of technology would provide such an understanding if the emphasis of this study had the purpose of helping citizens to understand their relationship to other humans and their environment.

Citizens need to understand the importance of social institutions in lessening the impacts of cultural-lags and their relationship to a democracy. These institutions may include the government, the family, religion, law, education and social services. A study of these institutions should also include emerging groups and associations that are both challenging and helping to redefine the tenets of a democracy. The overall purpose of this study should not only allow the citizen to understand the problems that have been overcome in a democracy, but to view the ideal of a democracy as a dynamic process of change and search for a more just and humane society.

Citizens should further be given the opportunity to understand how cultural differences have helped to create the human condition. Today, humans are living in a world where groups are becoming more and more interrelated. Moreover, the numerous inventions and innovations and styles of life created by individual groups can be a benefit to others. Each culture does not have to reinvent artifacts of technology or depend exclusively on its own human resources. This is not to suggest that a study of cultural differences should help to develop a universal culture. Rather, it is to help develop an understanding that cultural diversity is a valuable resource that should be preserved and extended.

The citizen in a democracy should additionally be acquainted with the means by which theoretical knowledge is discovered and applied to satisfy human needs and desires. The advantages of science and technology in providing basic human needs scarcely need to be written. Through their use, the quality of the human condition and the survival of the human species has been fostered over the last million or so years. Yet, numerous social scientists, futurists, environmentalists and political activists now believe that society is at the crossroad of survival and extinction. The danger of this extinction is believed to stem from a lack of understanding and decision making related to the uses of science and technology. Cutcliffe (1985) illustrated this view:

> Not to have an appreciation of mathematics, of science, of engineering is simply not to know human nature, not to know of heroic things that human beings have done and are doing in the world and to the world. . . .
>
> The practical value of scientific and technological understanding is not to create hundreds of thousands of instant technical experts on the problems surrounding [society] . . . but rather to expose citizens to the existence, and to introduce them to the workings, of science, engineering, and technology. As such, they will be sensitized to the complexity of the social context within which science and technology reside, perhaps even gaining some real insight into the nature of that complexity. . . . A public educated even as broadly as suggested above can thus respond intelligently to science and technology as factors in their personal, social, and political lives (pp. 12, 15).

Motivation for Learning

It has generally been accepted by educational theorists that intrinsic motivation is preferred over extrinsic motivation. However, when a student lacks the motivation to learn, the educator has a responsibility to provide an environment that encourages learning. Traditionally, education was based on an authoritarian model. In this model, learning was motivated by reward for desirable behavior and punishment for undesirable behavior. This model sometimes placed a greater emphasis on getting good grades than on learning.

Presently, the educational spectrum ranges from the authoritarian model to various models and assumptions that every student will learn if permitted to follow their interests. Perhaps a more generally accepted model is that of "assisted learning." Assisted learning is based on the premise that the student is guided to learn and not forced. It is important to note that this premise is based on the philosophical decision that education should help the individual to develop their latent faculties. Such a philosophical position does not attempt to organize education like a manufacturing assembly line, designed to impart clones of a pre-set mental pattern. Bigge and Hunt (1968) noted that the following concerns were important with regard to motivation.

- When learning is perceived by students as being relevant to their needs, they will generally be more interested and motivated to learn.
- When students develop goals, objectives and learning activities for the material being learned, they have a more personal involvement and increased motivation.
- An occasional failure in the learning process is not in itself a negative motivator. Too much has been made of the role of success. Uninterrupted successes may be as negative for the cause of learning as an uninterrupted series of failures. It is healthful to allow students to experience failures, provided the failures contribute to their learning.
- When motivation is created by extrinsic means, retention, understanding and transfer will be much less than when the material is learned intrinsically.
- When extrinsic rewards are used to build motivation, educators must be aware to the problem of students working for the rewards rather than learning.

The Role of Practice and Retention

Although some learning occurs with an insightful moment, other learning requires practice. If transportation technology educators are to help students learn, several important principles must be followed when considering the role of practice and retention. First, repetition does not teach. Practice, the type of process learning which has an experimental character allows students to qualitatively assess what and how they are learning. Through practice the student might ask themselves "How does this learning material relate to previously learned material?" "What oversights have I made?" or "How can I do better?" From this perspective, practice are those activities that allows the gradual development of learning to take place. The student is then able to progress to more advanced learning.

Practice may be either massed or distributed. Massed practice involves long periods of practice. With mass practice, fatigue and boredom can overcome the learner causing practice to become repetition. Distributed practice occurs through a succession of short practice sessions with periods of other activity or rest spaced between learning. This spacing in many instances facilitates the learning and retention process. It is common for some individuals to reach a plateau in the learning cycle. Having reached this plateau, it may be necessary for the technology education student to find quiet time or recreation activities to allow the subconscious to continue to work on the problem or activity. This quiet time or recreation may allow for illumination of the problem or a renewed effort toward the learning situation.

Evaluation

The purpose of instruction is to allow students to acquire the necessary knowledge and skills to perform specified competencies. Therefore, instruction should be followed with some form of evaluation. The most important reason to evaluate should be to determine whether each student has met the goals and objectives that educators have specified. Traditionally, technology educators have relied on examinations to make this determination. Technology educators are, however, finding other means of evaluating student achievement of specified objectives. These include the writing of objectives that allow students to demonstrate knowledge and skills needed outside of the school setting.

Assessment may also be used to help educators to determine the effectiveness of instructional activities. Activities must be redesigned if students fail to meet specific objectives after engaging in the experience. Thus, student performance provides the criteria as to the need for modifying or eliminating activities.

Assessment of Curriculum

Curriculum assessment may involve the examination of instructional programs, materials, teaching strategies, textbooks, audiovisual aids and the organizational and physical arrangements of an educational setting. This type of assessment may include all aspects of a teaching environment or a specific portion of a curriculum, such as audiovisual aids. While ongoing instructional programs are subject to assessment, curriculum assessment is usually associated with a new or innovative approach (Gay, 1980).

In addition to overall student performance, there may be other factors which are included in the assessment of curriculum. These factors might include the attitudes of students, teachers, administrators and parents with regard to the curriculum. These are important considerations. For example, how a technology educator feels about curriculum change may significantly affect teaching effectiveness. By determining the reasons for teacher dissatisfaction, remedies may be found that could bring about a change in teacher attitude and subsequently increase the effectiveness of the curriculum.

Another factor which should be considered in curriculum assessment is cost. Clearly, educational funding is not plentiful. New programs must be justifiable in terms of cost. A new curriculum is usually considered cost-effective if one or more of the following is true: a) it costs the same as other curriculum efforts but results in greater achievement; b) it costs less and has equal or greater student achievement; c) it costs more, but significantly increases achievement.

When performing a curriculum assessment, technology educators must consider the difficulty of comparing the effectiveness of one curriculum approach over another. Two curricula which are concerned with the same content may contain objectives which are very different. It may, therefore, be difficult to measure fairly or with any degree of validity the effectiveness of the new approach.

Assessment of the School

An assessment of the school involves an in-depth analysis of the entire educational program and all aspects of its infrastructure. This would include the schools stated philosophy, goals and objectives, the needs of the learner, the needs of society (in relation to the needs of the learner), content, process and techniques, facilities and equipment, academic services and student outcomes. The purpose of a school assessment is to determine the degree to which the school objectives are being met. The assessment may further be used to identify the strengths and weaknesses of the entire educational program. This information provides feedback for future direction and planned activities with regard to school resources. Based upon a school assessment, the decision might be made to eliminate or redirect resources to various needs.

In planning to perform an assessment of the school, Davis (1989) advocated a six step process to collect and evaluate the material gathered. This six step process included:

1. Focus the evaluation problem by defining the charge from the client and the constraints.
2. Identify various stakeholders and audiences.
3. Generate questions of interest to stakeholders.
4. Redefine and limit questions through negotiation with vested parties so the questions can be addressed.
5. Determine the methodology: Specify for each question the instrument or data source (new or existing), the sample from who data have been or need to be collected, the time frame for data collection (if gathering new data), the methods of analysis, and the intended use of the results.
6. Communicate the findings to stakeholders in ways that they can use the results (p. 17).

Assessment of Personnel

An assessment of personnel should include individuals who are directly or indirectly responsible for educational outcomes. This would include groups such as administrators, counselors and teachers. Again, the purpose of this assessment is to determine the degree to which educational outcomes are being achieved.

One of the reasons that this area of assessment has been slow to progress is that it is complicated and involves issues that are not readily defined. Teacher assessment can be used to illustrate this complexity. Teacher assessment has typically been based on observation of the teacher in the classroom by an administrator. In some situations, the educator may be asked to complete a self-study report. Another alternative is to have students assess the teacher on a number of criteria. Each of these methods, however, contain a number of problems which are a concern to both reliability and validity of the assessment devise (Gay, 1980).

First, the number of teacher observations is small. Often these observations may be made only once in a given year. This represents only a small sample of observed behavior. Secondly, there are outcomes of these observations that reduce their reliability and validity. Educators as well as students tend to act differently when they are being observed. Teachers may, therefore, teach better or worse as a result of nervousness or the student/observer interaction. Finally, there is concern over the rating form used. There is rarely any documentation of the reliability and validity of the rating form.

It is necessary then to work on how to assess teacher behavior. First, what are the objectives of this assessment and what specific teacher behaviors are to be assessed? It is further necessary to determine what distinguishes an effective teacher from an ineffective teacher? This question is concerned with teacher accountability. Ideally, teacher effectiveness should be judged in terms of student performance. Such an assessment has its own built in difficulties. The main question here is: To what degree can a teacher be held accountable for the achievement of students? This is a very challenging area of assessment.

In a keynote address of Technology Education Symposium VII, Maley (1985) provided some criteria by which Technology Educators might be assessed. These included a teacher and student emphasis in the:

- Use of the historical role of technology in human development;
- Study of the relationship between technological decisions and human values;
- Examination of the benefits and risks in choosing various technologies;
- Changes occurring in contemporary technology;
- Use of technology assessment as a means for influencing the choice of future technologies;

- Understanding and application of mathematics, science, social studies, and communication;
- Study of technology through the use of an exploratory and experimental laboratory;
- Examination of societal problems that are capable of a technological fix; and
- Use of interdisciplinary approaches to teaching and learning (pp. 6–9).

Assessing Student Performance

The assessment of student performance is often difficult for technology educators. The need for objective and precise data for student evaluations is also recognized by technology educators. In addition to being a prerequisite for the assignment of grades, student evaluations are also the basis for decisions concerning future educational and career plans. Data that is inaccurate can cause a misdirection of those student plans. Student performance is also a measure of teacher effectiveness. A comprehensive knowledge of what students can and cannot do, in conjunction with the stated objectives of the course, can provide transportation technology educators with a basis for evaluating their instructional strengths and weaknesses.

Transportation technology educators are also aware of the ethical considerations of assessing student performance. Are educators morally justified in applying absolute standards to a classroom of students when each is unique in terms of aspirations, background and personal commitment? Is it appropriate, for example, to pass a student who does not do well but exhibits maximum effort while at the same time passing a gifted student who is only working at a minimal effort? The need for accurate assessments of student performance must be weighted against the fact that educators are dealing with human beings and not mass manufactured production (Lorber and Pierce, 1983).

Clearly, there is no single assessment technique that can solve the problems associated with student evaluation. However, it is possible to use a variety of evaluation criteria and grading techniques that can allow transportation technology educators to feel more at ease with the assessment process.

Technology educators, like most other educators rely heavily upon paper and pencil examinations. Paper and pencil tests have been used successfully to pose the same problems to all students under the same test conditions. Such tests provide a reasonable basis of comparison for all students. Tests can be further used to sample a broad area of student knowledge or a specific area of learning.

Criterion, Domain and Norm-Referenced Tests

Assessing students to determine their abilities relative to the stated instructional goals involves comparing each student's demonstrated performance with preset standards or criteria. This type of assessment is known as criterion-referenced. The term criterion-referenced test simply means that the items on the test are referenced to a specified set of subordinate skills that make up a goal (Carey, 1988).

Transportation technology educators may also decide to use domain-referenced tests. In this type of test, the test items have been referenced to a domain of tasks. The domain of tasks are representative of the specific behavioral objectives identified by the instructor and the subordinate skills needed to accomplish those objectives.

Since criterion and domain-referenced assessments usually do not provide comparative data, norm-referenced tests may be used to determine how well individual students perform in comparison to other students. In this type of a test, each student's performance is compared with the average performance of students with similar characteristics (i.e., age or grade level). In order to achieve a high level of reliability and validity, norm-referenced tests will usually contain items that range in difficulty from simple to very difficult. The test items at either extreme may have little relationship to the original instructional intent. Many items are also included to differentiate between students than to differentiate between those who can and cannot demonstrate a specific competency (Carey, 1988).

Alternative Assessment Procedures

When transportation technology educators begin to use specific objectives and focus on the identified educational goals that students will be able to demonstrate, paper and pencil tests may receive less emphasis. Alternatives to traditional testing might include the more frequent use of construction projects, demonstrations, design activities, community projects, gaming, interdisciplinary studies, interviews, models, product testing and development and research and experimentation by students in the transportation technology laboratory. When technology educators develop activities that require subordinate skills, and when students demonstrate those skills through an alternative assessment procedure, evidence has been produced for the evaluation of the stated instructional objectives.

In using alternative assessment procedures, it is important that transportation technology educators specify to students the observable behavior that students will be able to perform as a result of the instruction or learning taking place. It may further be helpful to students to provide a model or checklist in order for them to obtain a mental picture of what is expected of them.

Implementing Curriculum Changes

The implementation of curriculum changes cannot be done by a single individual. It must be made as part of an institutional process for change, and the degree of change will probably be a function of the amount of commitment that the participants have given to the task.

Curriculum change in the transportation technology area may be instituted in two methods. The first, is to develop a small instructional unit to be integrated into the existing curriculum. While this method is relatively easy to do and less expensive in money, time and effort, it is incapable of making large scale changes that may be needed in a very traditional or non-technology based curriculum.

The second method is to use a systems approach to assessing the philosophy, goals and needs of the students and the community. After this assessment is completed, the assessors will begin to develop long-range plans for continuing the development and improvement of the instructional program. This is a much slower and more expensive method of implementing curriculum change. It may, however, be more desirable to a staff that has not had the experience in planning and implementing large scale curriculum changes.

Eiss (1970) provided some considerations that educators should be aware of in assessing and developing long-range educational plans. Several of the more important considerations are:

1. The entire school community should be involved in the developing process. This would include administration, faculty, board members, students, alumni, and influential members of the school community.
2. The curriculum development should begin with a critical examination of the current educational system, including its strengths and weaknesses. Faculty members, students and other interested parties should be involved in this process.
3. A tentative philosophy and long-range goals should be developed by the participants. The philosophy and goals should be open-ended in order that they may be changed easily when new ideas and more information are obtained.
4. Inservice education for the faculty is needed as soon as possible. One method of providing this inservice education is to have those involved in the assessment and development of the new curriculum develop small instructional units based upon the established philosophy

and goals. These instructional units should use a variety of teaching and learning strategies so that they may be further revised and tested.

5. Financial resources for the assessment and development of the long-range plans should be carefully monitored. This will insure that the project will not be cancelled at the last minute due to a lack of funds.

6. A tentative timetable should be developed for the completion of the long-range plans. The timetable and plans should include: a) preparation and evaluation of the goals and objectives, b) development of experimental units, c) inservice education, d) curriculum planning and development, e) evaluation of progress at each step of the curriculum development and f) plans for continuing the assessment and revision.

Developing and Assessing an Instructional Unit in Transportation Technology

As previously stated, if those involved in the assessment and long-range development process have not had experience in curriculum planning and revision, it may be helpful to begin with the development of several small curriculum units before revising the entire curriculum. The first step of this process is to select a unit topic. Eiss (1970) suggests that this might be some part of the instructional program that educators are having difficulty getting across to the students.

The second step would involve an analysis of the topic. In this analysis, the topic to be taught should be studied carefully and broken down into its component parts. The technology educator should then identify those aspects that the student will be expected to know and do upon completion of the unit. For example, upon completion of an alternative energy instructional unit, the technology educator would probably expect a student to be able to differentiate between various forms of alternative energy and be able to perform the mathematical calculations for an energy assessment of a residential dwelling.

Once those aspects that the student would be expected to know and do are identified, the technology educator should arrange the various component parts into a logical instructional sequence. Behavioral objectives are then written and criterion assessment items are identified to measure the attainment of the specified objectives. The technology educator should then develop a learning sequence to enable the student to master each aspect of the unit. These learning sequences may be developed and tested in an experimental manner. This would assure that they are effective in allowing students to progress.

Finally, the material should be assembled into a completed learning unit. It should then be implemented in an experimental fashion with individual students or small groups. Again, this would allow the technology educator to revise the unit and instructional procedures until it is effective in achieving its stated goals. Once this process of assessment and development has been successfully tried with different units and learning strategies, the faculty should be able to use the systems approach to the revision of an entire technology education curriculum.

Literacy in Technology Education

DeVore (1986) and Miller (1986) have noted that a technological society requires numerous forms of literacy. In a democratic society, citizen involvement in the decision making process is essential to a democracy. Daily, numerous public policy decisions are being based on scientific and technological issues. It is possible to find many instances in the local or national news where citizens are deciding, either through deliberation or default, the implementation of technical solutions to human problems. For instance, decisions at the local and national level are regularly made with reference to: agricultural production, energy generation and management, resource management, sustaining the environment, waste reduction and wildlife protection. An understanding of scientific and technological information is essential for an analysis of these and many other issues.

Schools throughout the United States of America have had limited success with curricula which would provide students with experiences in applying scientific and technological principles in problem solving situations. Jennings (1988) wrote: "Many youth lost the motivation to continue their education because of their experiences with school curricula that held virtually no connection with the real world and its rapidly advancing and highly technological living conditions" (p. 2). Waetjen (1985) also noted:

> The risk for our society is to underestimate the importance of the assessment of technological change or to assume that the assessment is entirely a scientific process. . . .

A central role of an education institution is to offer a curriculum that gives its students a basic understanding of the society in which they live. Proceeding from that premise, it is logical to assume that in a democratic, technological society, the curriculum would strongly reflect those characteristics.

> Almost all areas of the curriculum contain information about the democratic form of government in the United States. The same cannot be said about technology. People are becoming out of touch with a fundamental aspect of their society because our education institutions impart so little understanding of its technological base (p. 9).

To meet these challenges, the educational system within the United States has been moving through various stages of reform. In numerous instances (e.g., Boyer, 1983; National Commission on Excellence in Education, 1983; National Science Board Commission on Precollege Education in Mathematics, Science and Technology, 1983), these reforms have placed an emphasis on the study of science and technology.

The curriculum area of technology education has not been immune to these national changes. Technology education with its focus on 'technological literacy,' has provided a link in assisting students to understand, live and work in an advanced technological and information based society. The interdisciplinary nature of technology has also helped students to comprehend and apply science, technology and social science to the problems facing humankind.

If technology educators are to help students become technologically literate, further reforms will be necessary in the curriculum area. In addition to the suggestions made by Maley (1985), technology educators should further promote student understanding and application of the technical structure and operation of various technologies. It is clear that too many individuals do not understand the inner working of the major appliances and utilities that effect their lives. Consumers should be expected to use the various devices and systems of technology in a safe and efficient manner. They should further be able to make some rudimentary diagnostic procedures in the event that the device or system should fail.

Students should have a sociocultural understanding of technology. An understanding of the various applications and limitations of technology would help to diminish many of the negative aspects of technological development. In a democracy, citizens and consumers are continually being asked to make evaluations of the applications and limitations of technology to human wants, desires and problems. A curriculum that helps students to evaluate the appropriateness of various technological devices and fixes would go far in helping to create a more just and sustainable future.

Finally, students in technology education should gain an appreciation for and understanding of how scientists develop theoretical explanations of natural phenomena. Science has had a significant influence on society and the environment. As a means for understanding "why," science has become an interaction between the searching human mind and the physical world. Through scientific inquiry, we are able to observe things as they are, and events as they happen. Science further provides us with a process of ordering, classifying and establishing relationships. It is a process which allow scientists to recognize the Laws of Nature, and develop theories that helps us to understand and cope with our natural and human made world. Just as citizens are being asked to evaluate the appropriateness of technology, they are also being asked to evaluate the appropriateness, risks, value of, and test results from scientific research.

The curriculum area of technology education can go far in promoting technological literacy through a study of technology that contributes to an understanding of our technical means and empowering citizens to make rational decisions to life's challenges. Such a problem-solving curriculum will have to move beyond the paper and pencil tests that assess memorization of facts. It will require an interaction between the student and the educator by which both learning and assessments are negotiated prior to instruction or learning. This interaction would therefore help to promote student individuality, independence and development of social responsibility. In developing the technologically literate individual, the broad goals of a technology eduction program should allow students to develop their knowledge and intellectual skills, develop a commitment to the tenets of a democracy, strengthen their individual, group and political skills and develop an awareness of public policy issues and citizen involvement. Table 2 illustrates a conceptual framework for the promotion of technological literacy in technology education.

Conclusions

While the purpose of this chapter was to provide some means for assessing transportation technology curricula, it should be again stressed that there are no single set of assessment procedures that will work in every instance. Effective assessments are usually accompanied by a number of diverse and flexible assessment strategies that have been adapted to a particular group or institution. While assessment may be a response to external demands or audiences, its focus must remain with the educators and institution. Assessments may further serve multiple purposes, but the primary purpose should be for the improvement of student learning. Good assessments will require an enormous amount of data collection and assurances that the information gathered is valid, reliable and credible. Lastly, the costs associated with an assessment should be weighed against its potential benefits and side effects.

A CONCEPTUAL FRAMEWORK FOR PROMOTING TECHNOLOGICAL LITERACY		
GOALS		
Acquiring knowledge related to the use of science and technology	Developing life-long learning skills	Developing societal and ethical values
Appreciating the importance of science and technology on people, the environment and culture	Developing creative abilities and positive concepts of self-worth	Strengthening problem solving, decision making and value clarification skills
Apply scientific and technological concepts, processes and systems to the problems of human needs and desires	Apply tools, materials, processes and technical concepts of technology in a safe, efficient and responsible manner	Apply the concepts of technology assessments to human problems
CONTENT		
Concepts of science and technology	Systems and processes used by scientists and technologists	Interdependence of humans, science, technology, culture and nature
AREAS OF EMPHASIS		
Collecting data	Analyzing data	Hypothesis testing
Evaluating data	Obtaining conclusions	Making predictions
Problem solving	Technology assessments	Public policies
Local problems	Regional problems	Global problems

Table 2

REFERENCES

Aspy, D. N., & Roebuck, F. N. (1972). An investigation of the relationship between student levels of cognitive functioning and the teacher's classroom behavior. *The Journal of Educational Research, 65*(8), 365–368.

Baird, L. L. (1973). Teaching styles: An exploratory study of dimensions and effects. *Journal of Educational Psychology, 64*(1), 15–21.

Bigge, M. L., & Hunt, M. P. (1962). *Psychological foundations of education* (2nd ed.). New York: Harper & Row.

Boyer, E. L. (1983). *High school: A report on secondary education in America.* (The Carnegie Foundation for the Advancement of Teaching). New York: Harper & Row.

Carey, L. (1988). *Measuring and evaluating school learning*. Boston: Allyn and Bacon.

Cutcliffe, S. H. (1985). Understanding science, technology and engineering: An essential element of cultural literacy. *Federation Review, 8*(4), 10–15.

Davis, B. G. (1989). Demystifying assessment: Learning from the field of evaluation. In P. J. Gray (Ed.), *Achieving assessment goals using evaluation techniques* (pp. 5–20). California: Jossey-Bass.

DeVore, P. W. (1986, February). *Measuring technological literacy—problems and issues.* Paper presented at the meeting of the National Science, Technology, Society Conference: Technological Literacy, Baltimore, Maryland.

Eiss, A. F. (1970). *Evaluation of instructional systems.* New York: Gordon and Beach.

Gay, L. R. (1980). *Educational evaluation & measurement: Competencies for analysis and application.* Ohio: Charles E. Merrill.

Jennings, G. L. (1988, February). *Technology education: In pursuit of technological literacy.* Paper presented at the National Conference of the Association of Teacher Educators, San Diego, California.

Lorber, M. A., & Pierce, W. D. (1983). *Objectives, methods, and evaluation for secondary teaching* (2nd ed.). New Jersey: Prentice-Hall.

Miller, J. D. (1986). Technological literacy: Some concepts and measures. *Bulletin of Science, Technology & Society, 6*(2&3), 195–201.

National Commission on Excellence in Education. (1983). *A nation at risk: The imperative for educational reform.* Washington, DC: U.S. Government Printing Office.

National Science Board Commission on Precollege Education in Mathematics, Science and Technology. (1983). *Educating Americans for the 21st Century: A plan of action for improving mathematics, science and technology education for all American elementary and secondary students so that their achievement is the best in the world by 1995.* Washington, DC: Author.

Provus, M. M. (1971). *Discrepancy evaluation for educational program improvement and assessment.* California: McCutchan.

Rowntree, D. (1987). *Assessing students: How shall we know them?* New York: Nichols.

Stuffebeam, D. I., Foley, W. J., Gephart, W. J., Guba, E. G., Hammond, R. I., Merriman, H. O., & Provus, M. M. (1971). *Educational evaluation & decision making.* Illinois: F. E. Peacock.

Tough, J. (1976). *Listening to children talking.* London: Ward Lock.

Waetjen, W. B. (1985). The nature of our technological society. In *Technology education: A perspective on implementation.* Virginia: International Technology Education Association.

INDEX

— *D* —

— *E* —

— *F* —

— *G* —

— *H* —

— *I* —

— J —

— L —

— M —

— *T* —

— *U* —

— *V* —

— *W* —